The Triumph of Mercy

The Triumph of Mercy

Philosophy and Scripture in Mullā Ṣadrā

Mohammed Rustom

SUNY PRESS

Cover art by Mohamed Zakariya.

Published by State University of New York Press, Albany

Printed in the United States of America

For information, contact State University of New York Press, Albany, NY
www.sunypress.edu

Production by Diane Ganeles
Marketing by Michael Campochiaro

Library of Congress Cataloging-in-Publication Data

Rustom, Mohammed.
The triumph of mercy : philosophy and scripture in Mulla Sadra / Mohammed Rustom.
p. cm.
Includes bibliographical references and index.
ISBN 978-1-4384-4341-6 (hardcover : alk. paper)
ISBN 978-1-4384-4340-9 (paperback : alk. paper)
1. Sadr al-Din Shirazi, Muhammad ibn Ibrahim, d. 1641. 2. Islamic philosophy. 3. Sufism. I. Title.

B753.M84R87 2012
181'.5—dc23 2011038838

10 9 8 7 6 5 4 3 2 1

To Nosheen, for all her love and support

Contents

Acknowledgments

This book is based on a doctoral dissertation submitted to the University of Toronto's Department of Near and Middle Eastern Civilizations in the fall of 2009. Thanks go first and foremost to my thesis advisor Todd Lawson, who over the years has shared his vast knowledge of Islamic thought with me in unstinting measure. Not only did he see to it that each page of this study conformed to his rigorous academic standards, but he has, through all of my successes and failures, always been a gracious friend and supporter.

Apart from offering helpful comments on the present work at different stages of its gestation, I have also had the fortunate opportunity to learn from Sebastian Günther, Maria Subtelny, Shafique Virani, and the late Michael Marmura. Other teachers from whom I have greatly benefited include Talal Ahdab, Deborah Black, Richard Blackburn, Nasser Danesh, Thomas Robinson, Walid Saleh, and Liyakat Takim. In many ways, they have bestowed upon me the foundational tools necessary for the kind of undertaking presented here.

Seyyed Hossein Nasr's encouragement and guidance from the very outset of this project has been crucial, as has been the time William Chittick spent with me reading the works of Mullā Ṣadrā. Caner Dagli, Robert Dobie, Atif Khalil, Mohammad Hassan Khalil, Joel Richmond, Sajjad Rizvi, Kristin Sands, John Walbridge, and SUNY Press's two anonymous reviewers all provided essential feedback on various aspects of the present study. Nasrin Askari, Ryan Brizendine, Shiraz Sheikh, and my research assistant Rizwan Mohammad have kindly taken care of many nitty-gritty details related to the book, and a number of scholars sent along important references. Specific thanks in this regard are due to Peter Adamson, Jules Janssens, Farhana Mayer, Matthew Melvin-Koushki, James Morris, Gregor Schwarb, and Alexander Treiger.

Over the course of a decade of study at the University of Toronto, on the administrative side of things, Anna Sousa, Jennie Jones, and Elaine Genius have offered a helping hand every step of the way. At Carleton University, the support of my colleagues in the College of the Humanities in general, and Farhang Rajaee and Kim Stratton in particular, has made academic life all the better.

Research for this book was made possible through doctoral fellowships courtesy of the University of Toronto and the Social Sciences and Humanities Research Council of Canada, an Ontario Graduate Scholarship, and the Davidson Fund in Religious Studies at Carleton University. Carleton's Office of the Dean (Faculty of Arts and Social Sciences) administered a grant in order to commission the artwork which adorns the front cover. For facilitating my research in Iran, I would like to acknowledge the assistance of Hamid Mohammadi at the Iranian Embassy in Ottawa, Jalil Hosseini of the Tehran-based Organization of Culture and Islamic Relations, and Gholamreza Aavani, former director of the Iranian Institute of Philosophy.

A paragraph from the Introduction originally appeared in *Comparative Islamic Studies* 4, no. 1 (2008): 89, and a sixth of Chapter 1 in the *Journal of Qur'anic Studies* 9, no. 1 (2007): 128–31, 3. These materials have been reworked into the present book by kind permission of Equinox Publishers and Edinburgh University Press respectively.

Last, but certainly not least, heartfelt thanks go to my family. My parents have supported me from the start, and for this I am very grateful. Abbi, Ammi, my son Isa Ahmed, as well as my siblings, nieces, and nephews have all enriched my work in their own unique way. My wife Nosheen has made innumerable sacrifices and has always sought to create for me an ambience in which I could carry out my research. This book is dedicated to her.

Transliterations and Abbreviations

Transliterations

Arabic and Persian words, proper names, and book/article titles have been transliterated in accordance with the system employed by the *International Journal of Middle Eastern Studies*, with the exception that no distinction is made in transliterating consonants shared between Arabic and Persian. The names of authors who write in European languages in addition to Arabic or Persian have not been transliterated.

Abbreviations

Journals

BJMES = *British Journal of Middle Eastern Studies*
CB = *Les Cahiers de Byrsa*
CIS = *Comparative Islamic Studies*
DI = *Der Islam*
DSTFM = *Documenti e Studi sulla Tradizione Filosofica Medievale*
FADDS = *Faṣl-Nāma-yi Andīsha-yi Dīnī-yi Dānishgāh-i Shīrāz*
ICMR = *Islam and Christian-Muslim Relations*
IJAS = *International Journal of Asian Studies*
IQ = *The Islamic Quarterly*
IS = *Islam and Science*
ISt = *Islamic Studies*
JAAR = *Journal of the American Academy of Religion*
JIP = *Journal of Islamic Philosophy*
JIS = *Oxford Journal of Islamic Studies*
JMIAS = *Journal of the Muhyiddin Ibn 'Arabi Society*
JQS = *Journal of Qur'anic Studies*

KHNṢ = *Khirad-Nāma-yi Ṣadrā*
KN = *Kâr-Nâmeh*
MBSS = *Majallat Markaz Buḥūth al-Sunna wa-l-Sīra*
MIDEO = *Mélanges de l'Institut Dominicain d'Études Orientales du Caire*
MRR = *Mawlana Rumi Review*
MS = *Mediaeval Studies*
MW = *Muslim World*
PBSMS = *Proceedings of the British Society for Middle Eastern Studies*
SI = *Spektrum Iran*
SIs = *Studia Islamica*
SMT = *Studies in Medieval Thought*

Reference Works

DC = *Dictionnaire du Coran*, ed. M. A. Amir-Moezzi. Paris: Robert Laffont, 2007.
EI[2] = *Encyclopaedia of Islam*[2], ed. H. A. R. Gibb et al. Leiden: Brill, 1960–2004.
EI[3] = *Encyclopaedia of Islam*[3], ed. G. Krämer et al. Leiden: Brill, 2007– .
EJ[2] = *Encyclopaedia Judaica*[2], ed. M. Berenbaum and F. Skolnik. Detroit: Macmillan, 2007.
EQ = *Encyclopaedia of the Qur'ān*, ed. J. McAuliffe. Leiden: Brill, 2001–2006.

Introduction

The great German scholar of Islamic intellectual history Max Horten (d. 1945) published two important books on Muḥammad b. Ibrāhīm al-Shīrāzī (d. 1050/1640)—more commonly known as Mullā Ṣadrā—at the turn of the twentieth century.[1] Yet Horten's works on this towering figure of Islamic thought, as well as his other pioneering contributions to later Islamic philosophy and theology, did not receive the scholarly attention one would have expected. This is partly due to the fact that at the dawn of the twentieth century, the story of the earlier period of Islamic philosophy had not even begun to be told. There were indeed a number of general surveys (now outdated) on the history of Islamic philosophy, but the nature and scope of many early Muslim philosophers' teachings were still largely unknown. Horten's books on later Islamic philosophy and theology were, therefore, eclipsed by concurrent and later studies on some of the seminal figures in early Islamic thought, such as Fārābī (d. 339/950), Avicenna (d. 428/1037), Ghazālī (d. 505/1111), and Averroës (d. 595/1198).

Yet it was not always an interest in the history and development of Islamic thought which impelled scholars to take up its study. For many of these scholars—and not a few contemporary writers on Islamic philosophy—philosophical thinking in Islam only had life and/or interest insofar as it contributed to the development of Western philosophy. From the late nineteenth century to roughly the 1960s, Islamic philosophy was therefore primarily studied in order to understand its historical influence on the West. Since Islamic philosophy's historical contact with medieval Europe came to an end with the work of Averroës, this meant that the writings of some of the major authors of later Islamic thought, such as Shihāb al-Dīn Suhrawardī (d. 587/1191) and Ibn ʿArabī (d. 638/1240), had not been translated into Latin. There thus emerged a view of Islamic philosophy amongst Western scholars which saw it as no more than a conduit for transmitting knowledge from late antiquity to the late medieval period, but which in the process failed to extend and foster its own philosophical heritage.[2]

Apart from the question as to why medieval Muslims would be interested in the writings of antiquity in the first place, this view of the historical role of Islamic philosophy went essentially unchallenged for the first half of the twentieth century. But this old story of Islamic philosophy was slowly approaching its end. Between 1938 and 1952, the French Iranologist and philosopher of religion, Henry Corbin (d. 1978), who had already made a name for himself by introducing Heidegger to the French-speaking world,[3] published several groundbreaking books on Avicenna and Suhrawardī.[4] From 1953 to the late 1980s came a steady stream of pioneering publications on later Islamic thought carried out by Jalāl al-Dīn Āshtiyānī (d. 2005), William Chittick, Corbin, Toshihiko Izutsu (d. 1993), Hermann Landolt, Mehdi Mohaghegh, James Morris, Seyyed Hossein Nasr, Fazlur Rahman (d. 1988), and Sayyid Muḥammad Ḥusayn Ṭabāṭabāʾī (d. 1981). These scholars' contributions made it possible to discuss Islamic philosophical thinking on its own terms, and not just as an offshoot of the wider history of Western philosophy. They also helped pave the way for a substantially different picture of the development of philosophy in the heartlands of Islam post-Averroës.

This resuscitation of interest in later Islamic philosophy ensured that some of Islam's most important and time-honored scholars would be brought back into the spotlight. Amongst these figures, a good deal of attention was justifiably devoted to the writings of Mullā Ṣadrā, whose thought marked the highpoint of the school of Isfahan and revolutionized the discipline of Islamic philosophy for good.[5]

The past two decades have consequently witnessed a growing number of studies on almost every aspect on Ṣadrā's life[6] and thought.[7] While the bulk of scholarly attention has been devoted to Ṣadrā's philosophical works proper, his writings which fall under the category of the "transmitted" Islamic sciences (*al-ʿulūm al-naqliyya*) have not received the attention they rightly deserve.

The single largest body of texts which belong to this latter category are in the field of Qurʾānic sciences.[8] Ṣadrā wrote some sixteen works pertaining directly to the Qurʾān, three of which deal with certain theoretical aspects of his understanding of the sacred book. The remaining thirteen, which are undeniably attributable to him, are all in the field of Qurʾānic exegesis (*tafsīr*). They consist of ten independent commentaries upon individual chapters of the Qurʾān (all but one are complete), and three commentaries upon select verses.[9] Taken together, these writings mark the first time in the history of

Islamic thought that a philosopher had undertaken such a wide-scale commentary upon the Qur᾿ān. So significant were Ṣadrā's Qur᾿ānic writings that they themselves have been the subject of several lengthy, philosophical commentaries and glosses.[10] The two key figures in this regard are Mullā ʿAlī Nūrī (d. 1246/1830) and Mullā Hādī Sabziwārī (d. 1289/1873), whose works have played a pivotal role in the development of Islamic metaphysics in Iran from the Qajar period to the present.[11]

This is not to suggest that authors endowed with a penchant for philosophy before Ṣadrā were not concerned with the Qur᾿ān. As Alexander Knysh correctly suggests, in a civilization founded upon Qur᾿ānic principles, the Muslim philosophers could not but remain "loyal to their sacred book."[12] Thus, it comes as no surprise to read that the most prominent philosophers in Islam well before Ṣadrā took up the pen had commented upon the Qur᾿ān in one form or another.[13] We find many explicit Qur᾿ānic references and even "commentaries" on Islam's sacred text in the writings of al-Kindī (d. ca. 257/870),[14] the Ikhwān al-Ṣafā᾿,[15] Avicenna,[16] Averroës,[17] and Suhrawardī.[18] But unlike Ṣadrā, these philosophers' readings of the Qur᾿ān are limited to a handful of its *āya*s (verses) and shorter *sūra*s (chapters), and do not have an eye on the wider *tafsīr* tradition.

Ṣadrā's work on the Qur᾿ān should also be distinguished from *tafsīr*s which have philosophical content or are philosophical in nature, but ultimately belong to the mainstream genre of *tafsīr*. The greatest work belonging to this category is undoubtedly Fakhr al-Dīn al-Rāzī's (d. 606/1210) *al-Tafsīr al-kabīr* ("The Grand Qur᾿ān Commentary").[19] Ṣadrā's *tafsīr*s function as independent philosophical commentaries upon select verses and chapters of the Qur᾿ān that seek to engage the enterprises of Sufism, Islamic philosophy, and Shīʿī and Sunnī theology,[20] while also remaining in conversation with, but not bound to, the *tafsīr* tradition as such. He can thus avoid discussing the kinds of tangential issues that someone like Rāzī, qua Qur᾿ānic exegete proper, would have to address in his *tafsīr*.

In saying that Ṣadrā wrote philosophical commentaries upon aspects of the Qur᾿ān I do not wish to endorse the simplistic characterization that reduces his *tafsīr* compositions to nothing more than a set of philosophical "glosses" upon scripture.[21] Ṣadrā does not merely approach the Qur᾿ān as a thinker who seeks to justify his philosophical and mystical positions by using the Qur᾿ān's dicta. Rather, he finds within the Qur᾿ān the same vision of reality at which he arrived through the long and arduous process of study and self-purification. Thus, Ṣadrā's approach to the Qur᾿ān is philosophical because his philosophy is Qurʾānic.[22] The difference between his strictly-defined philosophical writings and his *tafsīr* compositions is that the former (although not entirely) are more concerned with explicating the nature of reality in purely philosophical terms. But when Ṣadrā approaches scripture, he is able to discuss the same themes he takes up in his philosophical works in more familiar "religious" language, as he is now operating within the framework of the Qurʾān's mythic structure.[23]

Since Ṣadrā only took up writing on the Qurʾān after his philosophical views had fully matured,[24] it is true that there is a great deal of unity to his works in the Qurʾānic sciences. At any rate, it is nevertheless problematic to attempt to understand his theoretical and practical scriptural hermeneutics by studying his different Qurʾānic works as if they were an organic whole.[25] For one thing, such an undertaking would easily occupy several lengthy volumes. At the same time, since Ṣadrā's writings on the Qurʾān span many different periods of his life and reflect different concerns, a study of this nature would not be able to communicate what is so unique about each of Ṣadrā's *tafsīr* works as texts sufficient unto themselves.[26] Each of his *tafsīr*s employ a range of varying sources, engage different questions, and, ultimately, present tightly-knit arguments that are reflective of the underlying objectives of the *tafsīr* in question.

With the above points in mind, the only way we can come away with an idea of how Ṣadrā's *tafsīr* reads as *tafsīr* is to focus on one work which typifies, but by no means exhausts, his understanding of, and approach to, the Qurʾān. This study therefore presents the first book-length attempt to explain, through a textual and analytical examination of one of Ṣadrā's *tafsīr* works, the manner in which philosophy and scripture interact with each other in his thought. For reasons which will be discussed shortly, I have chosen to devote my attention to Ṣadrā's commentary upon that Qurʾānic chapter which occupies central importance in Muslim daily life, namely the Fātiḥa.[27]

It is worth citing the Fātiḥa here, especially since its verses will resonate in many of the pages to follow:

In the Name of God, the All-Merciful, the Compassionate.
Praise is for God, Lord of the worlds,
the All-Merciful, the Compassionate;
Master of the Day of Judgment.
You alone do we worship, and from You alone do we seek aid.
Guide us upon the straight path—
the path of those whom You have blessed;
not of those who incur wrath, nor of those who stray.

Like every other Qur᾿ān-commentator before him, Ṣadrā extols the merits of the Fātiḥa.[28] We are told in the exegetical literature, for example, that this particular chapter contains the entire Qur᾿ān. This helps explain why ʿAlī b. Abī Ṭālib (d. 40/661) is famously known to have said, "If I wanted, I could write seventy camel-loads of commentary upon the Fātiḥa."[29] Ṣadrā's commentary on the Fātiḥa, generically entitled *Tafsīr Sūrat al-fātiḥa,* is clearly more modest. But that is not to say that it is not "weighty."

By the time Ṣadrā wrote the *Tafsīr Sūrat al-fātiḥa,* he had already penned over ten independent *tafsīr*s. He also had already written his most important theoretical work on the Qur᾿ān, the *Mafātīḥ al-ghayb* ("The Keys to the Unseen"),[30] whose name is inspired by Q 6:59 and is also an alternative title of Rāzī's aforementioned *tafsīr*. In this work, Ṣadrā fully outlines the theoretical and practical considerations involved in any act of scriptural interpretation. Thus, in the *Tafsīr Sūrat al-fātiḥa,* which is his last complete *tafsīr* composition (written less than a decade before his death),[31] we encounter a Mullā Ṣadrā whose thinking on scripture had crystallized. His commentary on the Fātiḥa thus represents his most mature attempt to comment upon scripture, a fact which is evident throughout this pivotal text. We find in this book a very comprehensive, internally coherent picture of a number of key metaphysical, cosmological, psychological, theological, and soteriological teachings squarely situated within the traditions of Islamic philosophy and theoretical Sufism. In short, Ṣadrā's *Tafsīr Sūrat al-fātiḥa* offers nothing less than a penetrating metaphysical commentary upon the Qur᾿ān's opening chapter.

It is important to note here that Ṣadrā's *Tafsīr Sūrat al-fātiḥa* does not give pride of place to his most important philosophical doctrines, that of the "fundamentality of being" (*aṣālat al-wujūd*) and its gradation (*tashkīk*).[32] Indeed, we find a similar phenomenon at work in Ṣadrā's strictly speaking non-philosophical treatises, such as his *Iksīr al-ʿārifīn* ("The Elixir of the Gnostics"). Commenting on the marked absence of *aṣālat al-wujūd* and *tashkīk* in this book, Chittick notes that the work can be said to articulate Ṣadrā's core philosophical ideas by presenting "an analysis of their implications in philosophic-religious terms."[33] It would then be safe to say that, although not an essential part of the *Tafsīr Sūrat al-fātiḥa,* these two concepts do indeed punctuate Ṣadrā's entire commentary since they constitute his general, underlying perspective which, in the context of this *tafsīr* work, is recast in the language of scripture and religious dogma.

Chapter 1 of this study seeks to outline Ṣadrā's Qur᾿ānic hermeneutics. I show that, although he wrote several theoretical works on the Qur᾿ān toward the end of his life, his thinking on the nature and function of scripture had already taken shape at an earlier phase in his career. But this is not to say that Ṣadrā does not lay out his hermeneutical theory in any one given work. As will be demonstrated, this indeed is the task he sets out for himself in the first chapter of his *Mafātīḥ*.

Chapter 2 brings this study's concern with Ṣadrā's practical hermeneutics to the forefront, as I turn my attention to his *Tafsīr Sūrat al-fātiḥa*. This chapter takes account of the sources and various intellectual traditions which inform the text and shape its discourse. I also outline the form and content of this *tafsīr* work. This chapter, therefore, sets the tone for the remainder of the book, which is concerned with critically assessing the *Tafsīr Sūrat al-fātiḥa*'s most salient teachings.

I offer a close reading of the teachings in metaphysics as laid out in the *Tafsīr Sūrat al-fātiḥa* in Chapter 3, demonstrating the manner in which Ṣadrā employs the structure and language of the opening verses of the Fātiḥa to mould his ontology into what Christian Jambet calls the "theophanic model"[34] of God's Essence and attributes, closely following the teachings of Ibn ʿArabī and his followers.

The chapter on metaphysics sets the stage for Chapter 4, which attempts to unearth Ṣadrā's unique cosmology of praise (*ḥamd*) and anthropology (taking their lead from the second and third verses of the Fātiḥa respectively), both of which admirably demonstrate the operative or practical dimension of his theoretical hermeneutics.

The verses of the Fātiḥa also prompt within Ṣadrā answers to two problems, both of which he solves by enlisting the help of Ibn ʿArabī. The first of these leads him to inquire into the nature of idolatry and its relationship to religious belief. In Chapter 5, therefore, I situate Ṣadrā's understanding of idolatry within the framework of similar discussions in later Islamic thought, demonstrating how his meditations upon Q 1:1 allow him to articulate his position concerning the "God created in beliefs." Not only does Ṣadrā show himself to be a faithful adherent of an important doctrine in later Islamic thought, but he also manages to tie this teaching into his explanation of the diversity of approaches to the Qurʾān.

The other issue which Ṣadrā attempts to tackle in the *Tafsīr Sūrat al-fātiḥa* is the question of whether or not God's mercy is open to all human beings in the afterlife, and, if so, how such a teaching relates to other scriptural statements which seem to indicate otherwise. The problem of soteriology, which Ṣadrā discusses in several of his other books, is the most characteristic feature of the *Tafsīr Sūrat al-fātiḥa*. After discussing Ṣadrā's treatment of this topic in his other writings in Chapter 6, in Chapter 7 I turn to his argument as laid out in the *Tafsīr Sūrat al-fātiḥa*, demonstrating the manner in which his ecumenical stance is a corollary to his doctrine of the fundamentality and oneness of being, especially when this idea is cast in the language of the Qurʾān in general, and the Fātiḥa in particular.

Three appendices accompany this study. Appendix 1 presents translations of some of the most essential texts from the *Mafātīḥ* in which Ṣadrā expounds his theoretical scriptural hermeneutics, thereby complementing my treatment of this topic in Chapter 1. Appendix 2 presents nearly fifty texts from the *Tafsīr Sūrat al-fātiḥa* in translation. Apart from the obvious usefulness of making excerpts of a noteworthy commentary upon the Fātiḥa available in English translation,[35] displaying these passages from Ṣadrā's *Tafsīr Sūrat al-fātiḥa* in one place also allows us to see how his ideas in this work unfold in their raw form. The final appendix presents the core texts from Ibn ʿArabī's *al-Futūḥāt al-makkiyya* ("The Meccan Revelations") which were reworked by Ṣadrā into the *Tafsīr Sūrat al-fātiḥa*. By juxtaposing, in translation, Ibn ʿArabī's originals with Ṣadrā's renditions, this appendix aims to demonstrate how significant Ibn ʿArabī's presence is in this *tafsīr* work, and how carefully Ṣadrā recasts Ibn ʿArabī's points in his own unique style and language.

1

Qur᾽ānic Hermeneutics

A thinker who wrote as widely and rapidly as Mullā Ṣadrā would naturally have drawn upon other authors' books, either by way of direct citation or indirect adaptation. Using the *Tafsīr Sūrat al-fātiḥa* as a case study, in the following chapter I will demonstrate just how indebted Ṣadrā's *tafsīr* is to the writings of his predecessors, amongst whom are some of the most important figures in Islamic thought. With respect to Ṣadrā's *Mafātīḥ,* which we encountered in the Introduction, we find many direct references to Ibn ʿArabī's *Futūḥāt* along with several references to Ghazālī's writings, particularly his *al-Munqidh min al-ḍalāl* ("The Deliverer from Error"). S. J. Badakhchani, following the contemporary Iranian philosopher and seminarian Ḥasanzādah Āmuli, suggests that a later section of the *Mafātīḥ* is nothing more than a translation of Naṣīr al-Dīn Ṭūsī's (d. 672/1274) Ismāʿīlī Persian eschatological work, *Āghāz wa-anjām* ("The Beginning and the End").[1] Although upon closer inspection the section in question is reworked by Ṣadrā with more attention to detail, this may be the first indication that Ṭūsī's "influence" upon Ṣadrā's philosophical teachings is more a result of his familiarity with Ṭūsī's work as an Ismāʿīlī thinker rather than as a Twelver thinker.[2] With respect to Ṣadrā's theoretical understanding of scripture as laid out in the *Mafātīḥ,* however, it would be incorrect to say that it has been influenced by the work of Ṭūsī or Ghazālī. The only directly discernable influence on Ṣadrā's scriptural hermeneutics in terms of its theoretical articulation can be traced back to the work of Ibn ʿArabī, as will be discussed in the present chapter.

I have shown elsewhere how internal references within Ṣadrā's oeuvre can help us answer questions concerning the chronology of his compositions on the Qurʾān and its sciences.[3] At times, however, such references can be misleading for the simple reason that Ṣadrā is known to have rewritten some of his earlier books, but which refer to texts that were definitively penned after the former works' completion (but before their revision). Although this kind of practice can often lead to a dead end with respect to dating particular texts within the Ṣadrian oeuvre, it is probably safe to assume that, on the whole, references to Ṣadrā's earlier writings in his later books are to be taken at face value. This is likely more true of later texts which noticeably modify or correct the positions and arguments mentioned in the earlier texts to which they refer.

It is with the above point in mind that we should seek to understand a remark in a fairly recent study by Sajjad Rizvi, who states that Ṣadrā's key theoretical works which deal with the Qurʾān, namely the *Mutashābihāt al-Qurʾān* ("The Ambiguous Verses of the Qurʾān"), the *Asrār al-āyat* ("The Secrets Behind the Qurʾān's Verses"), and the *Mafātīḥ* were written "as a preparation for his own incomplete mystical and philosophical commentary."[4] This observation is surprising because we know, largely based on the dating provided by Rizvi himself, that these three books were written after Ṣadrā had completed most of his *tafsīr*s.[5] With respect to the *Mutashābihāt* and *Asrār*, there is little in these two texts which would indicate that they were meant to function as preparations for Ṣadrā's *tafsīr*s. But with respect to the *Mafātīḥ*, Rizvi is not far from the mark.

The *Mafātīḥ*, like the *Mutashābihāt* and *Asrar*, was written toward the end of Ṣadrā's career. Unlike these two titles, the *Mafātīḥ*'s most significant discussions vis-à-vis the Qurʾān were originally a part of Ṣadrā's magnum opus, *al-Ḥikma al-mutaʿāliya fī l-asfār al-ʿaqliyya al-arbaʿa* ("The Transcendent Philosophy: On the Four Intellectual Journeys"), commonly known as the *Asfār*.[6] The section in question, namely Miftāḥ 1 of the *Mafātīḥ*'s twenty Miftāḥs or sections, deals with such topics as the nature of revelation and the different levels of the descent of God's Word and its correspondences to the inner layers of man's soul. Since the *Asfār* was written over a twenty-two year period (from roughly 1017/1608 to 1037/1628),[7] it is difficult to determine when the theoretical sections on the Qurʾān (later to be incorporated into Miftāḥ 1 of the *Mafātīḥ*) were written. But we can be sure that these relevant sections were written concurrently with if not before most of Ṣadrā's *tafsīr*s. Miftāḥ 1 of the *Mafātīḥ*, therefore, occupies a special place amongst Ṣadrā's writings on the Qurʾān.

Lord of the Heart

Miftāḥ 1 is complemented by another brief text which is not to be found in the relevant sections of the *Asfār*, namely the introduction to the *Mafātīḥ* itself. Taken together, Miftāḥ 1 and the introduction to the *Mafātīḥ* can, generally speaking, be said to encapsulate Ṣadrā's esoteric hermeneutical vision of the nature of the Qur'ān.[8] I will therefore turn my attention to Ṣadrā's pronouncements in the introduction to the *Mafātīḥ*, which will facilitate my analysis of Miftāḥ 1.

At the beginning of the *Mafātīḥ*, Ṣadrā tells his readers that he had been meaning to write this work for quite some time:

> For some time now I have longed to bring forth the Qur'ān's meanings. [With] my previous reflections I attempted to walk its roads and [by means of] the way stations of the pious explore its paths. In order to attain this goal I would consult my soul [*nafs*], casting aside the arrows of my own opinion.[9]

Ṣadrā says that he was reluctant to carry out this endeavor because of the weight of the task itself.[10] The passage above states explicitly that some preparatory work was required on the part of the author in order to undertake this task. These are the words of someone who had already written eleven independent commentaries upon various chapters and verses of the Qur'ān.[11] Shortly before this, Ṣadrā remarks that the work was written as the result of a spiritual experience which compelled him to bring forth what he knew of the Qur'ānic sciences. That this passage would precede the one cited above, where Ṣadrā expresses his wish to write the *Mafātīḥ*, may come as a surprise. It may come as even more of a surprise given that what follows the introduction, namely Miftāḥ 1, was written before the introduction to the *Mafātīḥ* itself, albeit in a much more condensed version. But the reasons for this are purely stylistic. The following lines are dramatic and compelling; they are written with vigour, a sense of urgency, and in mellifluous Arabic. They are, in effect, Ṣadrā's meditations after-the-fact, summarizing the end of his endeavors which he will go on to explicate in more or less straightforward fashion for the remainder of the introduction:

> A command has issued from the Lord of my heart [*āmir qalbī*], and a spiritual allusion has come forth from my innermost recesses [*waradat ishāra min sirr ghaybī*]. God's

> judgment and decision have come to pass and He has decreed that some of the divine symbols [*al-rumūz al-ilāhiyya*] become manifest, and that the matters related to the Qurʾānic sciences, Prophetic allusions, secrets of faith, flashes of wisdom, esoteric glimmerings connected to the wonders of the glorious revelation, and the subtleties of Qurʾānic interpretation be brought forth.[12]

The wording here is very important. Ṣadrā was commanded by the Lord of his heart to bring forth the "divine symbols," the "matters related to the Qurʾānic sciences," and the "subtleties of Qurʾānic interpretation." As it soon becomes apparent from the contents of Miftāḥ 1, the fulfillment of this command was articulated in discussions dealing with such phenomena as the Qurʾān's use of allusory language and the senses of scripture.

Ṣadrā also notes in the introduction that the *Mafātīḥ* was an inspired work, since it was the result of an "opening" (*fatḥ*):

> The Master of the holy realm of the Divinity [*ṣāḥib quds al-lāhūt*], the Owner of the Kingdom of the Dominion [*mālik mulk al-malakūt*], granted me a new opening [*fatḥ jadīd*], made the sight of my insight piercing with His light, revealing to my heart an opening which drew me near . . . .[13]

Ṣadrā further remarks that this opening granted him new knowledge of the "treasures of the symbols of the divine realities [*kunūz rumūz al-ḥaqāʾiq*],"[14] which, it will be recalled, he was commanded by the Lord of his heart to bring forth. This "opening" may be one reason why Ṣadrā would go on to incorporate the sections of the *Asfār* having to do with the Qurʾān into Miftāḥ 1. Yet this spiritual experience was also accompanied by a great burden of responsibility. Ṣadrā says, "I said [to myself] after this opening within myself [*fatḥ li-nafsī*], 'now is the time to begin mentioning the principles [*uṣūl*] from which the branches [of the Qurʾānic sciences] derive.'"[15] This approach would be characterized by its sapiential perspective and would not delve too deeply into matters pertaining to exoteric exegesis, such as the fine points of Arabic grammar. He notes that excessive concern with language is characteristic of the approach of the exoteric scholars who "have the outward [*ẓāhir*] and the legal aspects [*ḥadd*],[16] whereas we have the inward aspect [*bāṭin*] and the transcendent perspective [*maṭlaʿ*]! It has been said, 'He who comments [upon the Qurʾān] using his own opinion has concealed the truth [*fa-qad kafara*].'"[17] Ṣadrā then provides us with a theoretical definition of *taʾwīl*:

> As for *ta'wīl, it does not spare nor leave anything out* [*lā tubqī wa-lā tadhar*] [Q 74:28],[18] for it comes—thanks be to God!—as a discourse [*kalām*] in which there is no crookedness, nor do doubt or confusion assail it.[19]

Before this definition of *ta'wīl*, Ṣadrā lists some of the spiritual prerequisites which are absolutely necessary in order for one to penetrate the Qur'ān's symbols.[20] The interpreter is expected to do the following:

(1) Have patience and purity

(2) Continuously profess the *shahāda* or statement of God's oneness

(3) Undergo spiritual discipline

(4) Spend time in solitary retreat

(5) Abstain from the sciences and character traits of the common folk

(6) Learn the "science of swimming in the Ocean (*baḥr*)"

(7) Know the "language of the birds" (a reference to Q 27:16 and the allusive language of the Sufis)

(8) Understand the "language of the Dominion" (*malakūt*)

(9) Have access to the secrets of the "realms of the Divinity (*lāhūt*) and Invincibility (*jabarūt*)."

Although he does not elaborate at great length upon these conditions, nor is this exposition systematic, the point that Ṣadrā's wants to make is that without meeting these basic spiritual prerequisites, *ta'wīl* is impossible.

Yet he lays out another "condition" when it comes to interpreting the Qur'ān. He addresses his readers in the following manner:

> O intelligent, discerning one! If you want to investigate the science of the Qur'ān, the wisdom of God and the principles of faith—that is, faith in God, His angels, books, messengers, and the Final Day [cf. Q 4:136]—then you need to return to the guardians [*ḥafaẓa*] of the secrets of the Qur'ān and its meanings, seek out its folk and those who bear it, and ask the "people of remembrance" about its contents. As He—exalted is His name—says, *Ask the people of remembrance if*

> *you do not know* [Q 16:43], just as, with the rest of the arts and sciences, you would seek out their folk.[21]

It is the inner purity of the "people of remembrance" which makes them receptacles for the secrets of the divine book. They have died to themselves and live in God. To this effect, Ṣadrā cites an unnamed sage, and then, in the following order, Plato, Jesus, the Prophet, and ʿAlī. Commenting on ʿAlī's saying, "God loves courage, even if it be in the slaying of a snake," Ṣadrā says:

> There is no snake like your soul, so slay it and purify it of the stain of its false beliefs and ugly opinions; or, subjugate it until it becomes a *muslim* in your hand. First cast it aside like the staff of Moses, then pick it up with your right hand after it has returned to its primordial nature [*sīratihā al-ūlā*, cf. Q 20:21] and original disposition [*fiṭratihā al-aṣliyya*]. It shall then live an intellectual life, striving for the Return [*al-maʿād*] and the final abode [*al-mathwā*].[22]

Ṣadrā then advises those seeking knowledge of the Qurʾān but who do not have access to any of the "people of remembrance":

> O you in pursuit of the Real and the science of the First and the Last! If none of the folk of this kind—whom you can ask concerning the goal of the Qurʾānic sciences—are destined for you, then you should study this book. It contains beneficial principles [*al-qawānīn al-nāfiʿa*] pertaining to the knowledge of revelation, [and] is comprehensive in its foundations which allude to the secrets of *taʾwīl* [*al-muḥīṭ bi-qawāʿidihi mushīra ilā asrār al-taʾwīl*]. . . .[23]

The *Mafātīḥ*, therefore, does not introduce Ṣadrā's individual *tafsīr*s. Rather, it introduces the basic esoteric principles underlying these commentaries themselves. In other words, the *Mafātīḥ*, in keeping with its title, provides the keys which will allow one to access the hermeneutical perspective Ṣadrā adopts in his Qurʾān commentaries. And, more specifically, this perspective is most clearly articulated in Miftāḥ 1.

Although the introduction to the *Mafātīḥ* prepares us to read Miftāḥ 1 of the book's twenty Miftāḥs, we would need to look in every possible corner within the text to see how Ṣadrā's statements in the introduction relate to the remaining Miftāḥs (especially Miftāḥs

3–20). When Ṣadrā deals with, for example, God's attributes much later in the *Mafātīḥ*, we may have some idea of how his introduction can inform such a discussion, namely that the secrets contained within the Qur'ān reveal to the one who looks closely enough—that is, has the ability to "see"—the knowledge appropriate to a true understanding of God's attributes. The first Miftāḥ, on the other hand, follows quite smoothly from the *Mafātīḥ*'s introduction, and the implications of the discussions there are clearly discernable when juxtaposed with the stated intent in the text's introduction. It is, therefore, in the first Miftāḥ's directness that Ṣadrā's theoretical hermeneutics is best displayed. Indeed, most of the other parts of the *Mafātīḥ*, like the *Asrār* and to some extent the *Mutashābihāt*, function as elucidations on the points raised in the *Mafātīḥ*'s first Miftāḥ.

Etiquette and Understanding

I have thus far not discussed Miftāḥ 2 of the *Mafātīḥ*, which ostensibly contains a good deal of material on the Qur'ān. But, upon closer inspection, this part of the *Mafātīḥ* does not help us come away with a clearer picture of Ṣadrā's theoretical scriptural hermeneutics. Rather, it can be said to complement Miftāḥ 1, but even then only in derivative fashion. The first section of Miftāḥ 2 seeks to offer "allusions" (*ishārāt*) to the Qur'ān's "merciful purposes" (*al-aghrāḍ al-raḥmāniyya*) and "divine intentions" (*al-maqāṣid al-ilāhiyya*).[24] We learn here that the Qur'ān is fundamentally concerned with three things: the Origin (*mabda'*), the Return (*ma'ād*), and the path that one must take to his place of Return (*ṭarīq*). Significant for our purposes is the fact that Ṣadrā relates these same three realities to the structure of the *Sūrat al-fātiḥa* itself. This is because, as we will see later in this study, the Fātiḥa has traditionally been regarded as containing or "being" the entire Qur'ān. Despite these parallels, however, this section of Miftāḥ 2 is confined to a general discussion that highlights the major topics dealt with in the Qur'ān: theology, cosmology, psychology, anthropology, law, and eschatology.

A later section of Miftāḥ 2 deals with the use of one's opinion (*ra'y*) in understanding and interpreting the Qur'ān, while another discusses the Qur'ān's "ambiguous" (*mutashābih*) verses.[25] With respect to the former, it seems that Ṣadrā simply wishes to emphasize the fact that the intellectual effort to understand the Qur'ān, as well as the use of unveiling (*kashf*) for those who have access to this mode of knowing, are legitimate means to understanding the Word. As for the latter, nothing significant emerges here which cannot be found in Ṣadrā's other writings, particularly the *Mutashābihāt*.[26]

Certainly the most important aspect of Miftāḥ 2 is a section that outlines what we can call Ṣadrā's "practical" understanding of how to benefit from the Qur'ān. The title of this relevant part of Miftāḥ 2 tells us that the discussion is devoted to simply "alluding to the etiquette" that one must observe when trying to understand the Qur'ān. As Ṣadrā himself says, these guidelines provided here are taken from Ghazālī's famous *Iḥyā' ʿulūm al-dīn* ("The Revival of the Religious Sciences"), and can ultimately be traced back to earlier Sufi sources, particularly the *Qūt al-qulūb* ("The Nourishment for Hearts") by Abū Ṭālib al-Makkī (d. 386/996). Furthermore, it can be noted that the one significant departure from Ghazālī in Ṣadrā's listing is reworked from Ibn ʿArabī's *Futūḥāt*.[27] As given by Ṣadrā, then, these guidelines can be paraphrased in this manner:

(1) Understanding the gravity (*ʿaẓama*) of the Word

(2) Purifying the heart from sins and false beliefs

(3) Having presence of heart (*ḥuḍūr al-qalb*) and abandoning internal chattering (*ḥadīth al-nafs*)

(4) Pondering over (*tadabbur*) what is being recited

(5) Investigating the implications of the meanings of every verse

(6) Ridding oneself of those things which hinder one's understanding of the Word (*mawāniʿ al-fahm*), such as paying excessive attention to the correct written form and oral articulation of the letters of the Qur'ān, blindly adhering to the interpretations of Qur'ānic verses given by the scholars of one's own school of thought, being engulfed (*istighrāq*) in the niceties of the Arabic language, and rejecting those exegetical remarks which do not come solely by way of transmission (*naql*)

(7) Realizing that in every prohibition, command, promise and threat, it is the reader himself who is being addressed

(8) Feeling the impact of the message, which can be realized by making oneself feel insignificant before the

Qur'ān and even physically assuming a posture of meagerness and humility when one reads verses which speak of God's punishments or threats, and expressing joy and happiness when one reads verses where God's promises of forgiveness are mentioned

(9) Ascending (*tarraqī*) in degrees until one hears the recitation of the Word as coming from God, and not the self. There are three levels of "hearing the Word" (*samāʿ al-kalām*). They are, in ascending order, when the servant feels that he is facing God while reciting the Word, which is for the heedless (*ghāfilūn*); when the servant witnesses with his heart that God is addressing him while reading the Qur'ān, which is for the righteous (*ṣāliḥūn*) and appears to be an internalization of rule #7; when the servant sees the Speaker in the Word itself, which is for the those brought near to God (*muqarrabūn*)

(10) Understanding that those verses which condemn the wicked are being addressed to the reciter, but that those verses which praise the righteous do not include the reciter.

As is the case with Ṣadrā's aforementioned spiritual prerequisites for those who wish to do *ta'wīl*, he does not go into detail in his Qur'ānic writings on how these etiquette-related guidelines pertain to his work on *tafsīr* as a whole. In other words, we have no textual evidence to suggest that this was Ṣadrā's preferred method all or most of the time he approached the Qur'ān. Likewise, we cannot say that these guidelines amount in any concrete fashion to a set of rules that Ṣadrā lays down on how to interpret the Qur'ān. All that we can say with respect to these guidelines in Miftāḥ 2 is that they are informal rules of physical and spiritual conduct for those who wish to internalize the teachings of the Qur'ān.

More broadly speaking, we cannot even say that Ṣadrā's *tafsīr* compositions are guided by any kind of formal rules of interpretation, contrary to what some scholars have surmised.[28] As pointed out in the Introduction, each of his *tafsīr* writings is an independent work sufficient unto itself. And, by extension, each *tafsīr* assumes a different exegetical stance vis-à-vis the Qur'ān, as it is ultimately guided by the discussions Ṣadrā wishes to bring to light within the context of the *sūra* in question.

Without Miftāḥ 1, therefore, we are left with very little concrete information on how Ṣadrā actually understands the Qurʾān as such. Thus, for the remainder of this chapter, my discussion will be limited to Miftāḥ 1, except for instances in which relevant texts from Ṣadrā's other writings (such as the *Asrār*) help complete the picture of his scriptural hermeneutics as outlined in Miftāḥ 1. But before turning to Miftāḥ 1, an overview of Ṣadrā's ontology is in order, since its basic principles inform the entire argument of this section of the *Mafātīḥ*. Without taking this preparatory step, it will be difficult to appreciate the text's discussions concerning the intimate relationship shared between the Qurʾān and being. As will be seen shortly, Ṣadrā only makes this connection in relatively vague terms, and this is because he assumes that his readers will be able to relate his theoretical pronouncements on the nature of the Qurʾān to his ontology.

Concept and Reality

Ṣadrā distinguishes between two senses of being (*wujūd*): there is its concept (*mafhūm*), and then there is its reality (*ḥaqīqa*).[29] The reality of being, he says, is completely simple and indefinable, and is the most hidden thing. Following Aristotle's *Topics*,[30] Avicenna explains in his *Kitāb al-ḥudūd* ("The Book of Definitions") that in order for a thing to be defined, it must have a genus (*jins*) and differentia (*faṣl*):

> An essential definition [*ḥadd*][31] is a statement which denotes the quiddity of a thing, namely the perfection of its essential existence, which is what is actualized for it in terms of its proximate genus and its differentia.[32]

What is communicated in an essential definition, that is, when we know a thing's genus and differentia, is the quiddity (*māhiyya*) or the "what-it-is-ness" (that by virtue of which the thing is what it is) of its species.[33] Thus, when we bring together "animal" (genus) and "rational" (differentia), we are given the descriptive expression "rational animal." "Rational animal" conveys to us the quiddity of a particular species, namely "man," which is subsumed under the wider category "animal." By defining the species "man" as a "rational animal," man's quiddity or that by virtue of which man is a man (and not a horse, for example) is conveyed.

Being, however, has neither genus nor differentia, and thus is not susceptible to any form of definition. In other words, it cannot be defined since its quiddity cannot be conveyed.[34] Put differently, the reality of being cannot be got at since there is nothing about being which allows it to be subsumed into any general category (genus), let alone a more particularized category of the genus (differentia). Yet if the reality of being is indefinable and hidden, its essence or *anniyya*,[35] Ṣadrā tells us,

> is the most manifest of things in presence and unveiling,[36] and its quiddity the most hidden of them in conception and comprehension [*taṣawwur wa-iktināh*]. Its concept [*mafhūm*] is, of all things, the least in need of definition[37] and the most general of them in encompassment; its ipseity, in entification [*taʿayyun*] and individuation [*tashakhkhuṣ*],[38] is the most reified of all things that are reified since through it all things that are individuated are individuated, all things that come about come about, and all things that are entified and specified are entified, for it is individuated in its essence and entified in itself.[39]

Describing the reality of being in rhymed form, Sabziwārī famously puts it like this:

> Its concept is one of the most recognizable of things,
> but its reality lies in utter hiddenness.[40]

Being, Ṣadrā tells us, is actually "self-evident" (*badīhī*) in two respects: (1) by virtue of its simple givenness to us, which is tantamount to saying that the very fact or reality of being is itself self-evident;[41] and (2) its notion or concept. Turning our attention to the first of these two, we notice that being is the very ground of our experience of reality, and is therefore the most general and comprehensive of things, since it applies to all things. This explains why any predicate with which we can qualify being is itself subsumed under being. Indeed, Ṣadrā tells us that "it is not possible to perceive being through that which is more evident and more well-known than it."[42] Since being is so all-pervasive, any attempt to define its reality will end up in error, since one can only define being through what is more obscure than it.[43] If, for example, we speak of "horses" or "books," we can only do so with reference to existent entities, that is, entities that participate in some mode of being, even if these entities do not exist extra-mentally. In other words, the being of horses and books is what allows us to talk about them.[44]

Yet being's self-evidentiary nature is, in the final analysis, what veils it from us. It is the most proximate of things to us, and by the same token it is the most distant of them as well. This order of being's self-evidentiary nature is concerned with its reality as it is self-evident by virtue of its very givenness, although it cannot be defined because of its fundamental hiddenness, which obtains because of its all-pervasiveness and manifestness.

With respect to the other sense in which being is self-evident, namely its concept, we can make concrete judgments about its structure. As a concept, in other words, being is not entirely hidden from us. When, for example, we are presented with the statement, "This is a horse," the notion "horse"—which is an existent in one form or another—immediately occurs to the mind. This understanding of being is what Izutsu refers to as the "preconceptual" notion of being,[45] since it forms the basis through which we understand the world. In a sense, the preconceptual notion of being resembles the reality or givenness of being, although, as we have just seen, the givenness of being refers to the very fact of its apparentness in its hiddenness and its hiddenness in its apparentness. The preconceptual understanding of being, insofar as individual existents are conceived by the mind, is simply a preparatory stage in which the concept of being is self-evident to the mind based on the apprehension of a term or concept, such as "horse." The concept of being, on the other hand, again mediated by a concept such as "horse," is what Izutsu refers to as a "secondary elaboration" of the conceived object, which is to say that the image is "a step removed from the concrete and intimate kind of presence in the consciousness"[46] afforded to the mind by the self-evidentiary nature of being through the concept encountered by the mind.

Izutsu's distinction between the preconceptual notion of being and the concept of being does not, technically speaking, affect one important point: the concept of being, however conceived, is intimately linked to the existence of quiddities.[47] Thus, however we conceive of being, when we attempt to understand it conceptually, we must posit a quiddity, since being as the most self-evident concept can only be known through particular quiddities.[48] These quiddities "emerge" by virtue of being's gradational nature as particularizations, or what are known as specifications (*takhaṣṣuṣāt*),[49] individuations (*tashakhkhuṣāt*),[50] and modes (*anḥāʾ*) of being.[51]

Hence the reality of being is unknown, although its concept is self-evident. In other words, the self-evidentiary nature of the concept of being is itself a given. Applied to things, which is that to which the concept of being must necessarily attach, the only way being can be conceptualized is through its quiddity since quiddity is what allows for the "concept" of being to arise in our minds in the first place.

That is to say, the concept of being cannot arise out of a vacuum, but rather through being itself. If we were to attempt to conceptualize being without particular references, we would be inquiring into the reality of being, to which we have no access. The reality of being, therefore, is indefinable and inaccessible, although its concept—which is signalled in the first instance by quiddities—can be accessed and, from this perspective, "defined."

The Command's Descent

Early on in Miftāḥ 1, Ṣadrā employs several images to convey the significance of the Qur'ān. Some key points are made here which, when read in the context of Ṣadrā's treatment of the modes of descent of the Word, allow us to walk away with a clearer picture of his understanding of the nature of the Qur'ān. Alluding to an observation made in his introduction to the *Mafātīḥ*, Ṣadrā tells his readers that the Qur'ān, by its very nature, is meant to make human beings ascend. He notes that each of the Qur'ān's letters contains a thousand allusions and symbols, which is a fairly common trope in Sufi Qur'ānic exegesis. Ṣadrā likens the Qur'ān's letters to hunting nets which are outspread with meanings in order to capture the birds that are in the sky. The image used here, which Ṣadrā draws on in at least one of his *tafsīrs*,[52] is quite telling. Every bird (i.e., "human soul") finds its "sustenance" (*rizq*) in the Qur'ān, but very few of them will be captured by the Qur'ān's hunting nets. Most birds are contented with taking what little sustenance they need in order to get by, like those human beings who read the Qur'ān only to obtain particular types of knowledge, such as legal injunctions. These forms of knowledge, if followed, will grant human beings salvation.[53] But there are other birds who seek a different kind of sustenance from the Qur'ān. They hover over the Qur'ān's hunting nets, seeking their nourishment from the Qur'ān's letters and sounds since they contain the meanings of God's Word.[54] Since their sustenance in the deepest sense is contained in the Word itself and not just in its surface meanings, they immerse themselves within the Qur'ān's universe and become its "prisoners." These prisoners of the Qur'ān cannot but be captured by the Qur'ān's hunting nets, seeing as it is that they expend all their efforts grappling with its nets, but which, in the end, must necessarily overpower them.

In three instances the Qur'ān refers to itself as being or containing a "cure" (*shifā'*),[55] and the Prophet is reported to have said that "the Qur'ān is the cure."[56] We are thus not surprised to find references to the "hospital of the Qur᾿ān" (*shifā᾿-khāna-yi Qur᾿ān*) in Sufi literature.[57] Souls will naturally gravitate toward the Qur᾿ān since, as Ṣadrā remarks, it contains the cure to the greatest sickness which plagues the human condition, namely ignorance (*jahl*).[58] Hence, the deeper one is immersed in the Qur᾿ān, the more entangled he finds himself in its hunting nets, and the less ignorant he becomes. It is with this consideration in mind that we should read an important statement about the Qur᾿ān in one of Ṣadrā's early *tafsīr* compositions. Here, he employs several other images to convey the book's depth and significance. We find that ignorance, identified with blindness, is what keeps human beings fettered from attaining true life:

> Every one of its chapters is an ocean saturated with gems of meaning and exposition; rather, it is a celestial sphere filled with the stars of divine realities and essences. . . . The verses are shining stars which adorn and illuminate the heaven of guidance, prophecy, and sanctity [*walāya*], because of whose flashes and illuminations man and jinn attain unto *the last configuration* [*al-nash᾿at al-ukhrā*][59] [Q 53:47] and the abode of life, being freed from the darkness of blindness and deprivation, the punishments of the grave, and the fires of Hell.[60]

We have already seen how Ṣadrā refers to the Word of God as that by virtue of which man "ascends." By extension (and paradoxically), the less immersed/imprisoned one is in the Qur᾿ān, the more pinned down one is by other than it, which is tantamount to darkness, blindness, and ignorance. But what exactly is this book that contains the cure for the illnesses of man's existential condition and allows him to ascend? Drawing on another image, Ṣadrā alludes to the Qur᾿ān's nature by referring to it as a "rope" that descends from Heaven in order to save all those trapped in what Corbin would call the "cosmic crypt"[61]:

> The Qur᾿ān is God's firm rope [*ḥabl Allāh al-matīn*][62] which was sent down from Heaven in order to save those shackled in the cradle of satans and the abyss of those who have descended. It is one of God's lights [*nūr min anwār Allāh*]: it contains guidance for wayfarers, and through it one can ascend from the lowest of worlds to the highest way stations [*manāzil*] of the ʿIlliyyīn[63] and the most exalted levels of those seated upon *the seat of truth* [Q 54:55] and certainty. So read it, O impoverished one, and advance![64]

It is significant that Ṣadrā refers to the Qur'ān in the above-cited text from the *Mafātīḥ* as "one of God's lights." This reference, as we will see later in this study, is all the more important because of the emphasis placed in the *Tafsīr Sūrat al-fātiḥa* on the nature of light and its identity with God's Essence. In the present context, it is worth noting that Ṣadrā does not provide us with a clear-cut definition of the nature of the Qur'ān. All we have to work with are several stock images, and in each case Ṣadrā employs them, his intention is to convey the salvific role of the Qur'ān and not its nature as such. The reason he does not attempt to provide a definition of the sacred book for us seems to be because he wants to identify the Qur'ān with being. Although Muḥsin Bīdārfar[65] and Latimah Peerwani[66] insist that Ṣadrā does this explicitly, there is not one clear-cut text in his oeuvre which makes this point.

Yet Bīdārfar and Peerwani are not mistaken in their insistence on Ṣadrā's identification of the Qur'ān with being from one perspective, even if he does not explicitly make this connection. There is one text in Miftāḥ 1 in particular that provides us with a key piece to the puzzle. In the passage in question, Ṣadrā notes that the Qur'ān is one in its reality, but multiple in its levels of descent:

> Although the Qur'ān is one reality, it has many levels in its descent [*nuzūl*][67] and many names[68] in accordance with these levels. So in every world and configuration it is called by a name which corresponds to its specific station and particular rank.[69]

As was seen above, Ṣadrā's fundamental ontological stance is that there is one underlying reality, namely being, which in and of itself is indefinable. Yet we know of being through its many instantiations, all of which help define it in some limited fashion. The Qur'ān, likewise, cannot be defined, which is why Ṣadrā does not provide us with a definition of it, and limits himself to allusions of its true nature by employing symbolic imagery. Yet how is the Qur'ān one in its reality and multiple in its instantiations? The missing ingredient here, and which is essential to a proper understanding of Ṣadrā's Qur'ānic hermeneutics, lies in the function of God's Word.

Because the Qur'ān is God's Word, it is not to be identified with being as such. As we will see in Chapters 4 and 6 of this study respectively, being can, strictly speaking, only be identified with God's Essence (*dhāt*) and mercy (*raḥma*). The primary reason being cannot be identified with the Qur'ān is because the Qur'ān, by virtue of being God's Word, is itself an instantiation of being. That is to say, as soon as there is "movement" within being as such, it will necessarily be delimited and hence "defined" in some sense. On the other hand, Ṣadrā also insists that God's Word is to be identified with the divine Command *"Be!"* (Q 2:117):

> The Word is the High Spirit which is said not to fall under the shade of *"Be!"* because it is the same as the word *"Be!,"* which itself is the same as the Command, for *"Be!"* is God's Command [*amr*] through which things are existentiated.[70] There is no doubt about the fact that the Word [*qawl wa-kalām*] of the Real is above engendered things [*akwān*] and higher than them, since through God's Word, actuality [*fiʿl*], effectuation [*taʾthīr*],[71] and engendering [*takwīn*] occur. So how can God's Word fall under engendered existence [*kawn*]? He says, *God's Word—it is the highest* [Q 9:40].[72]

When God wills for His Word to emerge from its primordial silence and state of latency within the Essence, the Command sends out reverberations, which make up the "stuff" of the cosmos.[73] Yet the Word or Command[74] is "above" existent things, which allows us to understand why, in one sense, we can identify the Qurʾān—God's Word—with being. Since God's Word (*kalām*) is the first movement of being, that is, the first instance in which being makes itself known, it too is, in a sense, hidden and yet completely manifest. This explains why the cosmos only comes about through the Word and can be identified with it.[75]

Employing the language of theoretical Sufism, Ṣadrā identifies the cosmos with the articulation of the Breath of the All-Merciful (*nafas al-raḥmān*), a term based on a *ḥadīth*[76] and made popular by Ibn ʿArabī.[77] Ṣadrā identifies the Breath of the All-Merciful with expansive being (*al-wujūd al-munbasiṭ*) and the Real through whom creation takes places (*al-ḥaqq al-makhlūq bihi*).[78] Following Ibn ʿArabī, he likens this Breath to human breath. Just as human breath gives rise to articulated forms through the act of speaking, so too do the various levels of being take on concretized form within God's Breath, that is, through His act of speaking.[79] In other words, just as the forms of words become articulated in human breath (this being nothing other than the outward manifestation of an inward form), so too do the things which are formed within the divine Breath take on corporeal form through God's act of existentiation, effectively bringing the latent possibilities contained within God's "mind"[80] from potentiality into actuality.[81] God's Self-knowledge is thus made manifest (*iẓhār*)[82] through His Breath, bringing it from the Unseen to the seen until the Command is uttered.[83]

God's Command itself, however, has levels. For if this were not the case, then all of His Commands would have the same ontological status, which would mean that His Word would ontologically be on the same level as, for example, His creatures, who are lesser manifestations of the Word or Command. Strictly speaking, the Word consists of three levels: the highest, the mid-most, and the lowest.[84] God's Word at the highest level is referred to by Ṣadrā, following the wording of a well-known Prophetic supplication, as the Perfect Words (*al-kalimāt al-tāmmāt*):

> The highest level of the Word is the Word itself in terms of its principial purpose [*maqṣūd awwalī*], there being no other purpose beyond it because of the nobility of its existence, the perfection of its being, and because of its being the final goal [*ghāya*] of whatever is beneath it.[85] This is like God's originating the World of the Command through the Command *"Be!,"* and nothing else. These are God's Perfect Words [*al-kalimāt al-tāmmāt*] which are never exhausted, nor do they perish.[86]

Ṣadrā goes on to tell us that the highest form of the Word corresponds to the Originating Command (i.e., the world of the Decree, *qaḍā'*); the mid-most to the engendering Command (i.e., the world of temporal measuring out, *qadar*); and the lowest to the prescriptive Command.[87] The engendering Command must be obeyed, whereas obedience to the prescriptive Command is entirely man's choice. The engendering Command must be obeyed since human beings do not have a say in whether or not they will come to exist. The prescriptive Command, on the other hand, corresponds to God's rules as laid out in the religious law.[88]

The originating Command, being ontologically higher than both the engendering and prescriptive Commands, is of a completely different order. The intellective and disembodied forms of being which emerge from the Command are known as God's "Words." As intermediaries between God and His creatures, the function of these Words of God is to carry out His will in the created order.[89] Just as human commands—which proceed from human volition—come about through the function of our words, so too do the Perfect Words proceed from

God's Command.[90] And, just as the individual letters that make up the words of a human command arise spontaneously—that is, not gradationally—our words carry out our commands in a manner that is more primary than the actual objects of our commands. Likewise, God's Words embody His Command and are thus complete and perfect, since they come about as a direct result of the originating Command. That which is the object of the Command, namely the things in the cosmos (all of which come into being by virtue of the Command "Be!"), are thus weaker in being and less potent in effects than the Perfect Words themselves. Since these words are "Perfect," they inform the less perfect words, which are nothing but the shadows of the Perfect Words.[91]

God's Word is therefore the mode in which He reveals His will to the cosmos. His Word is the "stuff" of the cosmos since the cosmic order is nothing but the articulated form of the originating Command "Be!," which means that all the beings in the cosmos are simply instantiations of the Perfect Words which themselves are the primary instantiations of the originating Command. The highest level of God's Word, that is, His most principial Command which is identified with the Qurʾān, is therefore the prototype of being.[92] As the scroll of being, the Qurʾān's verses are everywhere, since they are entities of being which are to be found in the parchment of the cosmic order:

> Just as when the Command becomes an act, as in His saying *"Be!," and it is* [Q 2:117], when the Word becomes individuated [*tashakhkhaṣa*] and descends, it becomes a book.[93] The scroll [*ṣaḥīfa*] of the being of the created world is the book of God [*kitāb Allāh*], and its signs [*āyāt*] are the entities of the existent things [*aʿyān al-mawjūdāt*]: *In the alternation of night and day, and in what God created in the heavens and on earth, are signs for a people who are God-wary* [Q 10:6].[94]

The fact that the Qurʾān is the prototype of being explains why Ṣadrā does not attempt to define the Qurʾān's nature. The Qurʾān is not being as such, since, as the Word, it emerges through a delimitation of being. But, since it is the first delimitation of being, the Word of God cannot properly be encompassed.[95] It is, as the highest of the Perfect Words, the most inaccessible of them as well. Like the Intellect in Neoplatonism which contains all the archetypal forms and thus "is" the forms, so too can we say that the Qurʾān contains all of being and "is" being.

The Soul's Ascent

In his *tafsīrs*, Ṣadrā occasionally alludes to the correspondences which exist between the Qur'ān and man. He tells us, for example, that all of the Qur'ān's verses are "hidden shells containing valuable and precious pearls, every one of which corresponds to the soul of man."[96] As is the case with his other theoretical discussions concerning the Qur'ān, Ṣadrā's most important treatment of the correspondences shared between the Qur'ān and man is to be found in Miftāḥ 1 of the *Mafātīḥ*. In one key passage, he addresses a version of the famous Sufi doctrine of the Qur'ān's senses:

> Know that the Qur'ān, like man, is divided into a manifest [*ʿalan*] and hidden dimension [*sirr*], each of which has an outer [*ẓahr*] and inner [*baṭn*] aspect. Its inner aspect has another inner aspect known only to God: *and none knows its interpretation but God* [Q 3:7].[97] It has also been related in the *ḥadīth*, "The Qur'ān has an outer and inner aspect." Its inner aspect consists of up to seven inner dimensions [*abṭun*] which are like the levels of man's inner dimensions, such as the soul [*nafs*], heart [*qalb*], intellect [*ʿaql*], spirit [*rūḥ*], innermost mystery [*sirr*], and the hidden and most hidden [*al-khafī wa-l-akhfā'*].[98]

Although the above-cited text occurs quite late in Miftāḥ 1 and Ṣadrā does not develop it in any significant fashion, some of the earlier discussions in Miftāḥ 1 shed a good deal of light on his statement concerning the relationship shared between the Qur'ān and man. At the beginning of Miftāḥ 1, Ṣadrā makes the point that outward faculties will only be able to perceive the outward realities of things. The more outward and exoteric one's outlook, the more exoteric his vision of reality. Ṣadrā gives the example of Abū Lahab and Abū Jahl. Both of these individuals were eloquent in Arabic, yet neither of them saw the Qur'ān for what it was.[99] Their inner sight was blinded by the defilement of exterior forms, and hence their hearts were unable to perceive the truth of the Prophet's message.[100] The more one is immersed in outward forms, the less opportunity will he have to purify his inward state. The less purified his inward being, the less will he be able to perceive inward realities.

Yet Ṣadrā clearly does not limit his criticisms of exoteric individuals to the early enemies of Islam. There are many Muslim scholars who, despite their knowledge and formal learning of the Islamic sciences, when it comes to the Qurʾān, do not even "hear" one of its letters as they should be heard, and thus do not truly understand its words.[101] Ṣadrā makes it very clear that, when interpreting the Qurʾān, one cannot depart from conventions of the Arabic language, since this can only lead to mistaken interpretations of scripture.[102] At the same time, there is a difference between remaining faithful to the written Word and being confined by its most outward expressions (one of the *mawāniʿ al-fahm* in the etiquette-related guidelines listed in Miftāḥ 2). In his Persian work *Sih aṣl* ("The Three Principles"), which is anything but mild in its condemnation of the exoteric *ʿulamāʾ*, Ṣadrā makes his point clear:

> That which Zamakhsharī [d. 538/1144] and his likes understand from the Qurʾān is not, in reality, knowledge of the Qurʾān. Rather, it goes back to the sciences of lexicography, grammar, verbal expressions, and dialectical theology [*kalām*]. But knowledge of the Qurʾān is other than these sciences, just as the skin and husk of man is not man in reality, but only metaphorically. This is why, when one of the people of the heart [*aṣḥāb al-qulūb*][103] read [Zamakhsharī's *tafsīr*,] the *Kashshāf* ["The Discloser"], he said to its author, "You are one of the scholars of the husk [*qishr*]."[104]

The famous exegete Zamakhsharī and his likes are on the receiving end of Ṣadrā's criticisms here because they approach the Qurʾān through exoteric lenses, devoting the bulk of their reflections on scripture to issues related to grammar, language, theology, and law. The correspondence between the Qurʾān and man in this text is telling. Ṣadrā likens the outer reality of the Qurʾān to the outer reality of man, just as he likens the inner reality of the Qurʾān to the inner reality of man. The most superficial aspect of scripture is its husk, just as the most superficial aspect of man is his outward form or "skin."

Returning to Miftāḥ 1 of the *Mafātīḥ*, Ṣadrā again draws on the image of husks and outer coverings in discussing the relationship between the Qurʾān and man. This time, however, he juxtaposes the image with the necessary complement to the outward, namely the inward:

> The Qurʾān has degrees and ranks, just as man has levels and stations. The lowest level of the Qurʾān is like the lowest level of man:[105] the Qurʾān's lowest level is what is contained in the book's binding and covering [*jild wa-aghlāf*], just as the lowest rank of man is what is in the outer covering and

> skin [*al-ihāb wa-l-bashara*]. The husk of man attains nothing but the blackness of the Qurʾān and its sensory form. The man of the outward husk only perceives husk-like meanings [*al-maʿānī al-qishriyya*]. As for the spirit of the Qurʾān, its kernel [*lubb*],[106] and its secret, none but *the possessors of deep understanding* [12:111] [*ūlū-l-albāb*][107] perceive it. They do not attain this through knowledge acquired by way of learning and thinking. Rather, [they attain this] through God-given [*ladunī*] knowledge.[108]

In Ṣadrā's standard philosophical language, since being is a dynamic principle, the cosmic order is simply the flow of being through its self-individuation. Thus, being takes on different modes in accordance with the levels of intensity (*shidda*) and diminution (*ḍuʿf*) which it assumes through its self-concretization, meaning the more intense it is on its own scale of devolution the more of its true nature it manifests (and less of quiddity, which is "unreal"), while the less intense it is on its own scale of devolution the less of its true nature it manifests (and more of quiddity, which obscures being's reality accordingly).

As we saw earlier in this chapter, since the Qurʾān can in one sense be identified with being, like being it is both one and multi-leveled. Thus, the more one penetrates the Word of God, the closer one moves toward the undifferentiated aspect of being and hence the closer one moves toward unity. Since the Qurʾān's levels correspond to the levels of being, and Ṣadrā notes that the levels of man correspond to the levels of the Qurʾān, the more man penetrates being, the more "real" he becomes and the more he understands of the Qurʾān. Put differently, we can say that the more he understands the Qurʾān, the more intensely he "is."

In order to penetrate the Qurʾān's deepest levels man must therefore penetrate his own deepest levels. This can only be done when he engages in a *taʾwīl* of his soul, that is, when he causes his soul to return to its true Origin. The Origin is undifferentiated, which explains why, as Corbin suggests, *taʾwīl* is a metahistorical "event."[109] A return to one's Origin necessitates the crushing of the ego, at which time the self leaves the self and transcends time, space, and "history." Thus, the more one dies to the self, the deeper one becomes immersed in his true Self. The deeper one becomes immersed in his true Self, the deeper will he be able to penetrate being on the one hand, and the Qurʾān—the prototype of being—on the other.

Penetrating the veils of being is, as Ṣadrā notes elsewhere, akin to self-knowledge, which itself is tantamount to "being" and "presence."[110]

Another way of conceiving of self-knowledge is to say that it is akin to having knowledge of the heart.[111] To proceed from the husk of the Qur'ān to its kernel, one must be able to proceed from the husk of his own existence to its kernel, which is the heart. This heart-knowledge is tantamount to what Ṣadrā referred to in the last passage as "God-given knowledge." This type of knowledge allows one to read both the book of the soul and the book of God.[112] And since the human soul and the Qur'ān share such an intimate relationship, a completely refined soul shares an affinity with the Qur'ān in a principial manner.

As we have already seen, the Qur'ān is, as the Word of God, the first instantiation of the Command "Be!" In its originary unity, the Qur'ān contains the forms of all things within it, and is, from this perspective, akin to being. The individual words contained in the Qur'ān appear in the written text of the Qur'ān as collective words, just as all the existents in the cosmos are comprised of composite parts. But in the realm of the unseen, in the most unmanifest aspect of being, these collective words of the Qur'ān subsist on their own as individual letters.[113] The detached letters (*al-ḥurūf al-muqaṭṭaʿa*) in the Qur'ān, therefore, indicate something of the primordial nature of being, that is, before the full deployment of the Word. Indeed, for Ṣadrā, the detached letters are not only limited to the mysterious letter combinations at the beginning of some Qur'ānic *sūra*s.[114] Rather, they make up the entirety of the Qur'ān.

Ṣadrā's thinking here is clearly influenced by the famous Sufi martyr ʿAyn al-Quḍāt Hamadānī (d. 525/1131). In one key passage, which is reworked from ʿAyn al-Quḍāt's *Nāmahā* ("The Epistles"), Ṣadrā explains that the reason people do not see all the letters of the Qur'ān as detached is because they are too tied down to the husk of the book, which is another way of saying that they are confined to the husks of their own beings:

> Because the people of this world are in the station where forms are gathered and meanings separated [*al-jamʿiyya al-ṣūriyya wa-l-tafarruqāt al-maʿnawiyya*], they witness various letters as unified and letters which are of one species as numerous individual parts. Thus, when they look at the letters *He loves them, and they love Him* [*yuḥibbuhum wa-yuḥibbūnahu*] [Q 5:54], they see them as a unified species which is divided in its parts. However, those who have divested themselves of this world—for whom the veil has been lifted and the clouds of doubt and blindness have dispersed from the surface of their insight—[they] see

> these letters through inner sight in this way: *H-e-l-o-v-e-s-t-h-e-m* [*yāʾ-ḥāʾ-bāʾ-hāʾ-mīm*]. Then, when they ascend from this station to a higher station, they see them as tiny dots [*niqāṭ*].[115]

The higher one ascends the scale of being, the closer he ascends to the undifferentiated nature of being. Since the original Command was one Word, namely "Be!," the gnostic (*ʿārif*) is able to see the vast panorama of existence in its full potentiality, thus grasping the nature of things as so many individually differentiated species. At the furthest reaches of being, which is to say at the deepest level of the penetration of the Qurʾān and the human soul, the gnostic sees all things in existence as so many tiny traces of the divine Command.

2

Formal Considerations

In the previous chapter I outlined Mullā Ṣadrā's Qur'ānic hermeneutics in terms of theory. For the remainder of this book, I will closely examine how his hermeneutics relates to his work on the Qur'ān in terms of practice. The following chapters will therefore be concerned with Ṣadrā's last complete *tafsīr* composition, the *Tafsīr Sūrat al-fātiḥa*. But before determining the extent to which Ṣadrā's theoretical scriptural hermeneutics informs this *tafsīr*, some preliminary considerations are in order with respect to this work's sources and content. Thus, this chapter will address the following questions: (1) what are the sources for Ṣadrā's *Tafsīr Sūrat al-fātiḥa*?, and (2) how is the work ordered, and what are its contents?

The reason our first encounter with the *Tafsīr Sūrat al-fātiḥa* must entail a discussion of its sources is quite pragmatic: this text is a late work of Ṣadrā's and is a fine presentation of both the theoretical and practical dimensions of his teachings with reference to scripture. Since Ṣadrā was not writing or thinking out of a vacuum, we must be able to take account of those materials, figures, and ideas which make the text what it is. Failure to acknowledge the historical and intellectual background of the ideas in the *Tafsīr Sūrat al-fātiḥa* will impede us from understanding the influence exercised by the cumulative weight of the Islamic intellectual tradition upon Ṣadrā's thought. By extension, we will not be able to properly determine just what it is that Ṣadrā is doing that is so "unique" in this *tafsīr* at such a late stage in Islamic intellectual history.

Outlining the structure and content of the *Tafsīr Sūrat al-fātiḥa* is just as important as determining the work's sources. What the text is about and how its contents are ordered can tell us a great deal about Ṣadrā's practical hermeneutics. Like his philosophical treatises, he argues for similar points in this work, but within the context of a commentary upon the Qur'ān. Thus, the way arguments are formed, ordered, and delivered in this *tafsīr* gives us a good indication of how Ṣadrā situates his arguments within the context of the Qur'ān's universe of discourse and its interpretive traditions. Furthermore, since I will be closely examining Ṣadrā's most salient teachings in the *Tafsīr Sūrat al-fātiḥa* in the following chapters, outlining the work's content here will allow its less important, but by no means insignificant, features to emerge.

Texts and Sources

Those who are familiar with Ṣadrā's writings know that, in many ways, they can function as a resource for developments in the history of Islamic philosophy.[1] At the same time, engaging Ṣadrā's work gives one a sense of the grandeur of his historical range, synthetic abilities, and analytical mind. As Ibrahim Kalin describes it, "To read Ṣadrā is to read the history of how persisting philosophical problems can be re-discussed, restated, and reformulated in new contexts."[2] The task of determining the texts which Ṣadrā draws upon in his writings is therefore not an easy one. Ṣadrā at times incorporates expanded versions of discussions from his earlier writings into later works. And there is always the possibility, as we have already seen with respect to the *Mafātīḥ*, that some of his books contain reworked versions of texts written by other authors.[3]

In almost all of his writings, when Ṣadrā explicitly cites an authority belonging to the Islamic intellectual tradition, he often refers to him with such generic titles as "the realized gnostic" (*al-ʿārif al-muḥaqqiq*) or "the lordly knower" (*al-ʿālim al-rabbānī*). At other times, he will tell his readers the name of the book he is about to cite (as well as the chapter number, in some instances), but this does not necessarily make locating that particular passage any easier. With respect to Ṣadrā's *tafsīr*s in general, we are fortunate in that their editor, Muḥammad Khwājawī, has been able to identify many of their sources. Simple perusal through the notes to any of these *tafsīr*s will serve to indicate the vast range of materials drawn upon in each *tafsīr* text. But concrete judgments concerning Ṣadrā's sources for his *tafsīr*s cannot solely rely on Khwājawī's notes. With respect to the *Tafsīr Sūrat al-fātiḥa*, after subjecting it to very close textual scrutiny, a number of important points emerge which are not indicated in the editor's notes.

Qur᾽ān and Ḥadīth

Qur᾽ānic Verses

In the *Tafsīr Sūrat al-fātiḥa* we naturally find many citations from the Qur᾽ān. Out of the work's 182 pages, there are some 335 citations from or allusions to the Qur᾽ān, most of which Khwājawī identifies. So infused is Ṣadrā's worldview with the Qur᾽ān that he will seamlessly weave into the fabric of any given argument a number of Qur᾽ānic verses. It can also be noted that since the Qur᾽ān was second nature to Ṣadrā, in this work he at times inadvertently cites the Qur᾽ān incorrectly, or modifies its wording so that he can make his point within a particular context.[4] Apart from the verses of the Fātiḥa itself, Ṣadrā's most significant use of the Qur᾽ān in this *tafsīr* work occurs in the context of his treatment of God's mercy, to which I will turn in Chapter 7.

Shīʿī and Sunnī Ḥadīth

Just as Ṣadrā was the philosopher most concerned with the Qur᾽ān, so too was he the philosopher most concerned with Ḥadīth. For one thing, he left behind an incomplete philosophical commentary on al-Kulaynī's (d. 329/940-1) famous book of Shīʿī traditions, the *Kitāb al-kāfī* ("The Principles"),[5] and is known to have written several discrete commentaries on various other important Ḥadīths.[6] Ṣadrā's concern with "scripture" is, therefore, not only limited to the Qur᾽ān. To be sure, based on what we know of Ṣadrā's education, his interest in scripture is something which occupied him from early on in his life.[7]

As is the case with his other *tafsīr* works,[8] in the *Tafsīr Sūrat al-fātiḥa* Ṣadrā demonstrates a wide-ranging knowledge of Ḥadīth. He cites or alludes to some ninety-four traditions in total. Of these ninety-four traditions, twenty are of the "sacred" or *qudsī* type, that is, where God speaks on the tongue of the Prophet.[9] Of the twenty *ḥadīth qudsī*s cited, I have been unable to trace three of them.[10] The remaining seventeen are found in Sunnī and Shīʿī Ḥadīth literature, with eleven of them going to back to Sunnī sources,[11] one to a Shīʿī source,[12] and five to both Sunnī and Shīʿī sources.[13]

"Ḥadīth" in a Twelver Shīʿī context includes the sayings of the Prophet or *nabawī* traditions, and the sayings of Fāṭima (d. ca. 11/633) and the twelve Imams, or *walawī* traditions.[14] Yet Ṣadrā's usage of traditions in the *Tafsīr Sūrat al-fātiḥa* is not distinctively Shīʿī. Of the seventy-four non-*qudsī* traditions cited or alluded to, only three of them are sayings of the Imams,[15] all of which are to be found in Shīʿī sources. Of these seventy-four sayings, fifty-two go back to Sunnī sources,[16] nine to Shīʿī sources,[17] seven to both Sunnī and Shīʿī sources,[18] and six remain untraceable.[19]

Eleven of the fifty-two traditions from Sunnī sources which appear in this work come from the writings of the Sunnī authors whom Ṣadrā cites, namely Ghazālī, Rāzī, Ibn ʿArabī, and Ṣadr al-Dīn Qūnawī (d. 673/1274). Yet there are forty-one other traditions from Sunnī sources which Ṣadrā draws on, and does not seem to have a problem in doing so. Despite the astounding number of traditions from Sunnī sources which figure in the text, it does not seem that this alone calls Ṣadrā's Shīʿism into question, particularly if we take the following points into consideration: (1) after writing his *tafsīr*s, Ṣadrā would go on to pen the aforementioned incomplete commentary on Kulaynī's *Kāfī*; (2) the few times the names of the Imams, Shīʿī scholars, or books within the Shīʿī tradition are mentioned in the text, they are done so reverentially;[20] and (3) in one of his appendices to the *Tafsīr Sūrat al-fātiḥa*, he offers a novel Shīʿī reading of the Qurʾān's detached letters, taking them to spell the phrase, "ʿAlī is the path of truth to which we cling [*ʿAlī ṣirāṭ ḥaqq numsikuhu*]."[21]

What the absence of a heavy Shīʿī substrate to the *Tafsīr Sūrat al-fātiḥa* (and almost every other work in *tafsīr* by Ṣadrā) seems to indicate is that he was less concerned with reconciling his mysticism and philosophy with traditional Shīʿī dogma than he was with explicating his vision of reality, which could be done independent of particularly Shīʿī teachings. Indeed, it is for similar reasons that Hermann Landolt calls into question the specifically Shīʿī nature of Ṣadrā's thought in general.[22]

Philosophical and Theological Materials

Ṣadrā's Other Works

In the previous chapter it was argued that the *Mafātīḥ*, a very late work, occupies a special role amongst Ṣadrā's Qurʾānic writings as it lays out the esoteric perspective which informs his Qurʾān commentaries. It was also shown that, since the *Mafātīḥ* had its roots in an earlier text which was written concurrently with at least some of Ṣadrā's Qurʾān commentaries, the perspective argued for in the *Mafātīḥ* is certainly not an afterthought. With the advantage of hindsight, this perspective is fully explained and its implications entirely drawn out.

The question that remains is this: does the *Mafātīḥ* inform Ṣadrā's later works on the Qurʾān, and, if so, in what manner?

Turning to the *Tafsīr Sūrat al-fātiḥa*, we notice that, in the context of his treatment of such topics as the "Perfect Words," Ṣadrā explicitly refers to the *Mafātīḥ* five times.[23] The fact that the *Tafsīr Sūrat al-fātiḥa* mentions the *Mafātīḥ* several times allows us to perhaps safely conclude that it was written some time after the *Mafātīḥ*. This would explain why the *Tafsīr Sūrat al-fātiḥa* has a dimension of depth not to be found in Ṣadrā's other *tafsīrs*. From this perspective, we could say that Ṣadrā's primary source of inspiration for the *Tafsīr Sūrat al-fātiḥa* was his own *Mafātīḥ*.

With respect to his other writings, Ṣadrā refers to four titles in the *Tafsīr Sūrat al-fātiḥa*: *al-Shawāhid al-rubūbiyya* ("The Lordly Witnesses"),[24] the *Asfār*,[25] *al-Risāla fī l-ḥudūth al-ʿālam* ("Treatise on the World's Temporal Origination"),[26] and his glosses (*ḥāshiya*) on Ṭūsī's *Tajrīd al-iʿtiqād* ("An Exposition of Doctrine").[27] None of these well-known texts figure in this *tafsīr* in a significant manner, although, as will be made clear throughout the course of this study, there are instances in which Ṣadrā incorporates sections of his earlier writings into his commentary.

Avicenna and Suhrawardī

Although Ṣadrā discusses Rāzī's philosophical insights as they figure within the context of his *al-Tafsīr al-kabīr*, the only philosophical work to be explicitly cited by Ṣadrā in the *Tafsīr Sūrat al-fātiḥa* is by Avicenna.[28] In the context of his treatment of the different levels of certainty, Ṣadrā cites Avicenna twice,[29] both times from the ninth *namaṭ* or class (entitled *fī maqāmāt al-ʿārifīn*, "On the Stations of the Gnostics") of the section devoted to metaphysics in Avicenna's famous *al-Ishārāt wa-l-tanbīhāt* ("Remarks and Admonitions").[30] It is perhaps significant that Ṣadrā would cite this part of Avicenna's work, which belongs to a larger section (*namaṭ*s eight to ten) simply called "On Sufism" (*fī l-taṣawwuf*),[31] since Ṣadrā is known to have been critical of Avicenna for his lack of "spirituality."[32]

Ṣadrā says that through invocation and increased knowledge of and proximity to God, one will eventually become one of the "people of witnessing" (*ahl al-mushāhada*).[33] A common notion in Sufi literature is that what is actually witnessed cannot be spoken of or described, and thus only allusions (*ishārāt*) are possible. The apophasis invoked by Ṣadrā is linked with one of Avicenna's statements concerning the fruits of the spiritual life in which he says that this station cannot be described by ordinary language. Thus, although Ṣadrā makes use of a well-known philosophical work, he draws on its more "mystical" aspect in order to bolster an argument which is decidedly Sufi.

Suhrawardī does not explicitly figure in Ṣadrā's *Tafsīr Sūrat al-fātiḥa,* although he seems to identify him with the Stoics in one passage.[34] In what can be called an aside to his commentary upon the Fātiḥa (we will return to it later in this chapter), Ṣadrā responds to the view (known to have been defended by Suhrawardī) that being is merely a "rational construct" (*iʿtibār ʿaqlī*) by which being—not corresponding to anything in concreto because it is a secondary intelligible (*maʿqūl thānī*)—is grafted by the mind onto quiddities.[35]

Yet the most significant allusion to Suhrawardī is Ṣadrā's passing reference to one of the Illuminationist tradition's well-known technical terms, "lords of species" (*arbāb al-anwāʿ*).[36] Coined by Suhrawardī,[37] the term is equivalent to the Platonic Forms (*muthul*), which Ṣadrā prefers to use, not least for the reason that the Platonic Forms figure differently in Suhrawardī than they do in Ṣadrā.[38] Ṣadrā for his part does not dedicate a discussion to the Platonic Forms in this *tafsīr* work, nor are his references to the "lords of species" anything more than passing.

Schools of Kalām

Apart from a brief section dedicated to explaining and then refuting Jabirite and Qadirite positions on the formula (based on Q 16:98), "I seek refuge in God from Satan the accursed" (commonly referred to as the *istiʿādha*), Ṣadrā does not engage the views of any theological groups in the *Tafsīr Sūrat al-fātiḥa*.[39] He does, however, mention the Muʿtazilites' position concerning the "fixity" of quiddity, that is, that quiddities have the status of quiddities before their effectuation.[40] Zamakhsharī does appear in this *tafsīr* work, although his positions are not discussed qua Muʿtazilite thinker. Rather, Ṣadrā deals with him qua Qurʾān commentator.[41]

Other than Zamakhsharī, the only Muʿtazilite we directly encounter[42] in the *Tafsīr Sūrat al-fātiḥa* is the famous early figure Abū ʿAlī al-Jubbāʾī (d. 303/915), whose interpretations of the words "day of judgment" (*yawm al-dīn*) are given in the context of Ṣadrā's treatment of Q 1:4.[43] Jubbāʾī interprets the phrase to mean "the day of being rewarded for one's observance of the religion [*yawm al-jazāʾ ʿalā l-dīn*]."[44] There is nothing particularly Muʿtazilite about this interpretation, although one may speculate that Jubbāʾī's exegesis was carried out with two of the five fundamental Muʿtazilī principles in mind, namely God's justice (*ʿadāla*/*ʿadl*) and "the promise and the threat" (*al-waʿd wa-l-waʿīd*).

Sufi Texts and Authors

Ibn ʿArabī

Ṣadrā explicitly cites Ibn ʿArabī five times throughout the work,[45] reworks or cites texts from the *Futūḥāt*—without acknowledging their source—another four times,[46] paraphrases an author who cites Ibn ʿArabī's *Futūḥāt* once,[47] and refers to Ibn ʿArabī in passing once.[48] The texts from Ibn ʿArabī which Ṣadrā draws upon in the *Tafsīr Sūrat al-fātiḥa* range from his famous catch phrase, "he who does not have unveiling does not have knowledge,"[49] to more substantial materials with an eye to proving a particular point, such as the fact that God is the true object of worship in every act of worship.[50]

The most important issue that Ṣadrā addresses with recourse to Ibn ʿArabī's teachings is the question of God's mercy and its relationship to His wrath. Here, Ṣadrā is particularly concerned with the age-old theological problem of the existence of eternal suffering for finite actions, and how this is to be reconciled with the existence of a God who is purely merciful on the one hand, and who is unaffected by the wrong actions of His creatures on the other.

Turning our attention to the *Asfār*, we notice that he treats the problem of eternal suffering, but with an eye on resolving contradictory scriptural passages and with explicit recourse to the writings of Ibn ʿArabī and Dāwūd al-Qayṣarī (d. 751/1350). The section which corresponds to the question of eternal suffering in the *Asfār* is partly reproduced in the relevant section of the *Tafsīr Sūrat al-fātiḥa*. However, not only is the question of conflicting scriptural statements removed in the latter, but Ṣadrā cites some of the same texts from Ibn ʿArabī that he used in the *Asfār*. The only difference here is that these words reappear not as Ibn ʿArabī's, but as Ṣadrā's.[51]

The "School" of Ibn ʿArabī

There is no doubt that Qūnawī and his followers played a very important role in spreading the teachings of Ibn ʿArabī.[52] However, they tended to emphasize issues which may not have occupied a central role in Ibn ʿArabī's writings, or at least were not given systematic philosophical expression by him. Indeed, it is with Qūnawī that the rapprochement between the scripture-based language of Ibn ʿArabī's worldview and the technical discourse of Peripatetic Islamic philosophy begins to take place. From this perspective, it may even be more fitting to speak of the "school of Qūnawī" rather than the school of Ibn ʿArabī. Whatever term we give to the "school" which helped spread Ibn ʿArabī's ideas in Iran, Central Asia, Anatolia, and South Asia from the seventh/thirteenth century onward, one thing remains certain with respect to Mullā Ṣadrā: he found in the writings of Qūnawī and his followers a highly developed technical vocabulary which could suit his purposes in articulating his profound philosophical and mystical vision.[53]

There are three instances in which Ṣadrā cites an anonymous person(s) belonging to the school of Ibn ʿArabī, introducing him as "one of the people of God,"[54] "one of the unitarian gnostics" (*al-ʿurafāʾ al-muwaḥḥidīn*),[55] and "one of the verifiers" (*al-muḥaqqiqīn*).[56] Given the fact that the technical terminology of the citations clearly belongs to the developed form of theoretical Sufism, it is safe to say that these anonymous references belong to a member or members of the school of Ibn ʿArabī.

The only explicit reference we find in the *Tafsīr Sūrat al-fātiḥa* to a follower of Ibn ʿArabī is a short passage which cites Fakhr al-Dīn ʿIrāqī's (d. 688/1289) highly influential Persian work, the *Lamaʿāt* ("Divine Flashes"). The passage occurs in the context of Ṣadrā's treatment of the function of God's mercy on the Final Day. After citing an important passage from Ibn ʿArabī's *Futūḥāt*, Ṣadrā recounts an incident related by ʿIrāqī in the *Lamaʿāt* concerning Ibn ʿArabī's reply to a question posed by the early Sufi figure Abū Yazīd Basṭāmī (d. ca. 260/874) (for which see below).

The only other follower of Ibn ʿArabī who definitely figures in Ṣadrā's *Tafsīr Sūrat al-fātiḥa* is Qūnawī. Apart from an anonymous passage cited from Qūnawī's own commentary upon the Fātiḥa (Ṣadrā refers to him as "one of the gnostics"[57]), Ṣadrā draws on the same work toward the end of the text. Here, however, he offers a reworking of sections of the book, and incorporates them into his discussion concerning the levels of God's wrath.[58] Close comparison between the relevant part of Qūnawī's work with its corresponding section in the *Tafsīr Sūrat al-fātiḥa* reveals that Ṣadrā was able to recast Qūnawī's words in a manner not unlike his much more significant reworking of Bābā Afḍal's *Jāwidān-nāma* into his *Iksīr al-ʿārifīn*.[59]

Basṭāmī, Anṣārī, Ghazālī

Mullā Ṣadrā's thorough knowledge of the Sufi tradition did not stop with the writings of Ibn ʿArabī and his followers. As Carl Ernst has shown through his statistical analysis of the names of figures which appear in the *Asfār*, Ṣadrā was thoroughly familiar with the earlier tradition of Sufism as well.[60] This is also clearly evidenced in his commentary upon the famous Light Verse (Q 24:35), where a number of important early Sufi figures are cited, either explicitly or implicitly.[61]

Turning to the *Tafsīr Sūrat al-fātiḥa*, we find Ṣadrā drawing on the famous *shaṭḥ* or "ecstatic utterance" by Basṭāmī in which he says that even if God's Throne and all that it contains were to enter a corner of the gnostic's heart a thousand times, it would be unable to fill it.[62] This saying is cited some ten pages after the aforementioned incident related by ʿIrāqī, which runs as follows: upon hearing Q 19:85, "The day We muster the God-wary to the All-Merciful in droves," Basṭāmī let out a cry and asked how God will bring to Him those that are already with Him. Ibn ʿArabī responds to Basṭāmī's question with reference to the divine names, saying that those who are with Him will be taken "From the name 'the Compeller' to the name 'The All-Merciful,' and from the name 'the Overbearing' to [the name] 'the Compassionate.'"[63]

In another passage, Ṣadrā introduces an Arabic saying by the famous Ḥanbalī Sufi ʿAbd Allāh Anṣārī (d. 481/1089), referring to him with the honorific of the Sufi master Junayd (d. 297/910), namely "master of the tribe" (*shaykh al-ṭāʾifa*). Anṣarī is cited as saying that the different faces of God vis-à-vis mercy and wrath are actually a manifestation of mercy.[64]

We also find a reference in this *tafsīr* to "the books of the people of the heart."[65] Although this may be an allusion to the work of Ghazālī,[66] explicit references to Ghazālī total two. Ṣadrā demonstrates his familiarity with his *Munqidh* early on in the *tafsīr*, linking Ghazālī's observations concerning his pursuit of knowledge with his own point that the one who wishes to know the Qurʾān's meanings has to undergo very rigorous training.[67] Another instance in which Ghazālī figures in this text is through a citation from Rāzī's *tafsīr*, which cites Ghazālī's explanation of the different levels of the invocation, "There is no god but God."[68]

Ṣadrā's most extensive use of Ghazālī is to be found in his treatment of blessings (*niʿma*), which is prompted by the first part of Q 1:7. After a discussion concerning the nature of the Perfect Man (*al-insān al-kāmil*), the flow of Ṣadrā's *tafsīr* abruptly changes. Readers familiar with the eloquent prose and taxonomic approach of Ghazālī's *Iḥyāʾ* would immediately recognize the change in style. As Khwājawī rightly notes, the entire section is nothing more than a reworking of a section from book thirty-two of Ghazālī's *Iḥyāʾ*, the *Kitāb al-ṣabr wa-l-shukr* ("The Book of Patience and Gratitude").[69] Ṣadrā may have borrowed this section from the *Iḥyāʾ* because of the clarity with which Ghazālī treats the topic of blessings.

Shīʿī and Sunnī *Tafsīr*

Exegetical Notes within the Tafsīr Tradition

One of the most impressive features of Ṣadrā's work as a commentator on the Qurʾān is his clear mastery of both Shīʿī and Sunnī *tafsīr* literature. As we saw in the last chapter, Ṣadrā has some very harsh things to say about the exoteric Qurʾānic exegetes, whom he accuses of wasting their time in trivial details of lexicography and the like. Yet their contributions are nonetheless important, and Ṣadrā is fully aware of this. His engagement with questions in *tafsīr* seems to give his criticisms all the more credibility, since he is not simply rejecting something with which he is unfamiliar or ignorant. Ṣadrā wants his readers to know that he is well-versed in the *tafsīr* sciences, and that he is not satisfied with the enterprise as it is generally pursued in the books of scholars.

As a lead-in to further study, exoteric *tafsīr* is helpful, but it cannot give one access to truth. This is why Ṣadrā, for all his knowledge of *tafsīr* literature, devotes comparatively little space to it in his *tafsīr*s. He will often begin a discussion on a verse with the relevant exegetical remarks within the tradition. Once he has displayed his erudition and familiarity with the opinions of a number of scholars of *tafsīr*, he will then proceed to comment upon the Qurʾān in his usual philosophical and mystical manner.

In the *Tafsīr Sūrat al-fātiḥa*, Ṣadrā cites a number of various exegetical remarks which are often common to both the Shīʿī and Sunnī traditions. In this work we encounter a host of short interpretations on such topics as why the Fātiḥa is called "doubled" (*mathānī*);[70] the different but equal readings of the prayer to be found in Q 1:2 ("Praise is for God, Lord of the worlds"), which is known as the *ḥamdala*;[71] various positions on how one should read and understand the term *mālik* in Q 1:4;[72] different interpretations of the term *ṣirāṭ* found in Q 1:7;[73] and the views of the Qurʾānic exegetes on the identity of the *maghḍūb* and *ḍāllīn* mentioned in Q 1:7.[74] We also encounter a number of figures found variously within the genre of *tafsīr* literature: ʿAlī,[75] ʿĀṣim (d. 128/745), Kisāʾī (d. 89/805),[76] Ibn Kathīr (d. 120/737)[77] (not to be confused with the exegete who died in 774/1373), Ibn Masʿūd (d. 31/652),[78] Abū Ḥanīfa (d. 150/767), Ibn ʿAbbās (d. ca. 68/688),[79] ʿUmar b. al-Khaṭṭāb (d. 23/644), Ibn al-Zubayr (d. 73/692),[80] Ḥasan al-Baṣrī (d. 110/728), and ʿAbd al-Qāhir al-Baghdādī (d. 429/1037).[81]

ʿAyyāshī, Qummī, Ṭabrisī

Just as the Ḥadīth sources employed by Ṣadrā in the *Tafsīr Sūrat al-fātiḥa* are predominantly Sunnī, so too are his references from *tafsīr* literature. We only encounter two explicit and minor references to the famous Shīʿī Qurʾān commentator Muḥammad b. Masʿūd al-ʿAyyāshī (d. 320/932), who, according to Meir Bar-Asher's periodization of early Imāmī *tafsīr*, belongs to the pre-Buwayhid (r. 334/945 to 447/1055) school of Twelver Shīʿī scriptural exegesis.[82] Ṣadrā cites a *ḥadīth* from ʿAyyāshī's *tafsīr* in his treatment of the merits of the Fātiḥa, explicitly providing his name.[83] In the case of al-Ṭabrisī (d. 548/1154), a post-Buwayhid Shīʿī exegete,[84] he simply refers to a reading of the first part of Q 1:7 as having derived from the *Majmaʿ al-bayān* ("The Junction of Exposition"),[85] a reference familiar to any reader of Ṣadrā's *tafsīr*.[86] As for al-Qummī (d. 317/919), another important pre-Buwayhid Imāmī exegete, Ṣadrā does not mention his name, although Khwājawī traces one of Ṣadrā's grammatical discussions centered around the first part of Q 1:7 back to both Qummī and Ṭabrisī's *tafsīrs*.[87]

Zamakhsharī, Rāzī, Bayḍāwī, Nasafī, Nīsābūrī

In the *Tafsīr Sūrat al-fātiḥa*, Ṣadrā refers to Zamakhsharī on four occasions, two of which are rather insignificant.[88] One of the two significant references to Zamakhsharī is an allusion to his view—with which Ṣadrā takes issue—that God's ascribing mercy to Himself is simply a metaphor for His blessings to His servants.[89] Elsewhere, in a passage in which Ṣadrā offers his advice to those seeking knowledge of the Qurʾānic sciences, he refers to Zamakhsharī by name and is somewhat favorable. He notes that those who wish to know the specifics of the detailed discussions concerning the placement of letters in the *basmala* (the opening line of the Fātiḥa, "In the Name of God, the All-Merciful, the Compassionate"), should read Zamakhsharī's famous *tafsīr* work, since they will find such information there.[90] Although Ṣadrā goes on to praise the book for its unsurpassed linguistic analysis, it is clear from what follows that the linguistic sciences, like the other sciences not rooted in unveiling, are ultimately based on personal opinion and therefore fall short of the goal.[91]

The Ashʿarite theologian ʿAbd Allāh b. ʿUmar al-Bayḍāwī (d. ca. 685/1286) appears three times in the *Tafsīr Sūrat al-fātiḥa*. These appearances are all significant for one reason or another. In one passage, Ṣadrā seems to paraphrase a small portion of Bayḍāwī's commentary on the Fātiḥa in his *Anwār al-tanzīl* ("The Lights of Revelation"), but does not state that he is doing so.[92] In another passage, Ṣadrā prefaces his significant discussion concerning the Perfect Man and his relationship to the Qurʾān with a citation from the *Anwār*. In this citation, Bayḍāwī displays his philosophical know-how in explaining the meaning of the term *ʿālamīn* to be found in Q 1:2.[93] Ṣadrā then voices his disagreement with another one of Bayḍāwī's interpretations of Q 1:2 in which he argues that the verse indicates that all things are ordered and depend upon God.[94]

The *Madārik al-tanzīl* ("Understanding Revelation"), written by another Sunnī theologian, ʿAbd Allāh b. Aḥmad al-Nasafī (d. 710/1310), also figures in Ṣadrā's *Tafsīr Sūrat al-fātiḥa*. Because Nasafī for the most part presents a condensed version of Bayḍāwī's *Anwār*, it is difficult to determine whether or not Ṣadrā draws on the *Madārik* directly. But, since Ṣadrā is known to have had a copy of the first quarter of this text[95] and some of the specifically grammatical discussions are reminiscent of the style of Nasafī's *tafsīr*,[96] we cannot rule out the possibility that the *Madārik* in some manner or another figures in the *Tafsīr Sūrat al-fātiḥa*.

The most important exegetical source for the *Tafsīr Sūrat al-fātiḥa* is Rāzī's *tafsīr*, which Ṣadrā draws upon on four occasions. The first instance in which we encounter Rāzī is in Ṣadrā's treatment of the aforementioned formula standard to Islamic praxis known as the *istiʿādha*, where he relies heavily on the corresponding (but much longer and detailed) section in Rāzī's *tafsīr*.[97] Later in the text, Ṣadrā discusses how calling on God's names can also pose limitations upon the servant. One important passage here is a slightly reworded reproduction of Rāzī's arguments from his *tafsīr*.[98]

Another instance in which Rāzī appears in the *Tafsīr Sūrat al-fātiḥa* is in an albeit minor final appendix to the work, which, by Ṣadrā's own estimation, was meant to be a supplement to the text.[99] Ṣadrā says that this appendix is derived from the *tafsīr*s of Rāzī and Niẓām al-Dīn Nīsābūrī (d. 730/1329), who closely follows Rāzī's *tafsīr* in many places. Upon closer inspection, however, it turns out that all of the passages are actually from Rāzī's *tafsīr*.[100]

Rāzī also makes an appearance in this *tafsīr* work in the context of Ṣadrā's treatment of the levels of *dhikr*.[101] Ṣadrā cites Rāzī's meditation upon Ghazālī's explanation of the phrase, "There is no he but He" (*lā huwa illā huwa*). Ghazālī states that these words correspond to the station of the most elect of the elect (*akhaṣṣ al-khawāṣṣ*), and Rāzī says that he affirmed this point through scripture and demonstrative proof (*burhān*). Rāzī argues that the statement "There is no he but He" proves that God's effectuation (*taʾthīr*) does not take place by giving quiddities the quality of being, for if quiddities were given the quality of being, being, as a predicable quality, would itself require a quiddity.[102] Rather, God's effectuation is nothing more than the effectuation of quiddities, which are nothing before their instantiation, just as being is "nothing" before God gives it effectuation. One of the implications of this position is that essence precedes existence, and this gives Ṣadrā occasion to step in and defend his position on the fundamentality of being. The ensuing discussion does not directly pertain to the *Tafsīr Sūrat al-fātiḥa,* and functions as more of an excursus than a part of the commentary proper. Indeed, Ṣadrā makes it clear that the section in question is derived from some of his other works.[103]

Other Materials

Anecdotes, Maxims, Poems

Several anecdotes[104] and two maxims[105] are to be found in the *Tafsīr Sūrat al-fātiḥa,* most of which do not have any particular significance to the development of the work's main ideas. One anecdote which plays a somewhat important role in the *tafsīr* is taken from Ibn Hishām's (d. ca. 213/828 or 218/833) famous biography of the Prophet, in which ʿAbd Allāh Ibn al-Zabʿarī al-Sahmī raises an objection before the Prophet upon hearing Q 21:67. Ṣadrā uses this incident to explain how objects of worship other than God to which people may incline are themselves one of the "acts of Satan," and should thus be avoided.[106] He then contrasts people who incline to the acts of Satan with the perfect gnostics, who worship God without any delimitations of His reality.[107]

The only other significant anecdote in the *Tafsīr Sūrat al-fātiḥa* occurs shortly after the Ibn al-Zabʿarī narration, in which Ṣadrā explains the Prophet's method for elucidating the path of truth and the path of falsehood.[108] This is an important piece of information as it appears in Ṣadrā's text, since he gives it an interpretation to which many would object, tying it in as he does to the ultimate salvation of all human beings.[109]

It is well-known that Ṣadrā composed poems in Persian, and several of his books include citations from such important Persian Sufi poets as ʿAṭṭār (d. 618/1221) and Rūmī (d. 672/1273).[110] In some of his writings, Ṣadrā also displays his knowledge of Arabic poetry, and even tries his hand at composing his own verses. With respect to Ṣadrā's *Tafsīr Sūrat al-fātiḥa,* fourteen Arabic couplets appear in the text, twelve of which are anonymous citations of earlier materials.[111] Of these twelve anonymous couplets, two of them are important for Ṣadrā's understanding of the relationship between the Qurʾān, the cosmos, and the Perfect Man.[112] In two cases, Ṣadrā identifies the poet whose words he cites. The first of them is Labīd (d. ca. 41/661), one of the seven authors of the so-called "Suspended Odes" (*al-muʿallaqāt*) of pre-Islamic times.[113] The second is al-Maḥallī, a poet of the Banī Salūl tribe.[114]

The most significant couplet in the text, by an anonymous Arab bard, is slightly but significantly reworked by Ṣadrā from a longer poem to be found in a work by the famous geographer Yāqūt al-Ḥamawī (d. 626/1229).[115] It is a terse couplet that has to do with the different positions "the people of caprice" (*ahl al-hawāʾ*) take with respect to God, and how Ṣadrā does not fall into such traps because he has a single position in which he alone dwells.[116] The insertion of these verses occurs at a crucial moment in the text, where Ṣadrā distinguishes between the different types of knowers of the Qurʾān.

Structure and Content

A Note on Method

Mullā Ṣadrā is generally not always as systematic a writer in his *tafsīr*s as he is in his strictly philosophical writings. To be sure, there are plenty of instances in his *tafsīr*s where he digresses from the topic at hand. Such digressions may at times lead one to assume that the work in question lacks thematic unity.[117] What augments the difficulty in reading Ṣadrā's *tafsīr*s in general is the lack of helpful indicators of where the respective discussion is heading. The generic subheadings in these works may mislead one into thinking that the point under discussion is crucial to the text, which is often not the case.[118]

In my attempt to explicate the structure and content of Ṣadrā's *Tafsīr Sūrat al-fātiḥa,* I have not simply provided a diagram or description of the work's structure and then followed it up with a discussion of the content in each of its sections. Apart from being somewhat prolix, such an approach would present us with the same kind of confusion a reader of the original is bound to encounter when first reading the text, as it would not give us an adequate idea of how the work coheres as a whole. My approach, therefore, is to provide, as concisely as possible, an outline of the work's basic architecture alongside a summary of its contents.[119]

Tafsīr Sūrat al-Fātiḥa

Mullā Ṣadrā's *Tafsīr Sūrat al-fātiḥa* is 183 pages long. It consists of an introduction, eight parts or chapters with various subdivisions, and three appendices. Of the book's eight parts and three appendices, Ṣadrā only gives titles to parts one, six, and the first two appendices.

I have included these below, and have given my own titles to the text's unnamed sections. For reasons that will be made clear shortly, Ṣadrā devotes the bulk of his attention to verses one, two, six, and seven of the Fātiḥa.

***

Introduction
(*Tafsīr*, 1:1–3)

The introduction begins with a listing of several names traditionally associated with the Fātiḥa, and briefly discusses the question of whether or not it consists of six or seven verses. Ṣadrā announces in the introduction that the time has come to reveal the Qurʾān's meanings. He goes on to single out the Fātiḥa as the most special ray of God's lights, noting that it brings together the secrets of the Origin and the Return.

*

I seek refuge in God from Satan the accursed
Part 1: Seeking Refuge
(*Tafsīr*, 1:4–28)

This part of the work deals with the *istiʿādha,* which is normally recited before reading the Qurʾān but is not a part of it. Ṣadrā notes that his goal in this unexpectedly long section is to explain the *istiʿādha*'s intellectual meaning as opposed to its verbal meaning. To accomplish his goal, Ṣadrā discusses the different aspects of seeking refuge, which range from the one seeking refuge to why one seeks refuge. Taken together, Ṣadrā's treatment of the *istiʿādha* can be said to explore the theme of the reality of evil and man's weakness before it. Because man is so weak, he is constantly in need of God's help and mercy, the physical manifestation of which is voiced in the *istiʿādha*.

What emerges from Ṣadrā's explanations is significant to the development of the entire work. Several important points are made here concerning the function of the Perfect Words in the cosmos. The sections on cosmology in this section of the book, therefore, shed a great deal of light on the development of Ṣadrā's theoretical and practical hermeneutics.

An important digression in this part of the text, in part following Rāzī, is the brief discussion Ṣadrā devotes to the arguments of the Jabirites and the Qadirites concerning the efficacy of seeking refuge through the *istiʿādha* formula. Ṣadrā states that neither side will arrive at the correct answer unless God protects them and teaches them directly from Himself, which is precisely the message he would like to drive home: it is only with God's assistance that one can receive guidance, and hence the importance of the *istiʿādha* in eliciting divine aid.

*

In the Name of God, the All-Merciful, the Compassionate (Q 1:1)

Part 2: The Name and the Named

(*Tafsīr*, 1:29–72)

This section contains a full engagement with the philosophical and mystical implications of the divine name Allah, and a standard meditation on God's names the All-Merciful (*al-raḥmān*) and the Compassionate (*al-raḥīm*), noting, for example, that the former takes precedence over the latter (which will have important implications for what Ṣadrā will say later on).

After discussing the different types of approaches to scripture (i.e., outward and inward), Ṣadrā contrasts those people who are bound to particular fixed categories of interpretation and cannot go beyond them (i.e., exoteric scholars) with those who are not bound by any particular opinion, and who therefore get to the heart of the Qurʾān (i.e., the esoteric scholars). He ties this discussion into the point he is trying to make: just as there are different views of God, so too will there necessarily be different approaches to His Word.

Ṣadrā goes on to discuss how the name Allah is the first manifestation of multiplicity, acts as an isthmus (*barzakh*) between the Presence of Unity and the loci of the Command and creation, and unites all the contradictory divine names. We are then given a fairly standard explication of how multiplicity comes about in the cosmos by virtue of the different ruling properties of the divine names.

Ṣadrā's discussion of the divine names and the inaccessibility of God's Essence allow him to introduce two important themes: the gods of belief, and why only the Perfect Man worships God as God. These points are then linked with the author's treatment of the invocation/remembrance (*dhikr*) of God. We learn that the highest form of *dhikr* is invocation of the name "He" (*huwa*), which denotes the Essence Itself. One can only arrive at this practice after having realized that invocation of God's other names, such as the All-Merciful and the Gentle, lead us to particular aspects of His reality, the invocation of which ultimately entail limitations. This section leads Ṣadrā to respond to Rāzī's explanation of the invocation "There is no he but He," which then segues into an excursus in which Ṣadrā offers a condensed presentation, based on his other writings, of his position concerning the fundamentality of being and the non-reality of quiddities.

Ṣadrā ends this section with several comments upon the divine names the All-Merciful and the Compassionate. After discussing the fact that mercy really only comes from God and refuting Zamakhsharī's view that the ascription of mercy to Him is purely metaphorical, Ṣadrā introduces this book's most important ideas: the fundamentality of God's mercy, the accidental nature of His wrath, and how all human beings will ultimately end up in felicity.

*

Praise is for God (Q 1:2)

Part 3 (a): The Act of Praise

(*Tafsīr*, 1:73–78)

Ṣadrā begins this section by discussing the relationship between praise (*ḥamd*) and gratitude (*shukr*). Praise for God, we are told, is actually a type of speech, and is thus an "act." Since God's act is nothing but existentiation, being, insofar as it is "separate" from God, is an act of praise for Him. Thus, everything praises God, which means that each thing is both an act of praise and that which praises. The highest level of praise is the level of the Muhammadan Seal, which Ṣadrā connects here with the famous tradition in which the Prophet says that he will be given the "banner of praise" (*liwāʾ al-ḥamd*) on the Final Day.

*

Lord of the worlds (Q 1:2)

Part 3 (b): The Great Book and the Small Book

(*Tafsīr*, 1:78–82)

The discussion of the levels of praise, taken together with what Ṣadrā said earlier in Part 2 concerning the Perfect Man, informs what he says in this section. Here, Ṣadrā speaks of the correspondence between the macrocosm and the microcosm—the great book and the small book—which is prompted by his meditations on the second part of Q 1:2. It is in the context of Ṣadrā's treatment of the words *rabb al-ʿālamīn* that he refutes Bayḍāwī's interpretation of this verse, loosely tying it into his famous doctrines of substantial motion and the gradation of being.

*

The All-Merciful, the Compassionate (Q 1:3)

Part 4: Repetition of the *Basmala*

(*Tafsīr*, 1:82)

Since Ṣadrā dealt with the implications of the divine names the All-Merciful and the Compassionate in Part 1, this section is very short. He simply states that the occurrence of this verse here could be rhetorical and for purposes of confirming what came before it (i.e., Q 1.1). Or, it could be there to stress the *ḥamd* and *shukr* mentioned in the previous verse, which emphasize God's divinity (*ulūhiyya*) and man's servanthood (*ʿubūdiyya*).

*

Master of the Day of Judgment (Q 1:4)

Part 5: The Specification of Praise

(*Tafsīr*, 1:83–6)

Here, Ṣadrā discusses some of the grammatical and lexical usages of the term *mālik* or master. He then briefly relates how the verse in question conveys the principles of spontaneous, temporal origination and the gradation of being. Ṣadrā eventually goes on to explain how, in the next world, God's control of things will be made crystal clear because things will then exist in their full potentiality. Since a thing's existing in full potentiality necessitates that there be no receptacle for the locus of God's control, the actualized thing will itself become a self-evident manifestation of God's exclusive effective power.

The most important discussion in this part of the *tafsīr* is Ṣadrā's treatment of the modes in which *ḥamd* becomes specified in the cosmos as mediated by God's merciful qualities (recall that in Part 2 Ṣadrā says that *ḥamd* is both an act of praise and the act of existentiation—thus we see why mercy is identified with being and vice versa). This pivotal section not only elucidates what Ṣadrā says in Part 2, but it informs the most important discussions that come up throughout the remainder of the text.

*

You alone do we worship, and from You alone do we seek aid (1:5)

Part 6: The Precedence of Worship over Seeking Help

(*Tafsīr*, 1:87–97)

Just as Ṣadrā linked the function of *ḥamd* to his cosmology in the previous section, so too does he link *ḥamd* to worship in this section, although his treatment of the question here is quite circumspect. This is because Ṣadrā's main concern in this part of the *tafsīr* is to explain why the wording in Q 1:5 puts worship (*ʿibāda*) before seeking divine aid (*istiʿāna*). In other words, why does the verse teach people to say "You alone do we worship" before saying "from You alone do we seek help"? Ṣadrā offers several explanations for why the words "You alone do we worship" come first: they (1) are a way of admonishing the worshipper not to have self-interest in his devotions, (2) emphasize God's lordship and thus strengthen the servant's servanthood, (3) help avoid Satan's insinuations, and (4) allow one to realize his servanthood, which then leads to asking the Master for help. Furthermore, the precedence of "You alone do we worship" over "from You alone do we seek help" is similar to the Islamic testimony of faith, which puts servanthood over messengerhood, that is, it puts that which is lasting over that which is not, since servanthood does not end with the cessation of the world, whereas messengerhood does.

*

Guide us upon the straight path (Q 1:6)
Part 7: The Straight Path
(*Tafsīr*, 1:98–123)

In this part of the text, Ṣadrā offers several interpretations of the expression "the straight path" (*al-ṣirāṭ al-mustaqīm*). We are told, for example, that it can be the Qurʾān, Islam, God's religion, or the Prophet and the Imams. Ṣadrā's preferred understanding of the *ṣirāṭ*, which he states in the *Asfār* as well, is that it is made of the stuff of the soul itself.

Ṣadrā makes it clear that everyone is on a "path" to God, which is their straight path as determined by their primordial dispositions and modes of descent. Here, he anticipates several objections to this point. These objections have to do with why wrongdoers are punished if they are doing nothing but following their "path" (i.e., their natures); why the world should be created when all things eventually return to God; and why differences in peoples' primordial dispositions exist, and how these disparities do not compromise God's justice. Ṣadrā's responses to these objections lead him to the observation that although people are all on a straight path with respect to their essential natures (which he calls essential motion), they also have the ability to choose (which he calls volitional motion). Volitional motion allows people to freely choose their destinies within the confines of the possibilities presented to them by their essential natures.

*

The path of those whom You have blessed (Q 1:7)
Part 8 (a): The Nature of Blessings
(*Tafsīr*, 1:124–41)

Since a good portion of this part of the work is a reworking of a section of book thirty-two of Ghazālī's *Iḥyāʾ*, it is one of the least important in terms of the main ideas addressed by Ṣadrā throughout the text. The gist of the reworked section from the *Iḥyāʾ* is that true blessings have to do with felicity in the next world, although we can speak of blessings in this world as well. When Ṣadrā departs from paraphrasing Ghazālī, we learn that blessings are to be found everywhere, and that the entire universe is actually a theatre for God's blessings, all of which work in harmony with one another.

*

Not of those who incur wrath, nor of those who stray (Q 1:7)
Part 8 (b): God's Mercy and Wrath
(*Tafsīr*, 1:142–62)

Despite the fact that Ṣadrā reworks here passages from Qūnawī's *ʿIjāz* concerning the different levels and functions of God's wrath, the reworked passages from Ibn ʿArabī's *Futūḥāt* play a much more significant role. Situating the Qurʾānic image of God's "two hands" within the framework of a cosmology largely borrowed from Ibn ʿArabī, Ṣadrā demonstrates how God's mercy will triumph over His wrath for all creatures in the end. He also elucidates the manner in which the cosmos is pure beauty (again reworking a passage from Ibn ʿArabī's *Futūḥāt*), and describes how, as a mirror for the divine, the cosmos relates to the function of *ḥamd*. In a sense, this last section ties together many of the points Ṣadrā makes throughout the *Tafsīr Sūrat al-fātiḥa*.

*

Part 9 (a): On the Merits of the Fatiha I
(*Tafsīr*, 1:163–71)

Ṣadrā notes that he decided to include this section as a way of supplementing the points made in the *tafsīr* proper. This appendix draws links between the correspondences between the Qurʾān and the cosmos on the one hand, and the Fātiḥa and the Qurʾān on the other. Of course, the Perfect Man is equivalent to the Fātiḥa, as he is a transcription of the cosmos/Qurʾān, and this is a point that Ṣadrā is particularly interested in conveying here. Because the Fātiḥa contains everything, Ṣadrā says that the realized gnostics find in it what is contained in the entire Qurʾān. By extension, the Fātiḥa contains all that one needs to know about eschatology. Another theme covered in this appendix is the structural and doctrinal similarities shared between the Fātiḥa and the last two verses of the *Sūrat al-baqara*, which are traditionally known as the "closing verses" (*khawātīm*).

Part 9 (b): On the Merits of the Fatiha II
(*Tafsīr*, 1:172–3)

This brief section by and large charts what can be called the "inner itinerary" of man: as he recites the verses of the Fātiḥa, each verse corresponds to an aspect of his increasing psychological awareness of his existential situation. This is not unrelated to another discussion in this section in which Ṣadrā links the structure of the Fātiḥa to the circle of life: verses two to four deal with the Origin, five to six with the present world, and seven with the Return.

Part 9 (c): On the Merits of the Fatiha III
(*Tafsīr*, 1:174–83)

This book's final appendix is a collection of some of Rāzī's comments on the merits and structure of the Fātiḥa. Ṣadrā provides four discussions from Rāzī's *tafsīr* as a way of supplementing the book and listing more of the Fātiḥa's merits. Rāzī observes the importance of the number seven: there are seven verses of the Fātiḥa, seven sensory actions of the ritual prayer, seven levels of man's creation, and seven levels of the substance of his soul. He also discusses the symbolism of the ritual prayer's gestures, and explains how the *basmala* contains all that is needed to repel the devil's insinuations.

3

Metaphysics

In the introduction to the *Tafsīr Sūrat al-fātiḥa* Mullā Ṣadrā explains that, amongst the Qur'ān's "lights" (*lum'ān*), the Fātiḥa is particularly special. Despite its concision, it brings together the secrets of the Origin and the Return, as well as the states of people in the afterlife.[1] What is needed in order to understand the Word is submission, an attentive ear, God-wariness, and a pure heart:

> The light of guidance and the life of faith proceed from His lights [*lum'ān*], especially this *sūra* which, despite its concision,[2] contains all of the verses of the Qur'ān and the sum total of the secrets of the Origin, Return, and the states of creatures on the Final Day before the All-Merciful. So listen with the ear of your heart to the recitation of God's verses, and let the lights of the miracle of the Messenger of God penetrate your insides.[3]

Several points emerge from this important passage. Ṣadrā argues that the Fātiḥa contains the entire Qur'ān. A page earlier, we are told that the Fātiḥa is also called the "mother of the Qur'ān" (*umm al-Qur'ān*) because it contains all of the Qur'ān's meanings.[4] Since the Fātiḥa contains the entirety of the Qur'ān's meanings, it naturally brings together all of its inner teachings as well. The Qur'ān repeatedly informs its readers that they came from God and, after a short time of journeying on earth, will return to Him. From this perspective, it would not be an overstatement to say that the fundamental concern of the Qur'ān is the Origin, the Return, and the path to the Return, a point which Ṣadrā himself makes in the *Mafātīḥ*.[5] As soon as we speak of the Origin and the Return, what lies between them a fortiori becomes all the more important, since our actions in this world will determine the route of our return. Thus, Ṣadrā is calling our attention in this introduction to the all-encompassing nature of the Fātiḥa. As the Qur᾿ān's introductory chapter, it in a sense is a foreshadowing of what is to follow.

That Ṣadrā sees in the Fātiḥa the entire enfolding of the human drama is also made clear toward the end of the commentary, where there is an appendix in which he draws several links between the Fātiḥa's verses and their correspondence to the three "days" of man's life, that is, his Origin (Q 1:2-4 = morning), mid-way point (Q 1:5-6 = midday), and Return (Q 1:7 = night). Man's Origin corresponds to God's lordhood (*rubūbiyya*), since it was His will to bring him into existence; his mid-way point to his servanthood (*ʿubūdiyya*), since during his life on earth he should be concerned with worshipping God and purifying himself; and his Return to the science of the soul in the afterlife.[6] Thus, in the Fātiḥa, man has a roadmap which "brings together" all that he needs for his journey.[7]

Because the Fātiḥa is primarily concerned with the Origin and the Return, Ṣadrā spends a good deal of time discussing these two realities. In this and the next chapter, therefore, I will investigate the manner in which Ṣadrā tackles the first of these two topics. It will be shown how he presents us with a well-ordered and tightly argued picture of the nature of God, the manner in which multiplicity proceeds from Him, and the role of man in the cosmic scheme.

As noted in the previous chapter, Ṣadrā will normally discuss the grammar, derivation, and general meanings of certain key words which occur in the Fātiḥa. One would therefore expect him to devote some discussion to the first verse of the *basmala*. Yet in this *tafsīr* work, Ṣadrā pays little attention to the *basmala*. Consequently, we find none of the typical discussions in *tafsīr* literature centered around topics such as the grammatical points concerning the *basmala*,[8] the debate over the legality of reciting it in the ritual prayer (i.e., whether it is mandatory to recite or not),[9] and the question of whether or not it is specific to the Islamic community.[10]

Why Ṣadrā would choose to record the debates and discussions in *tafsīr* literature concerning other verses of the Fātiḥa but not the all-important *basmala* is unclear. What is even more surprising is that he devotes no attention to the Sufi interpretations of the *basmala* formula that we find in the works of such important authors as ʿAbd al-Raḥmān al-Sulamī (d. 412/1021),[11] Rashīd al-Dīn Maybudī (d. after

520/1126),[12] and ʿAbd al-Karīm Jīlī (d. 832/1428).[13] In fact, there is only one passing reference to the *basmala* formula in the entire work, and even this comes from the pen of Rāzī.[14]

Rather than engage any of the long-established exoteric and esoteric approaches to the *basmala* formula, Ṣadrā chooses to get to the heart of the matter, and he does so very quickly. After discussing the different types of knowers of the Qur'ān, he offers a long meditation on the nature of the name (*ism*) Allah. Since Q 1:1: begins "with" or "in" the name of God, the very structure of this verse seems to prompt within Ṣadrā several questions: how can God, who is beyond the reach of creation, also be accessible to creation? After all, it is God who begins with/in His own name, but why does this happen? What is the nature of that name of God with/in which He Himself begins? Questions such as these, although implicit, roam in the background as Ṣadrā introduces his detailed discussion concerning God's reality.

The Essence

In the *Tafsīr Sūrat al-fātiḥa* Ṣadrā says that God's Essence (*dhāt*) is beyond definition, description, name, denotation, and delimitation. In Its pure simplicity and uniqueness, It is only known to Itself, and forever escapes the grasp of the human intellect: "It has neither essential definition [*ḥadd*], nor name [*ism*], nor description [*rasm*], and intellectual perception does not have a way to It."[15] So beyond the grasp of human cognition is the Essence that all we can do is describe It as transcending our perception and understanding. Since it is quite commonplace in Islamic thought to identify God's Essence with Light (*nūr*), we can also say that the Essence is pure Luminosity and, thus, sheer Splendor, Plenitude, Perfection, and Infinity. The Essence therefore is forever out of our reach by virtue of Its own infinity, the measure and incomprehensibility of which we have some vague notion based on the fact that we have some concept of infinity. This is why Ṣadrā tells us that God's Essence, "in the intensity of luminosity [*shiddat al-nūriyya*], is beyond [our grasp of] infinity by virtue of [Its] infinity."[16]

Ṣadrā's language here is clearly indebted to Ibn ʿArabī and his followers' treatment of the divine Essence or the Absolute (*al-muṭlaq*).[17] At the same time, one will notice a direct parallel between Ṣadrā's treatment of God's Essence and his explication of the nature of *wujūd* or "being" as outlined in Chapter 1. The reason being can be said to be identical to God's Essence is because they both denote God's "reality."[18] Since God in His reality is completely hidden and inaccessible, and the terms "being" and "Essence" refer to this reality, they too are hidden and inaccessible, and therefore completely unknown.[19] Yet there is another sense in which being and God's Essence are one and the same reality: they are also the most evident of things, since there is nowhere that being and God's Essence are not to be found. To be sure, whatever can be said about being in purely philosophical terms can be said about the Essence in theological and mystical terms.

When Ṣadrā seeks to explain the notion of the Essence's accessibility, he employs the traditional language of theology and mysticism, just as he employs the standard language of philosophy in his explication of being's accessibility. Like the particularizations of being, the Essence's particularizations are to be found everywhere as well. In more poetic language, Ṣadrā refers to the modes of being as "drops of the ocean of the Necessary Reality."[20] In other words, the Essence, like being, can only make Itself known through particularizations of Itself, or what Ṣadrā calls "the rays of the sun of Absolute Being."[21] Once the Ultimate Reality becomes particularized, we can speak about It in more concrete and manageable terms. In other words, the vagueness which envelops all things disappears, in a sense, once we are able to delimit God's Essence.

Names and Their Loci

The Essence can only become delimited when we provide an essential definition of It. By defining It, we bring It into the scope of our own partial and limited frames of reference. Yet how can the Essence in Itself remain indefinable and inaccessible on the one hand, and definable and accessible on the other? As with a number of the crucial points made in the *Tafsīr Sūrat al-fātiḥa*, Ṣadrā addresses this question based on a statement made by Ibn ʿArabī in the *Fuṣūṣ al-ḥikam* ("The Ringstones of Wisdom"). In the text in question, Ibn ʿArabī says that God lies at the root of every definition given in the cosmos: "The Real is defined by every essential definition [*al-ḥaqq maḥdūd bi-kull ḥadd*]."[22] Ṣadrā affirms this point on the logic that since all things in the cosmos point to God, He is "defined" by all things in the cosmos.[23] Yet the God defined in the cosmos is not the Essence proper. With the concern of a theologian, Ṣadrā seeks to clarify Ibn ʿArabī's point:

> What was intended by "the Real" in Ibn ʿArabī's saying "The Real is defined by every essential definition" was that

> which is meant by [*mufād*] the word "God" [*Allāh*] from the standpoint of its universal meaning and intellectual concept, not from the standpoint of the reality of its meaning, which is the Essence of Exclusive Oneness [*al-dhāt al-aḥadiyya*] and the Unseen of the unseens [*ghayb al-ghuyūb*], since It has neither essential definition, nor name, nor description, and intellectual perception does not have a way to It.[24]

The distinction which Ṣadrā makes here between the Essence of Exclusive Oneness and the Unseen of the unseens[25] on the one hand and God on the other, corresponds to Ibn ʿArabī's well-known distinction between the Essence's Exclusive Oneness (*aḥadiyya*) and Its Inclusive Oneness (*wāḥidiyya*).[26] Many followers of Ibn ʿArabī couch the same dichotomy in different terms, referring to the levels of the non-entified Essence (*lā taʿayyun*) and the first entified Essence (*al-taʿayyun al-awwal*)[27] from which multiplicity proceeds, or the non-manifest and manifest faces of the Essence.[28] Whereas the non-manifest face of the Essence remains inaccessible and unattainable forever except to Itself, Its manifest face is that to which humans have access and to whom they return.[29]

The Essence must in one respect remain hidden, for if It were to be known even in Its hiddenness, It would not be absolute, but relative. That is, It would not remain completely unconditioned and therefore unknown if It were conditioned by the knowledge of a knower outside of It. Yet insofar as the Essence makes Itself known, It must make Itself relative in one sense. The only manner in which It can do this is by turning one side of Its face to the cosmos. In the language of Islamic theology,[30] the Essence makes Itself known through the divine names. As Ṣadrā puts it:

> With each quality, the Essence takes on a [specific] name—the names articulated in speech being the "names of the names" [*asmāʾ al-asmāʾ*]—and the multiplicity in them is in accordance with the multiplicity of the [names'] characteristics and attributes. This multiplicity is nothing but the standpoints [*iʿtibārāt*] of His unseen levels and His divine tasks [*shuʾūn ilāhiyya*],[31] which are "the keys to the unseen" [*mafātīḥ al-ghayb*, cf. Q 6:59] whose shadows and reflections fall upon existent things.[32]

The cosmos, therefore, is composed of the names of God. Since these names are nothing other than particularizations of the manifest face of the Essence, each name denotes a specific aspect of the Essence's relationship to the cosmos. Thus, the multiplicity introduced into the Essence is nothing other than Its own multiple standpoints and faces turned toward the cosmos, or what Ṣadrā calls, following Ibn ʿArabī and his school, the "divine tasks." As seen in the passage above, the divine tasks are a synonym for the expression "keys to the unseen." These terms refer to the multiplicity which comes about by virtue of the disclosure of the Essence's manifest face.[33] Once the Essence takes on different positions with respect to that which is strictly speaking outside of It, the names emerge with their own particularized qualities, which allow them to be distinguished from one another on the one hand, and from the Essence on the other. The level at which this takes place is what is denoted by the terms "divine tasks" and "keys to the unseen." Ṣadrā points out that it is the shadows and reflections of the divine tasks and keys to the unseen which fall upon existent things. These shadows are nothing but names which appear in the cosmos, and which Ṣadrā refers to as the "names of the names," a point which harks back to Ibn ʿArabī.[33] The names of the names are the tasks of the Essence found throughout the cosmos, which is to say that they are Its properties and traces.

Since the Essence must remain utterly hidden and inaccessible, how do the names come about from It without compromising Its fundamental obscurity? Again taking his lead from Ibn ʿArabī, Ṣadrā asserts that the names have no proper existence of their own. Rather, they are relationships formed between the Essence and the cosmos. Since they are relationships, no change is introduced in the Essence:

> All that is in the world of contingency is a form of one of the names of God and a locus of one of the tasks. So God's names are intelligible meanings in the Unseen Being of the Real [*ghayb al-wujūd al-ḥaqq*], meaning that the Essence of Exclusive Oneness [*al-dhāt al-aḥadiyya*] is that which the intellect has no way of conceiving, since were It to "exist" or occur to the intellect in order for the intellect to grasp It, these meanings would be divested from It, and the intellect would [be unable to] qualify It with itself. Thus, given Its unity and simplicity, the Essence of Exclusive Oneness allows for the predication of these meanings to It without there being an added quality [to It]. . . .[35]

Although the divine names are nonexistent entities in themselves, they do have a relative reality since they come about in relation to a particular face of the manifest Essence, which denotes a particular reality of God's Essence. As was seen in Chapter 1, the concept of being is known through particularizations of being. The particularizations of being can only be apprehended through quiddities, since quiddities, as entities entirely devoid of any reality, only emerge by virtue of the gradation of being. Likewise, each divine name denotes the Essence, but all the divine names are nonexistent entities.

It can be noted here that the divine names with respect to the Essence do not correspond, in philosophical language, to quiddities with respect to being. Although both the names and quiddities are actually nonexistent but take on a relative type of existence, the names serve as relationships between the manifest face of the Essence and the cosmos, whereas quiddities, although "relational" in one respect, are ultimately mental abstractions which emerge through the concretizations attendant upon the gradation of being.

That which corresponds to quiddities in Ṣadrā's philosophy to his explication of the unfolding of the Essence in his religious writings are the fixed entities (*al-aʿyān al-thābita*).[36] As Ibn ʿArabī tells us, the fixed entities are nothing but the objects of God's knowledge as they are known to Him forever. Whether God brings them into existence or not, the fixed entities never leave their state of fixity, and, hence, nonexistence. When and if they are brought into existence, they can only do so by virtue of the names.

As we saw in the above-cited passage, Ṣadrā says that "All that is in the world of contingency is a form of one of the names of God, and a locus of one of the tasks." The objects in the cosmos are loci of God's manifestation (*maẓāhir*), which is to say that they are receptacles which come about in accordance with their fixity. The loci are, in other words, nothing but the existentiated objects of God's knowledge "forever" known to Him (i.e., the fixed entities). In order for these fixed entities to emerge, the manifest face of the Essence must turn to them, and as soon as the Essence makes Its turn to these entities, relationships and, hence, names emerge between the manifest face of the Essence and the fixed entities, which at this later stage are to be understood as the names' loci. Thus, a quiddity corresponds to a fixed entity since they both denote the same thing: the particular reality of the entity in question, that is, its "what-it-is-ness." Like several other major figures of Islamic thought before him,[37] Ṣadrā explicitly makes this identification on more than one occasion.[38]

On account of the fact that the fixed entities denote the quiddities, we may be justified in asking what the divine names denote. In other words, do the divine names have an equivalent in Ṣadrā's philosophical system? Indeed, the function of the standpoint of the existent with respect to existence, which emerges as a result of the gradation of being and which determines the nature of the resultant quiddity, is akin to the function of the divine names in their relationality to the Essence on the one hand, and their colouring the loci[39] on the other. Technically speaking, however, the divine names do not figure in Ṣadrā's philosophical writings, since there is no direct conceptual equivalent in his philosophical lexicon.[40] This is perfectly understandable, since the divine names are theological categories and thus more appropriately belong to Ṣadrā's "religious" writings, which is why they figure so prominently in his *Tafsīr Sūrat al-fātiḥa*.

The All-Comprehensive Name

What prompted Ṣadrā's long meditation on Q 1:1 was the divine name Allah. According to a long-standing tradition in Islam, this name is unlike God's other names. Whereas each divine name denotes a specific aspect of the Essence's manifest face,[41] the divine name Allah does not function in the same way. Firstly, it does not denote any particular quality of the Essence, as, for example, *al-raḥmān* would denote the mercifulness of the Essence's manifest face, or *al-qahhār* would denote the dominating aspect of the Essence's manifest face. As the Islamic tradition suggests, Allah is a proper name (*ism ʿalam*). Since the name Allah signifies God's Essence but does not denote a particular quality of It, it is what the Sufi tradition refers to as an All-Gathering name (*ism jāmiʿ*), which is to say that it brings together all of the meanings of the divine names, each of which denote the Essence in a particular way.[42]

In keeping with a fundamental axiom of Ṣadrian metaphysics, "the simplicity of reality is all things [*basīṭ al-ḥaqīqa kull ashyāʾ*],"[43] the name Allah brings together all of the standpoints which the Essence assumes with respect to the cosmos in terms of the Essence's manifestness, since it is the one name which denotes the entire manifest aspect of the Essence on account of its being the first level of the Essence's self-unfolding:

> According to the great ones amongst the gnostics, the name "God" [*ism Allāh*] is an expression of the All-Gathering Divine Level [*martabat al-ulūhiyya al-jāmiʿa*] for all of the tasks, standpoints, descriptions, and perfections, within which all of the names and attributes—these being nothing but the flashes of His light[44] and the tasks of His Essence—are ranked. This Level marks the first instance of multiplicity

> to come about in existence, and[45] is an isthmus between the Presence of Exclusive Oneness [*al-ḥaḍra al-aḥadiyya*] and the loci of creation and the engendered Command [*al-maẓāhir al-amriyya wa-l-khalqiyya*].[46] In itself, this name brings together every contrary quality and opposing name, as you have already come to know.[47]

From the perspective that the Essence is everywhere, the names are to be found everywhere as well. And since the cosmos is saturated with the names, all that is in the cosmos denotes the name Allah. Taken as a whole, the entire cosmos names the Essence by naming the name Allah.

As all things in the cosmos name Allah, they can be said to "define" Him, since everything in the cosmos denotes an aspect of the reality of the name Allah which itself denotes the Essence. Since the name Allah brings together every other name, it is the least particularized of the Essence's particularizations and is, thus, the most entitled to being called the Essence's manifest face[48] simply because it is the "the first instance of multiplicity to come about in existence." The name Allah, therefore, corresponds to what we normally refer to as "God," that is, the God that is worshipped by people and to whom they will return in the next life.[49] Since any talk of the name Allah automatically brings us into the sphere of the ultimate end of religion, Ṣadrā's concern with Ibn ʿArabī's statement that the Real (*al-ḥaqq*)—a term that is synonymous with the name Allah[50]—is defined in every definition therefore becomes clear. In fact, Ṣadrā goes on to tell us that although the name Allah is defined in every definition, it itself cannot be exhausted in its meanings:

> The concepts [*mafhūmāt*] of all the divine names and their existential loci [*maẓāhir*], which are parts of the cosmos—both outwardly and inwardly—despite their multiplicity, [form] a real definition [*ḥadd ḥaqīqī*] in signifying God's name [*ism Allāh*]. It follows that all the meanings of the realities of the cosmos are a definition of God's name, just as all the meanings of the divine names define Him, except that it is possible for the human intellect to encompass [*iḥāṭa*] all the definitions of defined things in their particulars, as opposed to the meanings of the particulars of His definition, because these meanings cannot be confined [*ghayr maḥsūra*].[51]

The Essence of Exclusive Oneness, therefore, forever remains out of the reach of the cosmos by virtue of the fact that It does not turn Its face toward the cosmos. And when It does turn to the cosmos, what emerges are the names, which are not, strictly speaking, ontological entities but relationships. In fact, the name which denotes the manifest face of the Essence, namely Allah, cannot be exhausted and defined in its entirety, since, as Ṣadrā explains, this name brings together all of the names and hence all of the meanings in the cosmos.[52] Thus, although all things in the cosmos define God, they cannot confine Him through their act of definition, seeing as it is that they themselves are particularized definitions which "define" the whole.

4

Cosmology

After commenting upon the first part of Q 1:1 and devoting some discussion to God's attributes of mercy and compassion,[1] Ṣadrā turns his attention to Q 1:2, the first part of which reads, "Praise is for God [*al-ḥamdu li-llāh*], Lord of the worlds." Indeed, by the time we get to Q 1:2, we have already encountered God as He is in terms of His hiddenness and accessibility. According to Ṣadrā, Q 1:2 addresses another key point: the manner in which the cosmos comes about through the Supreme Reality.[2] The notion of "praise" (*ḥamd*) which figures in this verse is all-important for Ṣadrā, since it is the link between the manifest face of God and the cosmos, which is traditionally defined in Islamic texts as "everything other than God" (*mā siwā-llāh*).

In the context of his discussion on the *istiʿādha*, Ṣadrā returns to the theme of the nature of God's Word which he developed in the *Mafātīḥ*. After stating that God's Word is not of the order of the genus of sounds and letters, or of the order of the genus of substances and accidents, Ṣadrā reiterates his teaching that it comes about through God's Command. As the first existentiation from the manifest aspect of God, that is, as part of His Command, the Word is "Perfect." And since the realm of multiplicity and change emerges through the Perfect Words,[3] their emergence in the cosmos is gradational and not spontaneous. It is worth citing Ṣadrā's explanation here in the context of the *Tafsīr Sūrat al-fātiḥa* since it will help set the stage for his discussion of the cosmic function of "praise":

> There is a fine point [*daqīqa*] here: the origination of bodies—their substances, dark and other accidents, natures, and

> natural effects—is only gradational [*tadrījī*], [proceeding] bit by bit.[4] [This is] similar to motion, which is the exiting [*khurūj*] from potentiality into actuality. As for innovated things, their existentiation and exiting [potentiality and going] into actuality only obtains in one instant: *And Our Command is nothing but one, like the blink of an eye* [Q 56:5]. When the Command is like this, its origination from God resembles the origination of letters which only come to exist in one instant, that is, at that very indivisible moment.[5] Because of this likeness, their completion is their very beginning. That which comes about through the carrying out of His determination is called the "Word," and is described as "Perfect."[6]

The Act of Praise

Like his predecessors in the Qurʾānic exegetical tradition, Ṣadrā's commentary on Q 1:2 typically discusses the linguistic sense of *ḥamd* and how it relates to other cognate but structurally different terms, such as *madḥ* and *thanāʾ*.[7] He treats these discussions as more of a formality, perhaps because he would like to demonstrate how different his approach will be. This is clearly evidenced early in his commentary on Q 1:2.

Ṣadrā observes that for the people of unveiling, "'praise' is a kind of speech [*nawʿ min al-kalām*]."[8] Referring to his earlier treatment of the nature of "speech," he notes that speech is not that which is uttered by the tongue.[9] As we have already seen, God's Words arise from His Command. Speech is, thus, an act that comes about through the divine will. Since speech is an act and praise is "a kind of speech," praise is also a kind of act:

> The reality of praise, according to the verifying gnostics, is the act of making God's attributes of perfection manifest [*iẓhār al-ṣifāt al-kamāliyya*]. This could either be through words [*qawl*]—as is well-known amongst the masses—or it could be in act [*bi-l-fiʿl*], which is like God's praise for Himself and the praise of all things for Him.[10]

This passage is crucial for the distinctions Ṣadrā will set out to explicate for the remainder of his commentary upon Q 1:2. Praise, as an act, makes "God's attributes of perfection manifest." This can be done in one of two ways. Either the attributes of perfection are made manifest through words of praise, usually through the *ḥamdala*. Or, God's attributes of perfection are made manifest through the act of praise, which, Ṣadrā tells us, is akin to God's self-praise and the praise of all things for Him.

Insofar as God is the object of praise through speech, the praise that is allotted to Him in human speech may not bring about His attributes of perfection in a complete manner. This is because that which is denoted by words may actually differ from the word itself.[11] A human being can, for example, praise God with his tongue, but if his mind is not focused upon God at that moment, his praise of Him may be nothing more than an empty set of words. In fact, his act of praising God while something else is on his mind is akin to his praising that thing upon which his mind is fixated. But when God's praise is completely actualized, it is the very act of praise that does complete justice to His attributes of perfection.[12] It is, therefore, this second notion of praise which draws Ṣadrā's interest.

Ṣadrā says that the act of praise which brings about God's attributes of perfection is akin to God's praising Himself. But how does God "praise" Himself? This is made clear once we consider the wording of Q 1:2. In this verse, the speaker is none other than God, and He declares His own praise. While human praise, when done properly, can only bring about God's attributes of perfection by way of declaring them, God's praise for Himself, which is pure actuality, does more than simply "declare" God's perfection. As Ṣadrā tells us, God's praise for Himself is nothing but His act of bringing things into existence:

> God's praise for Himself—which is the most exalted level of praise—is His existentiation [*ījād*] of every existing thing. . . . His existentiation of every existent is "praise" in the infinitive sense, similar to the way speaking denotes beauty [of voice] through speech. The existent itself is "praise" in the sense of actualizing the infinitive.[13]

As was discussed earlier, the cosmos only comes about by virtue of the divine Essence's turning toward the fixed entities. But why did the Essence wish to bring about the cosmos? The Sufi tradition tells us that it is because It wanted to know Itself objectively, whereas before It had known Itself in a purely subjective manner.[14] And the manner in which God qua Absolute can know Itself objectively is by bringing Itself into the realm of relativity. The act of praise is therefore a form of existentiation primarily with respect to God's self-knowledge. By praising Himself, God proceeds from obscurity into apparentness, from hiddenness into manifestness. Yet God's praise for Himself necessitates that the objects of His knowledge become objectified, for it is through the objects of His knowledge that He can come to know Himself. Hence, praise pertains as much to God's objective self-awareness as it does to the existentiation of His creatures, for they are, in a sense, two sides of the same coin.

Since God, who is pure being, brings about the cosmos by praising Himself, each existent that arises out of His self-praise is itself a mode of that act of praise. As modes of the act of praise, or what Ṣadrā calls the specification (*takhṣīṣ*) of praise,[15] each existent is "praisified," meaning that each existing thing is both a form of praise and that which praises:

> In this sense, it is valid to call every existent thing "praise." And just as every existent is a "praise," so too is it a praiser [*ḥāmid*] because of its being composed of an intellectual constituent and a rational substance. . . . This is why this intellectual denotation has been expressed in the Qurʾān as "speech" [*nuṭq*]: *"God, the one who causes all things to speak, has caused us to speak"* [Q 41:22]. Likewise, every existent, with respect to the totality of its arrangement, is a single praise and a single praiser [cf. Q 59:24, 62:1].[16]

All things in existence, as specified instantiations of God's single act of praise, cannot but praise God because they themselves are acts of praise.[17] And the act of praise, as Ṣadrā pointed out, is the most complete manner in which God's attributes of perfection become manifest. "Praise," therefore, is "for God" (*li-llāh*) because existence belongs to Him.

The Muhammadan Reality

Just as every existent is a word of God proceeding from His Perfect Words which arise out of His Command, so too is each creature an act of praise which proceeds from God's self-praise. Yet there seems to be an ontological fissure here between God's self-praise and the emergence of the individual instantiations of this praise (i.e., the cosmos and its contents). As Ṣadrā demonstrated in the *Mafātīḥ*, the cosmos does not come about as a result of the Command, but through the intermediary of the Perfect Words, which can be understood as so many fragmented portions of the single Command "Be!" Since in the *Tafsīr Sūrat al-fātiḥa* Ṣadrā wishes to connect his cosmology of the Command and the Perfect Words with his cosmology of praise, there must be something that takes the place of the Perfect Words in his cosmology of praise. To be sure, although Ṣadrā does not make the connection explicit, he provides us with the missing link in the following crucial passage. Each existent in the cosmos is both an act of praise and praise itself, Ṣadrā explains, because

> the sum total [*al-jamīʿ*] is like one large man with one reality, one form, and one intellect. This is the First Intellect, which is the form and reality of the world, and is the complete Muhammadan Reality [*al-ḥaqīqa al-Muḥammadiyya al-tamāmiyya*].[18] So the most exalted and most tremendous level of praise is the level of the Muhammadan Seal, which subsists through the existence of the Seal [*al-martaba al-khatmiyya al-Muḥammadiyya al-qāʾima bi-wujūd al-khātam*] on account of the Prophet's arrival at the promised praiseworthy station in His saying, *Perhaps your Lord will raise you to a praiseworthy station* [Q 17:79]. So his hallowed essence is the utmost level of praise through which God praises Himself. This is why the Prophet has been singled out with the banner of praise [*liwāʾ al-ḥamd*],[19] and was called "praiser" [*ḥammād*], "most praiseworthy" [*aḥmad*], and "praised" [*maḥmūd*]. . . .[20]

By the time Ṣadrā wrote these words, it had become commonplace to speak of the Muhammadan Reality as the root and form of the world. Yet Ṣadrā's linking the level of the Muhammadan Reality with what he calls the "most exalted and most tremendous level of praise" is very telling in the context of his commentary on Q 1:2. In Sufi metaphysics, the Muhammadan Reality is nothing other than the eye through which God sees Himself objectively in the cosmos. It is thus a reality which, from the time God brought the cosmos into existence, has percolated throughout the generations and become particularized in God's many messengers and prophets sent to humanity. Since the Muhammadan Reality is the first thing created by God, it is the Word of God. As was seen above, God's Word only comes about by virtue of the Command. Indeed, there is a clear correlation between the act of praise and God's engendering Command (*al-amr al-takwīnī*). Just as God causes the cosmos to come about by saying "Be!," so too does He cause the cosmos to come about by praising Himself. And, just as the Perfect Words are the first entities to emerge by virtue of the Command, so too does the Muhammadan Reality emerge by virtue of God's act of self-praise. This parallel is all the more telling since the Command is a form of speech which produces that which is structurally related to speech, namely "words," just as the act of praise (*ḥamd*) produces something which is structurally related to it, namely that which is praised (*Muḥammad*). This interpretation is given further support by Ṣadrā's own statement, discussed earlier, that *ḥamd* is "a kind of speech."[21]

Although Ṣadrā states that the Perfect Words emerge through the Command, it is not incorrect to say that one single Word or Logos emerges from the Command. This is why he referred to that which emerges from the Command as "a Perfect Word." Since a Perfect Word is nothing but a fragmentation of the Command, one Word must logically precede the others. That Ṣadrā wishes to equate the Muhammadan Reality with the first Perfect Word is clear by his identification—which was well-established in theoretical Sufism several centuries before him—of the Muhammadan Reality with the First Intellect.[22]

Since the First Intellect is the first entity to come about in the cosmic order, and the act of existentiation is nothing other than the actualization of "praise," Ṣadrā describes the Muhammadan Reality as the highest level of praise through which God praises Himself. In other words, since God brings about the cosmos by praising Himself, the first entity to emerge as a result of this act of self-praise is the Muhammadan Reality. As the highest level of God's self-praise, the Muhammadan Reality is also the being that praises God most, which, as Ṣadrā explains, is why the person of the Prophet—who is the physical manifestation of the Muhammadan Reality—is given the "banner of praise" (*liwāʾ al-ḥamd*) on the Final Day.

The Perfect Man

After laying out the fundamentals of his metaphysics and cosmology, Ṣadrā then proceeds in the *Tafsīr Sūrat al-fātiḥa* to discuss what can be called his anthropology. Drawing on a well-known theme in later Islamic thought, he discusses the nature of the Perfect Man (*al-insān al-kāmil*). His treatment of this topic does not exactly follow his discussion of the Muhammadan Reality, since in explicating the nature of the latter he was more concerned with demonstrating the manner in which the Muhammadan Reality, as the highest level of praise, comes about through God's act of self-praise. At the same time, since the

Perfect Man is nothing but a particular manifestation of the Muhammadan Reality, it seems clear that Ṣadrā's treatment of the cosmology of praise was intended to serve as a lead-in of sorts to his treatment of the Perfect Man.

In introducing the notion of the Perfect Man, Ṣadrā takes his lead from a discussion on Q 1:2 in Bayḍāwī's *Anwār* where he discusses the different senses of the word *ʿālam* which figure in the verse.[23] Ṣadrā is particularly interested in demonstrating the manner in which man shares an intimate relationship with the cosmos by virtue of his very constitution. Just as the world contains signs through which God can be known, so too does man contain signs through which God can be known. Bayḍāwī explicitly says that gazing upon the cosmos and man are equal acts, since they share the same qualities.[24] Ṣadrā concedes that most people are created in a manner similar to the macrocosm, although he notes that most of them do not ever escape their animal natures and rise to the station of the intellect.[25] But how can man contain within himself, even potentially, the cosmos? In explaining this question, Ṣadrā draws on his earlier discussion of God's names and attributes:

> With respect to the point of view that man contains something of all that is in the macrocosm [*al-ʿālam al-kabīr*], it is because his perfect configuration [*nashʾatuhu al-kāmila*] is the locus of all the divine names and attributes and is the gathering place of all of the existential realities, as is known to those who assiduously pursue the signs in the horizons and within their selves.[26] So man is a prototype for all of what is in the cosmos. From this perspective, he is a small world [*ʿālam ṣaghīr*], which is why he is called the "microcosm" [*al-ʿālam al-ṣaghīr*]. . . .[27]

As was seen earlier, the cosmos is nothing but a synthesis of God's names, which themselves come about as relationships between the manifest face of the Essence and Its respective loci of manifestation. Just as the cosmos is the theatre for the manifestation of God's qualities, so too is man, who was, as the famous Prophetic tradition tells us, created upon the form or in the image (*ṣūra*) of Allah.[28] As mentioned earlier, the name Allah is an All-Gathering name since it brings together all of the divine names. It will also be recalled that the divine names are found throughout the cosmos, which, as Ṣadrā explained earlier in the *Tafsīr Sūrat al-fātiḥa*, as a whole "defines" Allah. Thus, created in the image of Allah, man contains all of the divine names within himself. Since the divine names are found throughout the cosmos, man also contains the cosmos within himself. But Ṣadrā does not just have in mind any man, since, as he notes, it is man's "perfect configuration" that is the locus of all of God's names and attributes. The man with a "perfect configuration" can only be the Perfect Man.

We saw at the beginning of the last chapter how Ṣadrā follows a long tradition of commentators upon the Qurʾān when he says that the Fātiḥa contains all things. It is in the context of his anthropology that he seeks to make the logical connection between the Fātiḥa and the Perfect Man:

> The relationship of the *Sūrat al-fātiḥa* to the entire Qurʾān is like the relationship of man—who is the small world—to the world, which is the great man. And just as the Perfect Man is a succinct book [*kitāb wajīz*] and an abridged transcription [*nuskha muntakhaba*] within whom is found all that is in the All-Gathering great book [*al-kitāb al-kabīr al-jāmiʿ*][29] . . . so too is the "opener of the book" [*fātiḥat al-kitāb*], within which, despite its brevity and concision, is found the sum total [*majāmiʿ*] of the aims of the Qurʾān and their secrets and lights. This All-Gatheredness [*jāmiʿiyya*] is not for the other Qurʾānic chapters, just as none of the forms of the world's parts have what man has with respect to [his bringing together] the form of the Divine Gatheredness [*al-ṣūra al-jamʿiyya al-ilāhiyya*].[30]

Since the Fātiḥa contains all things and man is potentially the entire cosmos, man potentially contains the Fātiḥa within himself. As a prototype of the cosmos, the Perfect Man is a microcosm. Likewise, as prototypes of the book of being, he and the Fātiḥa are "small books." Both the Perfect Man and the Fātiḥa share in common the qualities of gatheredness: they both bring together what is contained in the "big book," that is, the macrocosm. Since the Fātiḥa and the Perfect Man are identical, the Perfect Man contains within himself all of the Fātiḥa's secrets concerning the Origin and the Return.[31] This is an important point, for, as we will shortly see, it is from the perspective of the Perfect Man that Ṣadrā attempts to reveal some of the Fātiḥa's secrets.

5

Theology

In Chapter 3 I had the opportunity to evaluate the manner in which Mullā Ṣadrā recasts his ontology in his commentary on the Fātiḥa. It was shown that he was able to weave his distinctly philosophical position concerning the fundamentality of being into the fabric of his commentary in seamless fashion. This then allowed for a proper exposition of the *Tafsīr Sūrat al-fātiḥa*'s sophisticated cosmology of praise and its attendant anthropology, which was the focus of Chapter 4. I will now turn my attention to a theme addressed in the *Tafsīr Sūrat al-fātiḥa* which naturally follows the topics already covered in Chapters 3 and 4. By extension, the discussion introduced here is also a corollary of Ṣadrā's worldview when applied to the content of the Fātiḥa. I will highlight here how Ṣadrā attempts to shed light on Ibn ʿArabī's notion of the "God created in beliefs." To be sure, we still lack a comprehensive picture of Ṣadrā's theology (as understood here). Thus, apart from bringing to light some unknown aspects of Ṣadrā's teachings, this chapter will also demonstrate how influential Ibn ʿArabī has been upon these teachings.

From Outer to Inner

I demonstrated in Chapter 1 that Ṣadrā has very little patience for the more exoteric types of *tafsīr*, although he was thoroughly conversant in its methods. It is clear that Ṣadrā acknowledges non-mystical and non-philosophical scriptural exegesis as a legitimate enterprise, but he will rarely devote a lengthy discussion to account for why these approaches exist and how they ultimately tie into the wider picture of his metaphysics. One of the major exceptions to this is to be found in the *Tafsīr Sūrat al-fātiḥa*. Here, Ṣadrā attempts to explain why there are different types of readers of the Qur᾿ān, the exposition of which is closely linked to his treatment of the diversity of approaches to understanding God.

Since people take different positions with respect to God, they will obviously have different understandings of His Word.[1] According to Ṣadrā, this fact is itself proof of the Qur᾿ān's perfection. It, like God, is open to all types of readings, although not all interpretations are necessarily correct:

> Just as there are differences of opinion [*ikhtilāf wa-tafāwut*] in peoples' positions and beliefs concerning God—i.e., between the one who declares God bodily [*mujassim*] and the one who declares Him dissimilar [*munazzih*], the philosopher [*mutafalsif*] and denier of God's attributes [*muʿaṭṭil*], the one who ascribes partners to God [*mushrik*] and the one who declares Him one [*muwaḥḥid*]—so too are there differences of opinion between them in understanding [the Qur᾿ān]. This is one of the proofs of the Qur᾿ān's perfection, for it is a deep ocean in whose current most people drown, and from which none are saved except a few.[2]

One may either remain on the surface of an ocean or plunge into it. The deeper one goes, the more likely he is to reach its bottom and resurface with its hidden treasures. Likewise, there are many positions on God, but not all of them are correct since some of them are necessarily more superficial than others. It is only those who plumb the depths of being who can lay claim to understanding God, just as it is only those who plumb the depths of the ocean of the Qur᾿ān who can lay claim to understanding His Word.[3]

The point Ṣadrā is trying to make here would be difficult to understand without contextualizing his discussion. Before introducing the idea of the correspondence between different approaches to understanding God and the Qur᾿ān, he devotes some space to explaining how people have employed various linguistic tools in their attempts to comprehend the meanings of the Qur᾿ān's verses. Such people (whom Ṣadrā, in keeping with the long-standing Sufi tradition, refers to as the *ahl al-ʿibāra* or "the people of outward expressions")[4] are used by God for a higher purpose. God has effectively set them up to learn these partial sciences (*al-ʿulūm al-juz᾿iyya*), rooted as they are upon the Qur᾽ān's linguistic forms only. These people thus act as servants (*khawādim*) and instruments (*ālāt*) for the true purpose behind the Qur᾽ān, namely man's perfection.[5] Human perfection, Ṣadrā assures us, is not attained through outward, formal learning. Although outward knowledge is a necessary preparatory step for most seekers of truth, it cannot in and of itself lead to that truth.[6] Thus, the more outward forms of learning related to the Qur᾽ān exist as a means of facilitating a deeper understanding of the book.

In Sufi *tafsīr*, the term *ʿibāra* is often juxtaposed with the term *ishāra*, a word denoting the allusion to or indication of something which, by virtue of its depth, escapes outward expression.[7] Expressions, in other words, deal with the outer form of a deeper reality which can only be denoted by allusions. Because of the limitations of language and discursive thought (to which language is intimately tied), we can only allude to the Qur᾽ān's inner realities. Thus, if the ocean of the Qur᾽ān has outward expressions (i.e., its surface and waves), it also has an inner reality (i.e., its hidden pearls). In the following passage, Ṣadrā relates this basic exoteric/esoteric dichotomy in the cosmos to several cosmic realities and explains the fundamental difference between those concerned with the outer and inner dimensions of the Qur᾽ān:

> Expressions are like the enshrouded dead person, whereas allusions are like the subtle, recognizing, knowing [faculty] which is man's reality. Expressions come from the World of the Visible [*ʿālam al-shahāda*], whereas allusions come from the World of the Unseen [*ʿālam al-ghayb*]. Expressions are the shadows of the unseen, just as man's individuation [*tashakhkhuṣ*] is the shadow of his reality.
>
> As for the people of outward expressions and writing [*ahl al-ʿibāra wa-l-kitāba*], they have wasted their lives away in acquiring words and foundations, and their intellects have drowned in trying to grasp expositions and meanings. As for the people of the Qur᾽ān and the Word [*ahl al-Qur᾽ān wa-l-kalām*]—and they are the people of God [*ahl Allāh*] who have been singled out for the divine love, lordly attraction, and Prophetic proximity—God has facilitated the way for them and accepted from them few works for the journey. That is because of the purity of their intentions and their hearts.[8]

Since God's being encompasses outward and inward realities, like the readers of the Qur᾽ān, it will necessarily be comprised of people who swim on the surface of its ocean and those who plunge into its depths. Those who plunge into its depths are the "people of God," just as those who plunge into the Qurʾān's depths are the "people of the Qurʾān." As we have seen earlier in this study, modes of being (*anḥāʾ al-wujūd*) are darker, murkier, denser, and more shadow-like (i.e., manifest more essence) the lower they stand on the scale of being. The higher they stand on its scale, the less concretized they are, which is to say the less defined they become by their own outward forms or "expressions." As modes of being, the more individuated they are, the less shadow-like their natures, meaning they manifest more being, more depth, more "allusion," and less "expression."

At the beginning of Chapter 3 we saw that Ṣadrā refers to the Qurʾān as being one of the rays of God's light. Elsewhere in the *Tafsīr Sūrat al-fātiḥa* he refers to it as "one of the flashes of His Essence."[9] Since God's light pervades the cosmos, all of the latter's contents, in one form or another, reveal the light of God's being. However, some things reveal this light more clearly than others. This is to say that some things can either convey the nature of this light by their very existence, or they can play a subtler role by way of alluding to this principial Light of which all things are merely rays.[10] Since being and the Qurʾān are two sides of the same coin, the most outward forms of knowledge of the Qurʾān, like the most outward forms of knowledge of God, are less real and furthest from that form of knowledge only accessible to the people of the Qurʾān.

Idols of Belief

Approaches to the Qurʾān which are confined to the surface necessarily limit the Qurʾān's treasures from emerging. As has been seen throughout the history of Islamic thought, such a tendency is often an extension of, and/or something that informs, a more exoteric approach to scripture. It would be an unhelpful exercise on our part if we were to attempt to determine whether one's reading of scripture colors one's understanding of reality, or whether one's understanding of reality informs one's reading of scripture. This is because these approaches are not mutually exclusive, as they both seem to inform one another.

In Ṣadrā's case such a question becomes all the less important since he sees the Qurʾān as the prototype of being (from one perspective). It is perhaps for this reason that in his *tafsīr*s, Ṣadrā will often not draw as explicit a link between approaches to scripture and approaches to God. Thus, when he discusses the nature of idolatry in the context of the *Tafsīr Sūrat al-fātiḥa*, he takes it for granted that his discussion is as much concerned with understanding the verses of the Qurʾān as it is with understanding the nature of God.

In texts of Islamic thought, particularly Sufi writings, it was commonplace to say that concern with anything other than God was tantamount to idolatry. One of the first authors to make an explicit connection between self-absorption and idolatry was the early master of moral psychology al-Ḥārith al-Muḥāsibī (d. 243/857), who spent a good deal of time demonstrating the manner in which *riyāʾ* (religious ostentation) acts as what the Prophet referred to as a hidden form of idolatry (*al-shirk al-khafī*).[11] This hidden form of idolatry can manifest itself in a variety of forms. This explains why in Sufi literature we come across many synonyms for the hidden idolater, amongst which are such pejorative titles as "form worshipper" (*ṣūrat-parast*)[12] and "habit worshipper" (*ʿādat-parast*).[13]

If preoccupation with the idols of the self is a form of idolatry, then surely the intellectual constructs of God conjured up by the self can also be called "idols." Although this idea lurks in the background of numerous Sufi texts, the first explicit, theoretical discussion of the notion of "idols of belief" is to be found in the work of Ibn ʿArabī, who spoke of the "God of one's belief" (*al-ilāh al-muʿtaqad*) and "the God created in faiths" (*al-ilāh al-makhlūq fī l-ʿaqāʾid*).[14] As he famously (and controversially) puts it, "Neither [the worshipper's] heart nor eye ever witness anything except the form of his belief concerning God,"[15] and "there are none but idol worshippers."[16] After Ibn ʿArabī, a number of authors took up this idea, particularly the great Persian sage Maḥmūd Shabistarī (d. 740/1339).[17]

By the time we get to Mullā Ṣadrā, references to the "idols of belief" or the "God created in faiths" would have been immediately recognizable as having derived from Ibn ʿArabī and his school. This was the case with a number of important terms, such as the Oneness of Being (*waḥdat al-wujūd*) and the Perfect Man. Ṣadrā's writings are replete with discussions of these terms.[18] But when it comes to the notion of idols of belief, the only extensive discussion he devotes to it is to be found in the *Tafsīr Sūrat al-fātiḥa*. The section in this *tafsīr* where Ṣadrā takes up the question occurs in the context of his treatment of Q 1:1.

After explaining the nature of the divine names and how they relate to the All-Gathering name Allah, Ṣadrā ventures into a fairly detailed explanation of the fact that most people do not worship God as He should be worshiped (here he freely draws on his *Tafsīr Āyat al-kursī* or "Commentary on the Throne Verse"). Confined as they are to their own methods and intellectual constructs (like the people of expressions' approaches to the Qurʾān), they fashion and carve God in their own image and according to their own beliefs. Having crafted an image of the deity with their own interpretive tools, He then becomes fit for their worship:

> Most people do not worship God insofar as He is God. They merely worship the objects of their beliefs in accordance with what they have formed for themselves as objects of worship. In reality, their gods are those imaginary idols which they form [*yataṣawwarūna*] and carve [*yanḥitūna*] with the power [*quwwa*] of their intellectual or imaginary beliefs.[19]

Like Ibn ʿArabī, Ṣadrā closely follows the Qurʾān's wording when discussing the idea of "carving" an idol.[20] Whereas the people of Abraham carved an idol out of physical matter, those who worship the objects of their beliefs carve idols out of the "stuff" of their soul. As Ṣadrā puts it, these objects of belief are "formed and sculpted" through man's use of his imagination and intellect, or what he also refers to as the "hands" of man's intellect.[21]

Idolatry, therefore, is not only worship of a physical image or even preoccupation with other than God. It is also to conceive of God in accordance with one's own selfish whims and desires. Since a mental image of God cannot be God as such, it can only be an object of one's belief, created by the self for the self. Because this is the case, there is no difference between those who worship physical idols and those who worship the God of their beliefs:

> A believer amongst the veiled ones—those who create the divinity in the forms of the object of their belief and nothing else—only worships a god on account of what he creates within himself and forms [*taṣawwara*] using his imagination. In reality, his God is created for himself and sculpted with the hand of his controlling power [*bi-yad quwwatihi al-mutaṣarrifa*]. So there is no difference between those idols which are taken as gods [externally] and his God, owing to the fact that they are all created for the self, whether they be external or internal to it.[22]

Why do people create idols? Ṣadrā, again following Ibn ʿArabī, offers an explanation. He says that an idol is taken as an object of worship simply because of the belief on the part of the one worshipping the idol that it is divine, and therefore worthy of worship:

> External idols are also only worshipped because of their worshipper's belief in their divinity. The mental forms are the objects of their worship essentially, and the external forms are their objects of worship accidentally. Thus, the objects of worship of every idol worshipper are nothing but the forms of his beliefs and the caprices [*ahwāʾ*] of his soul, as has been alluded to in His saying, *Have you seen the one who takes his caprice for his god?* [Q 65:23]. Just as worshippers of bodily idols worship what their hands have created, so too do those who have partial beliefs concerning God worship what the hands of their intellects have gathered.[23]

Ṣadrā acknowledges in this passage that it is essentially "caprice" which incites one to fashion an idol. This caprice forms into a mental image first, and then, in the case of a physical idol, is made into a physical image. Whether the image remains physical or mental, the God created by the self and for the self is only worshipped because the self considers it to be divine. Thus, what the self ultimately worships is nothing but its own whims and desires, since an idol—whether physical or mental—is nothing but a projection of the self. Since one's caprice is a projection of the content of the self, when one forms an idol one is really only worshipping oneself. All beliefs in which God is delimited by the self are nothing but constructions of the self. This explains why one believes in the divinity of the idol which he himself creates: the image is "divine" because it is proximate to the self, which is to say that it is like the self.

From another perspective, it is God's self-disclosures (*tajalliyāt*) which determine a servant's object of worship. Since some of God's names predominate over others in each individual, it is these divine names that become the servant's object of worship. In other words, by delimiting God with his intellectual and imaginal faculties, the servant necessarily brings within his field of worship certain qualities of the divinity to the exclusion of others. Most people, therefore, worship God from behind the veil of some of His self-disclosures. But because God's self-disclosures are perpetually different, perspectives on Him, that is, idolized delimitations of His true nature, will naturally be different as well. Depending on which self-disclosure veils the servant, he will deny God in His other self-disclosures because he is unable to recognize anything as divine other than the idol that he has created for himself. This, according to Ṣadrā, is the height of displaying poor etiquette (*adab*) toward God:

> From this veiling, differences amongst people in matters of belief come about. Thus, some of them anathematize others and some curse others, while every one of them affirms for the Real what the other denies, thinking that what they opine and believe is the highest form of exaltation of God! But they err and display bad etiquette toward God, while they think that they have attained the highest rank in knowledge and etiquette![24]

The Religion of the Perfect Man

If people are idol worshippers who must necessarily limit God according to their own specifications, thereby allowing some of God's self-disclosures to be operative within them rather than others, what does this mean with respect to their fate in the afterlife? Are those who deny God in all of His self-disclosures condemned "forever" for their idolatry? In one passage, Ṣadrā juxtaposes God's true servants with those who are servants of their own opinions and caprices. He implies here that the latter are unable to love and seek God by virtue of their self-imposed limitations on knowing God's true nature. But then he says that by virtue of God's mercy and compassion, those who do not worship Him as He truly should be worshipped are nevertheless upon a path of guidance facilitated by God:

> The Real, out of the perfection of His compassion [*ra'fa*] and mercy [*raḥma*] toward His servants, the all-encompassing nature [*shumūl*] of His benevolence [*ʿāṭifa*], the unfolding [*inbisāṭ*] of the light of His being toward the contingent things, and the self-disclosure [*tajallī*] of the [manifest] face of His Essence to the existent things, made for each of them a likeness [*mithāl*] which they could imitate, a refuge [*mathāba*] toward which they could strive, a path which they could traverse, a direction toward which they could aspire, a *qibla* with which they would be satisfied,[25] and a law in accordance with which they could act. He says, *For everyone there is a direction toward which he turns, so vie for the good. Wherever you are, God will bring you all together* [Q 2:148]; *For each of you We have made a law and a way* [Q 5:48]; *Each party rejoicing in what is with them* [Q 30:32].[26]

As I will demonstrate in Chapter 7, Ṣadrā's notion of the path specific to each individual mentioned in this passage has the utmost importance for his soteriology. For our purposes at the present moment, we can note that this passage also provides us with an added nuance to Ṣadrā's stance on how people see their created idols as "divine." From one perspective, it is because of their caprice that people fashion an idol of God. But from another perspective, it is because God allows Himself to be delimited so that they can serve Him in a form suitable to their natures.

Ṣadrā also acknowledges the possibility of there being a group of individuals who do not confine God to their own intellectual and imaginary constructs, and who thus follow God as He should be followed.[27] The religious positions taken by most people are always in accordance with their caprices, or what they love. But the position of the people of God is in accordance with their object of love, namely God.[28] Since God is their only object of love, they can be completely sincere toward Him in their "religion."[29] From this perspective, their religion *is* God, and they are effectively "the servants of the All-Merciful" (*ʿibād al-raḥmān*) mentioned in Q 25:63.[30] Significantly, the only time in the *Tafsīr Sūrat al-fātiḥa* that Ṣadrā makes an explicit personal claim occurs in the context of his treatment of the religion of the people of God. At a climactic moment in the text, he injects the following verse:

> Those who love out of caprice take diverse positions.
> As for me, I have a single position, and dwell in it alone.[31]

Himself one of the "people of God" or "servants of the All-Merciful," Ṣadrā is able to lay claim to a special position (*madhhab*) when it comes to conceptualizing and worshipping the divinity. Unlike people who delimit God according to their own needs, Ṣadrā's position allows him to worship God in all of His multiplicity, thereby always showing proper etiquette to God because of his perpetual affirmation of Him in all of His self-disclosures. This quality, Ṣadrā reminds us, only belongs to the Perfect Man. Since the Perfect Man does not deny God in any of His self-disclosures, He is able to witness Him in everything, and recognize Him in every form:

> As for the Perfect Man, he knows the Real in every object of witnessing [*mashāhid*] and religious rite [*mashāʿir*], and he worships Him in every homestead [*mawṭin*] and locus of manifestation [*maẓhar*].[32] So he is the servant of God [*ʿabd Allāh*] who worships Him in all of His names and

> attributes. On account of this, the most perfect of human individuals—Muhammad, God bless him and his family—was given this name. Just as the divine name [Allah] brings together all the names—which are unified because of the Exclusive Unity of All-Gatheredness—so too does its path bring together the paths of all the names, even if each of these paths are specified by a name which sustains its locus, and each locus is worshipped and its straight path particular to it is traversed from that perspective.[33]

The path of the Perfect Man is the path of the name Allah, which naturally entails that those traversing it not delimit God in any fashion. The path of the name Allah brings together all of the other names. Since each divine name is a delimitation of the Essence, it manifests a delimited and therefore particularized form of God's true nature. Particularized forms of God result in idols and particular forms of worship. Since the name Allah contains all of the other names, its path contains all of the other particularized paths to God.

The one on the path of the name Allah has thus transcended physical idolatry. And to the extent that it is humanly possible (recall Ibn ʿArabī's statement that "there are none but idol worshippers"), he has also transcended what Corbin calls "metaphysical idolatry."[34] By virtue of having smashed "the idols of the age of ignorance,"[35] such an individual is able to behold that formless form which contains all forms. Since the Perfect Man can only perceive the formless with the heart, that is, his instrument of spiritual "cognition," the heart itself must be formless. Only by being nothing can one contain everything. The pure heart, which is no-thing because its function is merely to act as a perfect mirror in which God sees His own formless form, is thus not possessed of any forms and is itself formless.[36]

Free of human limitations and having transcended divinizing only particular self-disclosures of God to the exclusion of His other self-disclosures, the gnostic is able to perceive God in any of the forms in which He discloses Himself. When he looks at the cosmos, which is created upon the form of God's beauty, he cannot help but see Him. The gnostic thus gazes upon God within the multiple refractions of forms in the mirror of the cosmos, beholding His beauty in all things, in every object of worship, and through every form of belief. He is thus in love with the cosmos, since it is nothing other than his Beloved:

> It has been reported that God is beautiful and He loves beauty. He is the artisan of the cosmos and brings it into

> existence in His form [*shākila*], as He says, *[Say:] "everyone acts according to their form"* [Q 17:84]. . . . So the entire cosmos is of the utmost beauty because it is a mirror for the Real. This is why the knowers become enraptured by it and the verifiers realize love for it. For He is the object of gaze in every eye, the beloved in every form of love, the object of worship in every act of worship, and the Final Goal in both the unseen and the seen. The entire cosmos prays to Him, praises Him, and glorifies Him.[37]

This passage draws an important link with Ṣadrā's cosmology of praise. The Perfect Man is able to see the manner in which all things in the cosmos are modes of praise for God, and by virtue of this fact, nothing appears to him as ugly. Rather, as the passage states, the cosmos is "of the utmost beauty." As the mirror in which the divine Beloved's face is reflected in all of its unitary multiplicity, the Perfect Man also understands the teleological purpose of the cosmos: not only is it the arena in which God manifests Himself in His multiplicity; it also signals, by its very nature, that all of its contents—which are so many modes of praise—must return to the Object of all praise and glorification.[38] But the minute we speak of a return of all modes of praise to their Object of praise, we are naturally faced with a much wider problem: if all things come from God and return to God, then do they not all, in their being reabsorbed back into God, end in a state similar to their origin? In order to understand how Mullā Ṣadrā approaches this question, I now turn my attention to his soteriology.

6

Soteriology I

In Islamic thought, the basic principle that all human beings will return to God after their bodily deaths has, for the most part, been a given. Yet according to both the Qur᾿ān and Ḥadīth, the return to God is not the same for all individuals. The fortunate are promised Paradise and the unfortunate are promised Hell. This basic picture of Islam's anthropology of the next life, however, has posed some serious difficulties for a number of leading Muslim thinkers. By the second/eighth century we already encounter important debates in Islamic theology concerning the question of not only the cessation of Hell as a place of torment, but also whether or not Hell itself was/is eternal.[1]

Despite the fact that both Sunnī and Shī῾ī theologians have generally maintained the eternal nature of Hell and its torments,[2] in later Islamic thought we find several coherent arguments, all based upon statements in the Qur᾿ān and Ḥadīth and amongst thinkers of very different intellectual persuasions, in favor of the cessation of punishment in Hell. Amongst the most influential authors who upheld such positions, we can mention Ibn ῾Arabī,[3] Ibn Taymiyya (d. 728/1328),[4] and the latter's student, Ibn Qayyim al-Jawziyya (d. 751/1350).[5] We are also told that the first Ottoman Shaykh al-Islam and important interpreter of Qūnawī, Muḥammad b. Ḥamza al-Fanārī (d. 834/1431), believed that punishment in Hell would eventually come to an end.[6]

Ibn ῾Arabī seems to have been the most unequivocal on the question of the cessation of punishment in Hell, even arguing that Hell's flames will become a source of pleasure for its inhabitants, a position which has aptly been described as "sweet torment"[7] and "infernal felicity."[8] Although Ibn ʿArabī's argument in this regard is quite unique, rooted as it is in his metaphysics, he does not seem to have been the first Islamic thinker to uphold the view that Hell would become a place of comfort. According to Shahrastānī, the famous *adīb* al-Jāḥiẓ (d. 256/868) believed that since Hell's inhabitants will not be chastised in the Fire eternally, they will eventually end up becoming a part of the Fire's constitution.[9]

By the time we get to Mullā Ṣadrā, therefore, the problem of the cessation of punishment in Hell (and the possibility of mercy for all) had already been almost a millennium in the making in texts of Islamic thought. But what distinguishes Ṣadrā's approach to the question of the eternality of Hell from the likes of an Ibn Taymiyya is that Ṣadrā, like Ibn ʿArabī before him, roots his treatment of the problem as dealt with in scripture within the wider framework of his ontology.

Since scripture and being for Ṣadrā are one and the same reality, it is all the more fitting that scripture would also detail the ultimate return of all things to God. Thus, since all things come from the God, who is the Source of all beauty and goodness, so too must they return to Him, enveloped by His goodness and beauty. This means that Hell, which is a place of torment, anguish, suffering, and distance from God must be finite; for all creatures, regardless of their actions, must return to their original home. Indeed, such a position seems to be the logical outcome of the wedding of religious eschatological teachings with an ontology that posits absolute oneness as the basis for the multiplicity in the cosmos. This is why we find similar discussions amongst a number of medieval Christian theologians. The ancient Christian doctrine of *apokatastasis* or "restoration," which has its roots in the New Testament (i.e., Acts 3:21), was upheld by such important figures as St. Clement of Alexandria (d. 216), Origen (d. 254), Gregory of Nyssa (d. ca. 395), and John Scottus Eriugena (d. ca. 877).[10] We also find similar discussions in Jewish mysticism. As Moshe Idel notes, the famous Spanish mystic and disputed author of the Zohar, Moses de Leon (d. 1305), is known to have believed in the finite nature of punishment in Hell. He argued that since the soul is a "part" of God, it is impossible for God to punish Himself eternally.[11]

Despite the fact that we have a relatively comprehensive picture of Ṣadrā's eschatology, especially with respect to the "bodily" nature of the Return,[12] how his doctrine of "salvation" fits into his eschatology has received very little attention. This is quite surprising, owing to the fact that, as will be seen in the present chapter, this is a question which occupied Ṣadrā from early on in his career. The first mention of Ṣadrā's soteriology is to be found in Nasr's seminal English article on him written over four decades ago.[13] In that article he notes that Ṣadrā upholds the view that Hell's punishments will eventually come to an end, and that all human beings will return to God in a state of felicity. A decade later, in his study of Ṣadrā's *Zād al-musāfir* ("Provisions for the Wayfarer"), Āshtiyānī also noted the presence of this idea in Ṣadrā's writings.[14] The appearance in 1981 of James Morris' English translation of one of Ṣadrā's more popular works may have complicated matters, since in that text, Ṣadrā seems to take a different stance on the question.[15]

In Khwājawī's book on Ṣadrā published in 1987,[16] he notes that Ṣadrā does not treat the problem specifically; rather, he states the different views on the issue and is aware of the position of the school of Ibn ʿArabī. Khwājawī then goes on to cite several passages, all in Persian translation, of Ṣadrā's treatment of the problem. In all cases cited, Ṣadrā is portrayed as siding with the position that punishment in Hell is eternal for those who did not believe in God's unity. In the process, however, Khwājawī overlooks a number of important passages within Ṣadrā's oeuvre which clearly complicate the author's cut-and-dry presentation of the problem.[17] Lurking in the background of Khwājawī's discussion, and the relevant section in Jad Hatem's more recent study,[18] is a failure to clearly distinguish between two important issues, namely the problem of the eternality of Hell on the one hand, and the question of the ultimate felicity of all humans on the other. As we will soon see, this distinction lies at the heart of Ṣadrā's soteriology.

The most detailed treatment we have to date of Ṣadrā's soteriology can be found in Naṣīrī's monograph on Ṣadrā's *tafsīr* works,[19] although he too falls into the same aforementioned pitfall as Khwājawī and Hatem. Naṣīrī also agrees with Khwājawī's view that Ṣadrā ultimately does not support the notion that Hell is a pleasurable abode.[20] Unlike Khwājawī, his presentation of Ṣadrā's soteriology is more thorough in that he cites a good variety of relevant passages from Ṣadrā's *tafsīr* writings.[21] Yet, in the final analysis, Naṣīrī's explication remains unsatisfactory. This is because he does not examine Ṣadrā's *Tafsīr Sūrat al-fātiḥa*, which presents us with the summit of Ṣadrā's soteriological doctrine. At the same time, since the *Tafsīr Sūrat al-fātiḥa* contains Ṣadrā's most mature exposition of the nature of Hell, a number of his other non-*tafsīr* and *tafsīr* works which feature his soteriology, and which were penned before and inform the *Tafsīr Sūrat al-fātiḥa*, are not taken into account by Naṣīrī. Thus, before attempting to understand Ṣadrā's fully-developed soteriology in the *Tafsīr Sūrat al-fātiḥa,* we need to trace its development throughout his career. It is this task to which we shall now turn.

The Nature of Things

Ṣadrā first addresses the question of the problem of eternal punishment in Hell in his *al-Mabdaʾ wa-l-maʿād* ("The Origin and the Return"). This text is Ṣadrā's first full-length book and was completed in 1015/1606,[22] which places its composition in the period of his retreat in Kahak. Although this is Ṣadrā's earliest book, it already represents his mature thinking, and is written, like every other work which follows this one, from the perspective of the fundamentality and oneness of being. Indeed, the date of its completion coincides with the commencement of the *Asfār,* a project which Ṣadrā did not complete until much later.[23]

In the context of his discussion of common mistakes amongst people when it comes to interpreting eschatological realities, Ṣadrā introduces another mistaken belief to which most people adhere, namely the fact that (a) grave sinners (*ahl al-kabāʾir*) will reside in Hell for eternity (*khulūd*), and (b) God's mercy will never reach them. In refuting this belief, Ṣadrā calls attention to the fact that such a perspective both engenders despair amongst those aspiring toward God and contradicts the primary purpose of revelation, which is to facilitate for man a path to salvation:

> They do not know that God's mercy is all-encompassing [*wāsiʿa*], that His forgiveness takes precedence, and [that] the shortcoming is from us. They do not realize that this opinion is one of the things on account of which man despairs of God's mercy and thus diminishes in [both his] desire for the pleasures of the Garden and in [his] awe of the chastisements of the Fire. For those seeking God, heading towards Him, and longing to meet Him, having little desire and awe makes the path leading to God and His Dominion [*malakūt*] distant.
>
> Every belief and position [*iʿtiqād wa-madhhab*] which is inconsistent with God's mercy and guidance and makes the path [*ṭarīq*] leading to Him distant is undoubtedly false. For such a position is inconsistent with the establishment

> of revealed religions [*sharā'i'*] and contradicts the sending of messengers and the revealing of scriptures, since the purpose behind all of these is nothing but to lead creatures close to their Lord's mercy by way of the nearest of paths [*aqrab ṭuruq*] and the easiest of means [*aysar wajh*].[24]

This passage is significant for a number of reasons. Not only does it give us a window into Ṣadrā's earlier thought on the question of eternal suffering, but it also provides us with a clear picture of his view of the purpose of religion and revelation. As we will see in the next chapter, it is not without purpose that Ṣadrā ends this passage by saying that the purpose behind revelation is to provide for human beings the "nearest of paths" and "easiest of means" to their Lord's mercy.

Furthermore, it was noted above that by this point Ṣadrā had espoused the position of the fundamentality of being. *Wujūd* for Ṣadrā, it must be remembered, is identified with *raḥma*, as is the case with Ibn 'Arabī.[25] This explains why, as Ṣadrā says in no uncertain terms, any position which goes against the basic teaching of God's mercy is false, for such a position would be tantamount to negating being itself, which is impossible.

The Essential and the Accidental

The *Tafsīr Āyat al-kursī* is the next work in which Ṣadrā attempts to tackle the problem of eternal suffering in Hell.[26] This text, which is actually a commentary on Q 2:255-7, was completed some seven years after the *Mabda'*.[27] It is, therefore, one of Ṣadrā's first *tafsīr* compositions.[28] Like the *Mabda'*, this early book already shows a mature Ṣadrā at work. But with respect to the issue of eternal suffering in Hell, he does not spell out the implications of his position as one would perhaps expect.

Ṣadrā broaches the soteriological problem late in the work in the context of his refutation of the Mu'tazilite, Kharijite, and Zaydite belief that those Muslims who are grave sinners (*ahl al-kabā'ir*) will suffer in Hell eternally.[29] Hell is the eternal abode, he tells us, not of believers, but of nonbelievers and those who have false beliefs and defiled rational souls.[30] By extension, Ṣadrā also wants to refute those who try to simply dismiss the issue of Hell's eternal nature and maintain that the people in Hell will end up in Heaven after they have been thoroughly purified of their sins.[31] Ṣadrā is not pleased with this position as he does maintain that Hell, as well as "suffering" in it, is eternal.

Ṣadrā then attempts to answer the objections people have with eternal punishment in Hell.[32] The main problem is that this view seems to contradict the fact of God's fundamental mercy (a point that Ṣadrā also made in the *Mabdaʾ*, as we have already seen), and the fact that a famous *ḥadīth qudsī* says that God's mercy outstrips His wrath.[33] At this point he explicitly draws on Qaysari's *Sharḥ al-Fuṣūṣ*,[34] where the author makes the important observation that since God has the attribute mercy, it is not becoming of someone with that quality to inflict punishment forever.[35] Next, Ṣadrā cites a text from Ibn ʿArabī's *Fuṣūṣ* where he says that the final issue of the people of the fire, even if they are in the fire, is pleasure, as the fire's form will become cool and safe for those in it just as the fire became cool for Abraham when he was thrown in the fire by his people.[36]

With respect to the next world, Ṣadrā also tells us that what is intense pain for one person might be extreme delight for another, which is also the case in this world. That is why, in the next world, one person's chastisement might be someone else's pleasure.[37] At any rate, regardless of whether one believes suffering in Hell to be eternal or not, it is clear that the angels and minions (*zabāniya*)[38] of Hell who reside there do not suffer in it.[39] These arguments would not convince a scholar confined to the purely outward dimension of scripture, however, and Ṣadrā is well-aware of this.[40] What is needed in order to come to his standpoint, where the eternal nature of Hell is upheld alongside "suffering" therein, is the authority of unveiling (*kashf*). Since this is the standpoint from which Ṣadrā addresses the issue, he also insists that his positions are in keeping with the inner teachings of the Prophet.[41]

This is the extent to which Ṣadrā offers his own insights on the issue of eternal chastisement in Hell in the *Tafsīr Āyat al-kursī*. For the remainder of his discussion he cites an important section from Qayṣarī's *Sharḥ*.[42] It is worth summarizing Qayṣarī's main points here since they will go on to inform Ṣadrā's fuller exposition of the problem of soteriology in the *Asfār* and, in a sense, the *Tafsīr Sūrat al-fātiḥa*.

Following Ibn ʿArabī, Qayṣarī says that both Hell and Heaven will be inhabited by people in conformity with their natures. Those in Hell will reside there for so long that they will eventually forget about pleasure. Thus, their state of perpetual punishment will become a form of pleasure, which will then engender a state of rest and contentment in them. There are several *ḥadīth*s upon which Qayṣarī draws to make his point, the most important one being the aforementioned *ḥadīth qudsī* where God says that His mercy outstrips His wrath.

It will be noted that I have been referring to Ṣadrā's belief in the eternal nature of punishment in Hell as "suffering." This is because Ṣadrā in the *Tafsīr Āyat al-kursī* upholds a position which will continue to resurface almost as a leitmotif in nearly all of his subsequent discussions of this particular problem. This is the view that there is no contradiction between something being (eternal) chastisement from one perspective, and pleasure or comfort from another perspective. This idea is taken from Qayṣarī, who states that "the existence of something as chastisement in one respect does not negate its being mercy in another respect."[43]

There is no doubt that a much more substantial engagement with the question of eternal chastisement in Ṣadrā's writings is to be found toward the end of the *Asfār*. It is highly likely that the treatment of the problem in the *Asfār* takes place after Ṣadrā's discussion in the *Tafsīr Āyat al-kursī*. We can make this assumption on the following grounds: apart from the obvious chronological considerations, the *Asfār*'s presentation of the problem is also much more nuanced, and Ṣadrā attempts to engage the issue in a more straightforward manner.

Ṣadrā tackles the question of the eternal nature of suffering in Hell in the last *safr* of the *Asfār* (the section dealing with psychology and eschatology) under the subheading, "On How the People of the Fire Abide in the Fire Eternally" (*fī kayfiyyat khulūd ahl al-nār fī-l-nār*).[44] He begins this section by saying that the question of eternal chastisement is a theologically difficult problem, and one concerning which there are differences of opinion, both amongst the exoteric scholars (*ʿulamāʾ al-rusūm*) and the people of unveiling (*ahl al-kashf*).[45] He summarizes the position of those who believe that God's chastisement is not eternal. They maintain that since all people are created with yearning (*ʿishq*) for existence and longing for its perfection, the essential end of all is their source, which means that they all end up in goodness because all things seek God and yearn to meet Him as He is the source of love and longing.[46] There are indeed obstacles on the way to Him, but they are not eternal, for if this were the case then people would be unable to search for what is good.[47] To this effect, Ṣadrā cites a well-known Prophetic tradition which states that those who love to meet God, God loves to meet them, whereas those who dislike to meet Him, He dislikes to meet them.[48] Then Ṣadrā says that since love is essential and disliking is accidental, the people who love to meet God do so as a result of an intrinsic quality (*bi-l-dhāt*), whereas those who dislike to meet Him do so in an accidental manner (*bi-l-ʿaraḍ*).[49]

As for those who uphold the view that Hell and its chastisement are eternal, Ṣadrā explains their position, playing as it were the role of devil's advocate (no pun intended). He states that without sin, pain, and difficulties the order of the cosmos would become corrupted, and this would nullify God's wisdom. Thus, the order of things can only be upheld through the existence of lowly and base things. Since divine wisdom demands that there be different ranks, levels, and preparednesses of people, His decree requires that some of these people be felicitous and some wretched.[50]

Ṣadrā clearly does not favor this position. In fact, he says that since each party—whether felicitous or wretched—comes about by virtue of God's will and in accordance with a particular divine name, they will still return to their essential natures. Returning to one's essential nature itself entails delight and bliss. But the contrary qualities of the divine names must still obtain. Be they the names of beauty (*jamāl*) or majesty (*jalāl*), God's names must always have their respective loci in which they can manifest His infinite self-disclosures.[51]

Ṣadrā cites a passage from Ibn ʿArabī's *Futūḥāt* which states that people will enter either Heaven or Hell on account of their actions and will remain in their respective abodes by virtue of their intentions. Although this means that there will be people in Hell who are eternally tormented, Ibn ʿArabī says that this torment will be agreeable to their natures, meaning their "torment" will actually be pleasure. This is primarily because, as another version of the aforementioned *ḥadīth qudsī* says, "My mercy triumphs over My wrath."[52] This means that God will not simply punish His servants without allowing mercy to overcome wrath in the end. In fact, Ibn ʿArabī asserts, were the people of Hell to enter Heaven, they would feel pain because its "pleasures" would not be agreeable with their natures.[53] It is worth citing one of Ibn ʿArabī's more detailed explanations of this point. The passage occurs in the context of his discussion of the two forms of chastisement in Hell which are mentioned in the Qurʾān, namely Fire (*nār*) and Bitter Cold (*zamharīr*):

> The person of a cold constitution will find the heat of the Fire pleasant, and the person of a hot constitution will find the Bitter Cold pleasant. Thus Gehenna brings together the Fire and the Bitter Cold—because of the diversity of

> constitutions. What causes pain in a specific constitution will cause bliss in another constitution that is its opposite. So wisdom is not inoperative, for God keeps the Bitter Cold of Gehenna for those with hot constitutions and the Fire for those with cold constitutions. They enjoy themselves in Gehenna, for they have a constitution with which, were they to enter the Garden, they would suffer chastisement, because of the Garden's equilibrium.[54]

Ṣadrā also cites a passage from Qayṣarī's commentary on the *Fuṣūṣ* in which he states that God's chastisement is not eternal. Rather, it is there to purify people, just as gold and silver are placed in fire in order to separate base metals from pure substances.[55] Thus, chastisement in Hell is there insofar as humans need to be purged of the base characteristics which they acquired on earth and which prevent them from being in God's company.

There is clearly a contradiction in the reports cited by Ṣadrā. Ibn ʿArabī says that the chastisement is eternal, but that it is somehow pleasurable for those subjected to it because it is agreeable with their natures. Qayṣarī, on the other hand, says that punishment in Hell is simply there to purge people of their sins, and, once purified, they will no longer be chastised. Ṣadrā assures us that there actually is no contradiction between these two accounts. People can simultaneously be punished eternally and yet this punishment can come to an end:

> If you say that these statements which indicate that the cessation [*inqiṭāʿ*] of chastisement for the people of the Fire is inconsistent with what I have just said concerning the lastingness of pain for them, I say [the following]: I do not agree that these are inconsistent with one another [*munāfāt*], for there is no inconsistency between the non-cessation [*ʿadam inqiṭāʿ*] of eternal chastisement for the people of the Fire and its cessation for each of them at one moment.[56]

What Ṣadrā means by this statement is not altogether clear. We know that he is trying to defend a position which reconciles the idea of some form of abiding punishment in Hell with God's all-encompassing mercy. Several pages later, he clarifies his point. He says that the statements of the "people of unveiling" regarding the cessation of punishment in Hell are not inconsistent with those Qurʾānic verses which speak of chastisement in Hell. Much like the Kabbalist doctrine of transmigration (*gilgul*), which sees at the root of the transmigration (and therefore punishment) of souls an act of God's mercy,[57] Ṣadrā again draws on Qayṣarī's statement that something can both be chastisement and mercy at one and the same time.[58]

How, then, can something be punishment and mercy at one and the same time? Although he alluded to a solution earlier when he spoke of the intrinsic and accidental qualities with respect to those loving/disliking the meeting with God, Ṣadrā returns to this question later on in the text. He cites Ibn ʿArabī's meditation on the fact that since God created people for the sole purpose of worshipping Him, their innate disposition (*fiṭra*) is to only worship Him.[59] As Ibn ʿArabī argues elsewhere, one of the verses upon which this argument is based is Q 17:23, "And your Lord has decreed [*qaḍā*] that you worship none but Him." For Ibn ʿArabī, the "decree" in this verse is not merely prescriptive (*tashrīʿī*) but engendering (*takwīnī*), meaning that it is in the very nature of things, based on the divine decree, that God be the only object of worship in the cosmos.[60] Thus, when people worship gods other than God they do so because of their belief that their worship will bring them closer to God, which explains Q 39:3, " 'We only worship them to draw us closer to God.' "[61]

Since God's creatures ultimately worship none but Him, albeit in different forms, they all truly uphold their primordial covenant with God that they would worship none but Him. Ṣadrā notes that behind all forms of worship lies essential worship, and that that which is accidental, that is, what comes about by virtue of man's choices made during his life, must be accounted for. Thus, the human constitution (*nashʾa*), which is accidental and animal, will face torment whereas the substance related to man's soul (*jawhar nafsānī*) will not undergo corruption.[62] This means that the lowly qualities which a person acquires during his stay on earth will eventually be effaced through torment and chastisement in the afterlife. After this period of torment, he will return to his innate disposition. As for the one who had incorrect and false beliefs concerning God, his suffering will also come to an end, but he will be unable to return to his innate disposition (*fiṭra*) and will thus be "transferred to another innate disposition."[63]

Yet by virtue of the economy of the divine names there are some who must indeed reside in the fire, that is, who have been destined to come under the purview of God's names of majesty and wrath. Ibn ʿArabī takes his lead from two important texts, one a verse from the Qurʾān and the other a *ḥadīth*. Q 7:36 refers to the "people of the fire" (*aṣḥāb al-nār*) as residing in it eternally (*hum fīhā khālidūn*). The Prophet says that "none will remain in the Fire except for those who are its folk [*al-ladhīna hum ahluhā*]." The fact that these references in scripture refer to the people of the Fire as being "people" and "folk" gives Ibn ʿArabī cause to explain his position on why punishment in Hell is a good thing for its inhabitants: since Hell was always meant to be their home and is therefore suitable to their natures, were they to leave it, they would suffer immensely because of departing from their homestead.[64] As we saw earlier, this means that were the "people" or "folk" of the Fire to be taken out of Hell and led into the Garden, they would actually suffer pain because their constitutions would not be suited to the joys of the Garden. The reason their constitutions are not suited to other than the Fire, Ibn ʿArabī tells us, is because God has given them a constitution which is only suitable for residence in Hell.[65]

Ṣadrā stands in complete agreement with Ibn ʿArabī concerning the pleasurable nature of residence in Hell. At the same time, he notes that he considers Ibn ʿArabī's interpretation of the terms *aṣḥāb* and *ahl* used in the aforementioned Qurʾānic verse and *ḥadīth* to be weak. Ṣadrā understands the terms *aṣḥāb* and *ahl* to have relational meanings, which is to say that they do not indicate "residence."[66] He then seems to disagree with Ibn ʿArabī again, noting that the only way the people of the Fire's departure from their homestead could be an intense chastisement would be if by "departure," the "natural homestead [*al-mawṭin al-ṭabīʿī*] is meant."[67] Although Ibn ʿArabī speaks of a constitution being given to the people of the Fire so that they can bear and derive pleasure from its torments, it is unclear whether there is any real disagreement here between Ṣadrā and Ibn ʿArabī's positions. This is because they both indicate that Hell will, in one manner or another, be a necessary permanent abode for some people whose natures will be made suitable for it. Ibn ʿArabī refers to this nature as a "constitution," while Ṣadrā refers to it as a "natural homestead."

Where Ṣadrā stands in clear agreement with Ibn ʿArabī is on how Hell will become agreeable:

> There is no doubt that the entry [into Hell of] the creature whose end is that he should enter Hell—in accordance with the divine lordly decree—will be agreeable [*muwāfiq*] to his nature and will be a perfection of his existence. For the end, as has been stated, is the perfection of existents. The perfection of something which one finds agreeable to his nature [*al-muwāfiq lahu*] is not chastisement with respect to him. It is only chastisement with respect to others who have been created in higher ranks.[68]

If Ṣadrā is in fact disagreeing with Ibn ʿArabī, it could have to do with the particular details of how this "natural homestead" comes about. If this is the case, then Ṣadrā understands Ibn ʿArabī to say that the people of the Fire take up residence in it after their natures have been made agreeable to it, whereas Ṣadrā's position is that the "natural homestead" of the people of the Fire has always been, by virtue of the divine decree, the Fire and nothing else. Since Ṣadrā understands the Fire to be the natural homestead for some people, it is a form of perfection for them in accordance with the principle of substantial motion, namely that all things are constantly moving toward their substantial perfection as they ascend the scale of being. The most important point which emerges from this discussion is that Ṣadrā sets forth an argument for how punishment in Hell can be eternal, while not compromising the fundamentality of God's mercy.

Yet what, exactly, does Ṣadrā mean when he speaks of "the creature whose end is that he should enter Hell?" The reason Hell comes about, Ṣadrā will go on to say, is because of the configuration of the cosmos itself. The cosmos is nothing but differentiated modes of God's engendering Command. Hence, the duality which emerges in the cosmos is a natural and necessary result of the dispersion of God's Word which becomes fragmented the further it falls away from its Source. The two "rivers" which proceed from the Ocean of Oneness, therefore, account for the ontological roots of both good and evil.[69]

Because Hell exists by virtue of the "left" side of the river, and insofar as the "left" represents God's names of wrath and majesty, it must necessarily manifest God's qualities of wrath.[70] Although the river branches off into two, it comes from the same source of water. This source of water is nothing other than God's mercy, which for Ṣadrā, as we have already seen, is a synonym for being.

By the time we get to the *Asfār*, therefore, Ṣadrā is mainly concerned with reconciling the problem of eternal suffering in Hell with God's mercy. In fact, in the relevant sections of the *Asfār*, he relies mostly upon Ibn ʿArabī's *Futūḥāt*. Yet in one of these sections Ṣadrā rephrases a key passage from the *Futūḥāt*, which could be read as an attempt on Ṣadrā's part to explain why God's mercy must prevail.[71] Reproduced on the following page are the text from the *Futūḥāt* and the same text cited by Ṣadrā in the *Asfār*. Ṣadrā's alterations to the text of the *Futūḥāt* have been indicated in bold.[72]

***Futūḥāt*, 3:25 (Beirut)**

The two abodes will be populated, and mercy will outstrip wrath and *embrace all things* [Q 7:156], including Hell and everyone within it. God *is the Most Merciful of the merciful* [Q 12:64], as He said about Himself. We have found in ourselves, who are among those whom God has innately disposed toward mercy, that we have mercy on all God's servants, even if God has decreed in His creating them that the attribute of chastisement will remain forever with them in the cosmos. This is because the ruling property of mercy has taken possession of our hearts. The possessor of this attribute is I and my peers, and we are creatures, possessors of caprices and personal desires. God has said about Himself that He is *the Most Merciful of the merciful*. So we have no doubt that He is more merciful than we are toward His creatures, while we have known from our own selves this extravagant mercy. So how could chastisement be everlasting for them when He has this all-inclusive attribute of mercy? God is nobler than that. This is all the more true because rational proofs have affirmed that the Author is neither benefited by acts of obedience nor harmed by acts of opposition; that everything flows in accordance with His decree, His measuring out, and His judgment; and that the creatures are compelled in their choosing.

***Asfār*, 9:352–3**

The two abodes will be populated—**that is, the abodes of felicity and fire**—and mercy will outstrip wrath and *embrace all things* [Q 7:156], including Hell and everyone within it. God *is the Most Merciful of the merciful* [Q 12:64]. We have found in ourselves **[that we] are** among those **who have been innately disposed towards mercy. Since God has decreed it in His creation, He will remove the attribute of chastisement in the cosmos. God has given this quality, and the giver of perfection has more claim to it.** The possessor of this attribute is I and my peers, and we are **servants,** creatures, possessors of caprices and personal desires. **There is no doubt that He is more merciful than we are towards His creatures. And He** has said about Himself that He is *the Most Merciful of the merciful*. So we have no doubt that He is more merciful than we are towards His creatures, while we **know** from our own selves this **extravagance. You could say that** rational proofs have affirmed that the Author is neither benefited by acts of obedience nor harmed by acts of opposition, that everything flows in accordance with His decree **and His measuring out,** and that the creatures are compelled in their choosing. **So how could chastisement be everlasting for them?**[73]

In Ṣadrā's important addition to the *Futūḥāt* text, "God has given this quality, and the giver of perfection has more claim to it," the quality in question here is, of course, the mercy toward which God has allowed some to be predisposed. This insertion at least gives us a window into why Ṣadrā feels so strongly about mercy encompassing everyone in the end. But by far Ṣadrā's most important alteration to this passage is where he has "Since God has decreed it in His creation, He will remove the attribute of chastisement in the cosmos"[74] for Ibn ʿArabī's, "even if God has decreed in His creating them that the attribute of chastisement will remain forever with them in the cosmos." The effect produced in Ṣadrā's reading is that those who are innately disposed toward mercy simply act in conformity with the nature of God's will, namely that He does not wish for chastisement to persist in the cosmos. This alteration therefore illustrates the point that Ṣadrā would like to make: it is in the very nature of the divine decree that all things end in mercy and that chastisement comes to an end, the knowledge and realization of which is the exclusive purview of those who have been innately disposed toward God's mercy.[75]

For Ibn ʿArabī, the attribute of chastisement must remain in the cosmos by virtue of the distribution of the divine names. This is something that Ṣadrā would not disagree with. But why then does he alter the passage to make it seem like chastisement will not at all remain in the cosmos? This could be because, as Ṣadrā and Ibn ʿArabī see it, the root of "chastisement" is actually mercy, and from this perspective, the attribute of chastisement qua pain and punishment must eventually perish. It can again be recalled that since the root of the cosmos is being and being and mercy are the same reality, all that is accidental to being must eventually come to an end. Likewise, since wrath is accidental to mercy, so too must it come to an end.

7

Soteriology II

Ṣadrā's treatment concerning the ultimate fate of human beings in the afterlife is quite consistent in the *Mabda*ʾ and the *Asfār*. The most important point we walk away with from his discussion in the *Mabda*ʾ is that the purpose of religion is to lead people back to God's mercy through the shortest route possible. In the *Asfār*, Ṣadrā argues that it is in the nature of things itself that there be mercy and wrath, and that, ultimately, all things must devolve on God's mercy. In elucidating his point in the *Asfār* Ṣadrā draws quite freely on Ibn ʿArabī's soteriology. It will also be recalled that he recasts an important point in the *Futūḥāt* to read not that both mercy and chastisement will persist in the cosmos, but that only mercy will persist. Upon closer inspection, this reading of Ṣadrā's is not incongruous with Ibn ʿArabī's point. This is why he seems to use Ibn ʿArabī's soteriology to justify his position that there is no incongruity between calling a thing mercy and punishment at one and the same time.

Yet in neither the *Mabda*ʾ nor the *Asfār* does Ṣadrā attempt to explain his soteriology as such. We know from these two texts that he takes a number of positions for granted. But he does not present us with a coherent argument for how mercy will triumph in the end. What we have, rather, are tidbits of information which, when pieced together, give us a glimpse into Ṣadrā's reflections on the issue. It would be extremely difficult to draw any concrete conclusions from Ṣadrā's earlier pronouncements concerning soteriology other than the fact that he upholds a position that all creatures will end up in God's mercy, despite the outward appearance of punishment for some of them (which, at any rate, is in accordance with the divine will).

Turning our attention to the *Tafsīr Sūrat al-fātiḥa*, we find a much more detailed and internally coherent explication of Ṣadrā's soteriology. In a sense, Ṣadrā's discussions in this text have in mind the relevant sections of the *Mabda'* and the *Asfār* (as will become clear shortly, this is more true for the latter). Yet he also draws some important connections between ideas in these texts against the backdrop of his commentary on the Fātiḥa. It is as if Ṣadrā is prompted by the verses of the Fātiḥa to redress his treatment of soteriology, and by virtue of the unity of this Qur'ānic chapter, is compelled to bring unity to his ideas on the issue.

In his commentary upon the Fātiḥa, Ṣadrā returns to an important point to which he alluded in the *Asfār*, namely that mercy is essential whereas wrath is accidental.[1] Freely employing the language and symbolism of scripture to state his point, he introduces the problem of mercy's essentiality in philosophical yet familiar terms:

> Know that God's mercy embraces all things with respect to existence and quiddity. So the existence of wrath, in terms of the entity of wrath [*'ayn al-ghaḍab*], is also from God's mercy. For this reason, His mercy outstrips His wrath, since being is that very mercy which encompasses [*shāmila*] everything, as He says, *And My mercy embraces all things* [Q 7:156].[2] Amongst the totality of entities and quiddities—all of which the existential mercy [*al-raḥma al-wujūdiyya*] reaches—are the entities of wrath and vengeance. Through mercy, God gives existence to the entity of wrath, so its root is good, as is what results from it, such as pain, sickness, tribulation, trial, and the like. . . .[3]

Since all things arise from being and return to being, they are nothing in and of themselves, which means that their qualities are at best accidental. Things which seem to be evil, such as sickness or pain, spring up therefore within being, but by virtue of being's diminution and not its perfection. Yet since they are modes of being, their source is good, even if they bring along with them some temporary harm. This temporary harm and perceived evil is a necessary part of the structure of reality, which, by its nature, is graded and multilevel. The multilevel nature of the stratification of being entails that those modes of being which come about at the lower end of the scale of being be more dense, dark, tenebrous, material, and hence "evil." Thus, sicknesses and tribulations are simply depravations of being. Stated another way, they are "non-existence."[4]

In non-philosophical language, we can say that since things arise out of mercy through the Breath of the All-Merciful and return to mercy,[5] whatever negative qualities that become attached to them must naturally peel away. Creatures who return to God with negative qualities encounter God's wrath. And just as negative qualities are accidental, so too is the quality of wrath which they encounter. Wrath only arises out of mercy, which means that God's wrath is nothing but His mercy. However, because wrath is one of God's qualities, like mercy, it must embrace all things.[6] But because God's mercy outstrips His wrath, the essentiality of mercy will necessarily outstrip the accidentality of wrath. This is why Ṣadrā, following Ibn ʿArabī (but not acknowledging his source), says very early on in the *Tafsīr Sūrat al-fātiḥa* that "the end for all is mercy."[7] Despite the fact that the end for all is mercy, Ṣadrā insists that the routes individuals take to return to their Source of mercy are radically divergent.

Paths to Mercy

In the context of his commentary on Q 1:6 Ṣadrā makes a number of important statements which shed a great deal of light on remarks made earlier in the *Tafsīr Sūrat al-fātiḥa*. Following his meditations on the path or *ṣirāṭ* made in the *Asfār*,[8] Ṣadrā says that each individual has a path that he must traverse, and which ultimately leads him to God:

> Know that the path is not a path except through one's traversing it. An allusion has been made to the fact that every creature is heading towards the direction of the Real, towards the Causer of causes [*musabbib al-asbāb*] in an innate manner of turning [*tawajjuh gharīzī*] and a motion of natural disposition [*ḥaraka jibilliyya*]. In this motion of natural disposition, diversion and fleeing from what God has fixed for each of them cannot be conceived with respect to them. God takes them by their forelock, as He says, *"There is not a creature except that He takes it by its forelock. Verily my Lord is upon a straight path"* [Q 11:56].[9]

This path that an individual traverses belongs to him in an "innate manner of turning" and is a "motion of natural disposition." The path, therefore, is traversed in accordance with what Ṣadrā identifies as the *fiṭra* in the *Asfār*. Yet it would seem that, despite the fact that everyone is heading to God in an innate manner of turning, there are nevertheless differences amongst them in the route of their return, and, ultimately, their final fate.

Understanding these different routes taken by people to their destination (which is in accordance with their innate disposition and to which they innately turn) can only be made sense of once we have understood the nature of the path itself. The path, according to Ṣadrā, is, from one perspective, nothing other than the human soul:

> On the Day of Resurrection, and according to the view of the people of insight who have been overcome by witnessing the configuration of the afterlife, it is spread out for you as a sensory bridge [*jisr maḥsūs*] extended over the surface of Hell, its start being in [this] place, and its end being at the door of Paradise. Whoever witnesses it will know that it is of his design and building, and that it is an extended bridge in this world over the surface of his Hell in the fire of his nature, within which is the shadow of his reality.[10]

Ḥasanzādah Āmulī seems to stop short of suggesting that Ṣadrā borrowed the idea of the soul being the path from Ṭūsī's *Āghāz wa-anjām*.[11] Yet, as with all ideas which Ṣadrā derives from his predecessors, they take on a completely different character by virtue of his unique philosophical outlook. One important principle of Ṣadrā's doctrine of substantial motion—which can be said to implicitly lie at the heart of Islamic teachings on the Origin and the Return[12]—is that the very idea of change occurs within the category of substance itself. Indeed, this is an important departure from traditional Aristotelian substance metaphysics.[13] Ṣadrā tells us that the soul is "corporeal in temporal origination and spiritual in subsistence [*jismāniyyat al-ḥudūth wa-rūḥāniyyat al-baqāʾ*]."[14] As the underlying stuff of the human totality, the soul partakes in substantial motion, or what Ṣadrā also calls "essential motion" (*ḥaraka dhātiyya*)."[15] Since the very substance or essence of the soul partakes in motion, the distance it traverses is nothing other than itself.[16] Thus, the higher the soul ascends the scale of being, the more real it becomes, meaning the more it strips itself of its materiality and returns to its true nature.[17]

One of the implications of the identification of the soul with the path is that, because all of one's actions in this world are imprinted upon the soul, the nature of the human soul itself determines the route one will take in his journey back to God. The state of the soul, in other words, will become imaginalized in the next world, thus creating a pathway for man to his ultimate place of residency. The soul extends from Hell to Paradise by virtue of the fact that Hell for Ṣadrā is, from one perspective, nothing other than the corporeal world in which the soul is pinned down by matter.[18] If the soul cannot rise beyond the prison of corporeality, it will end up in Hell, that is, it will remain in its fallen state. Souls which have become fully actualized will on the other hand enter Paradise, which was/is their original home.[19]

Man, Ṣadrā tells us, gradually proceeds from the most manifest to the most inner, or from the most dense to the most subtle, "until he ends at his homestead which has been fixed for him by God."[20] The idea that man's destiny is inextricably linked to his place of return is something we have already seen in the *Asfār*. In the context of the *Tafsīr Sūrat al-fātiḥa*, Ṣadrā attempts to answer the problem of how, if everyone simply follows their instinctive nature and original disposition in accordance with the divine decree, the wicked amongst them will be punished while the righteous will be rewarded. He says that there is a difference between being distant from God but nevertheless felicitous, and being proximate to Him by way of the removal of intermediaries.[21] Yet it could be asked that if everyone is created with the disposition of love and desire for God, how can there be differences amongst humans with respect to these types of proximity and distance?[22]

These differences amongst creatures, Ṣadrā tells us, exist because souls are not created with the same innate disposition: some souls are more disposed toward purity than others, whereas others are more disposed toward murkiness. In the material realm, various factors in the world also have an effect upon the reason for why souls are so disparate. At the same time, while all creatures are created upon the path of uprightness (*ʿalā nahj al-istiqāma*), it is their choices which cause them to end up in either proximity to or distance from God.[23] Despite these points, Ṣadrā concludes that, ultimately, these souls differ because of "the preeternal decree."[24]

God's preeternal decree is what determines a soul's starting point, and, by virtue of the limitations imposed upon a human being by virtue of his inborn capacity, his ending point as well. This explains why Ṣadrā is adamant that each soul has its own mode of return back to God which is specific to it alone. As he puts it, every soul comes from "a specified point of origin [*maʿdan makhṣūṣ*] amongst the spirits' points of origin [*maʿādin al-arwāḥ*]," which necessitates that each soul comes from a point of origin unique unto itself.[25] Since for Ṣadrā the point of one's origin is also the point of one's return, the place of return is also specific for each individual. If the point of origin and place of return for each soul is different, then surely the path that each soul treads along—namely what it becomes, for the soul is the path itself—will be different. When humans ask God to guide them along the straight path in Q 1:6, therefore, they ask for nothing but guidance upon their own path, which will lead to their felicity.[26]

The foregoing considerations seem to be on Ṣadrā's mind from early on in the *Tafsīr Sūrat al-fātiḥa*. In a very crucial passage which occurs in the context of his discussion of the different paths of belief, Ṣadrā identifies the word *ṣirāṭ* with the word *sabīl*.[27] Drawing on a passage from his *Tafsīr Āyat al-kursī*, he makes a subtle distinction between the different paths available to an individual and the path appropriate for him:

> It is just as He says, *And do not follow the paths* [al-subul], *for they will divert you from His path* [sabīlihi] [Q 6:153], that is, the path which is for you contains felicity and salvation, for if this were not the case, then all paths would lead to Him, since God is the end-point of every purpose and the Final Goal [*ghāya*] of every endeavor.[28] However, not everyone who returns to Him will attain felicity and salvation from dispersion and chastisement. For the path to felicity is one: *Say: "This is my path* [sabīlī]. *Upon insight I call to God myself and those who follow me"* [Q 12:108].[29]

This statement requires some clarification. It is significant that Ṣadrā draws on Q 6:153 to make his point. The verse distinguishes between "paths" and "His path," and then Ṣadrā glosses the latter by saying "the path which is for you contains felicity and salvation [*al-sabīl al-latī lakum fīhā al-sa'āda wa-l-najāt*]." But then Ṣadrā surprises us. He goes on to say that the path that is particular to an individual brings felicity and salvation. Had this not been the case, then all paths would lead to God. But by virtue of the nature of being, we know that all paths do in fact lead to God. What Ṣadrā seems to have in mind here is that since each individual has a path to God specific to him, the other paths which are available to him are not actual options in terms of his return to God. He has the option to tread upon them, but the truth is, in accordance with his innate disposition, there is only one path that is open to his soul and it is that path that he must follow. Ṣadrā then says that not everyone who returns to God will attain felicity. This is because, in accordance with the divine decree, there are some who must end up in misery and wretchedness and some who must end up in felicity. Thus, while all souls return to God, some meet His names of beauty and others His names of majesty.

Yet there is a further complication: Ṣadrā clearly does not have in mind a cut-and-dried presentation of the nature of the afterlife where some end up in bliss and others suffer eternally.[30] As we have seen, he seeks to retain the truth of scriptural statements concerning infernal punishment; but, by virtue of the all-embracing character of God's mercy, he argues that this punishment is actually a form of comfort. Since the name Allah is the All-Gathering name, every servant, Ṣadrā reminds us, must return to Him. The different grades of individuals, whether felicitous or wretched, will become differentiated through their encounter with the name Allah.

According to a *ḥadīth qudsī*, on the Day of Judgment, after the angels, prophets, and believers have all interceded, only the intercession of the Most-Merciful of the merciful (*arḥam al-rāḥimīn*) will remain.[31] The names Most-Merciful of the merciful or All-Merciful (*al-raḥmān*), therefore, are commonly associated in texts of Islamic thought with divine intercession and human salvation. Ṣadrā tells us that since the All-Merciful is the one name that will intercede on behalf of all people, those who meet God's names of majesty in the next life will eventually come face-to-face with God as the All-Merciful (note their affinity at Q 17:110), a name which will subsist amongst His servants for all of eternity:

> As for the other paths, all of their goals is God [*Allāh*] firstly. Then the All-Merciful [*al-raḥmān*] will take over for Him [*yatawallāhu al-raḥmān*] at the end, and the property of the All-Merciful will subsist amongst them for eternity. This is a strange affair! I have not found anyone upon the face of the earth who knows it as it truly should be known.[32]

For Ṣadrā's part, although he had not come across any of his contemporaries who had known the truth of the ultimate salvation of human beings as it "truly should be known," it is safe to assume that he did not count himself amongst them. Indeed, the rest of the *Tafsīr Sūrat al-fātiḥa* assumes the soteriological picture laid out in the above two passages.[33]

Divine Hands and Feet

We have already seen how Ṣadrā speaks of the fundamental rootedness of all things in God's mercy. All things come from God and return to Him. Since the Source of all things is mercy, they will all return to their Source. But insofar as creatures are not with their Source, they are in the realm of multiplicity. Mercy, like being, becomes fragmented as it spreads throughout the cosmos and, to use a Platonic term, "shares" itself with the rest of the cosmic order. The further a thing is from its Source of mercy, the less mercy it will manifest, just as the further a thing is from its Source of being, the less being it will manifest. In the language of Islamic theology, we can say that the equilibrium of the divine names necessitates that God's names of beauty be complemented by His names of majesty.

Employing the imagery and language of Ibn ʿArabī and his followers, Ṣadrā speaks of the structure of the cosmos in terms of God's "two hands." As the *ḥadīth* tells us, God has two hands and they are both blessed and "right."[34] But not each hand manifests the same attributes. One hand gives preponderance to God's attributes of mercy and the other to His attributes of wrath.[35] From this perspective, we can speak of God's "left" and "right" hands, or the divine qualities which manifest leftness and rightness:

> Know that the ruling property [*ḥukm*] of the divine wrath is the perfection of the level of the grip of the left hand [*qabḍat al-shimāl*], for although both of His hands are holy, blessed, and right, the ruling property of each of them—leftness [*shimāliyya*] and rightness [*yamīniyya*]—is in opposition to the other from their respective standpoints.[36]

Just as two human hands are in opposition to each other, so too are the qualities denoted by God's two hands. Each of God's two hands is nothing other than a corollary of the different types of souls which have come about through the downward flow of the river of being.[37] Thus, the properties of each hand manifest themselves in accordance with the attributes of the people who fall under their sway: there are some who uphold God's oneness and give Him His rights of lordship, whereas others do not.[38]

Because God's hands are both "right," they are naturally both good. This idea again accords with a point Ṣadrā made in the *Asfār* and to which he returns in several places in the *Tafsīr Sūrat al-fātiḥa*: despite the outward appearance of a thing as wrath and punishment, inwardly, it is pure mercy.[39] This does not mean that both of God's hands are equal. Insofar as His hands are different and there are differences amongst His creatures, those who do not maintain the rights of lordship will be held responsible for their negligence. The general outcome will nevertheless be mercy.[40] With this point in mind, Ṣadrā offers a reading of Q 39:67. The verse states that the entire earth will be in God's grip on the day or resurrection, and the heavens will be folded in His right hand. Ṣadrā understands this to mean that all things will be enfolded back into God's mercy, despite the disparity amongst creatures with respect to their place of return.[41] That is to say, the scroll upon which the entire cosmic drama was written will simply be rolled back up and returned to its original Author.

Ṣadrā devotes much more time to God's feet than he does to His hands. This is partly because any talk of God's "feet" in Islamic thought automatically calls to mind two other important Qur'ānic symbols, namely His Footstool (*kursī*) and Throne (*ʿarsh*). The image of God's two feet as sources for the diversity in the cosmos therefore allows Ṣadrā to explain how multiplicity and opposition result from harmony, and how wrath and mercy become fragmented from mercy itself. The Throne is the seat or locus of mercy in accordance with the divine Command "Be!" In Q 20:5, the All-Merciful is seated upon the Throne.[42] While the All-Merciful sits on the Throne, His feet are placed upon the Footstool. Taking his lead in all likelihood from Ibn ʿArabī's *Futūḥāt*,[43] Ṣadrā explains this phenomenon as follows:

> When God created the Throne, He made it the locus of the establishment of existential mercy and the Unity of the Word of existentiation, which is the saying *"Be!"* [Q 2:117]. And He created the Footstool, and the Word was divided into two matters—Command and creation—so that He could create a pair of everything. . . . The two feet were let down onto the Footstool until the Word of the Spirit became divided in the Footstool, for the Footstool is the second in form and shape after the Throne. From the Footstool, two shapes came about in the body of the natural world. So the two feet were let down onto the Footstool, and each foot alighted in a place. One place was called the "Garden" and the other "Hell."[44]

The Footstool ontologically stands at a level lower than the Throne and also acts as the locus through which the polarity of God's divine names (symbolized by the two feet) become operative in the cosmos.[45] Although the two feet existed before they came to rest upon the Footstool, the Footstool is what allows the feet's properties to become actualized, that is, materialized. It is clear from Ṣadrā's discussion concerning the path of the soul that the place into which each foot alights is the Garden and the Hell of the soul respectively, since the path traversed by the individual will ultimately lead him back to his own reality, namely to Heaven or Hell.

Since the cosmos and all that it contains came about by virtue of the All-Merciful extending His two feet and allowing their properties to take on corporeal form, what will happen when the cosmos will cease to exist? Quite naturally, the cosmos will cease to exist when the All-Merciful draws up His feet, thus having all properties in the cosmos—whether they manifest God's attributes of wrath or mercy—return back to their Source of mercy. Ṣadrā makes this point in beautifully poetic language. It can be noted that the same passage will also be found in the relevant section in the *Asfār*. However, the account of the folding of the legs of the All-Merciful figures differently in both texts. For one thing, in the *Asfār*, Ṣadrā does not provide as detailed an account as he does in the *Tafsīr Sūrat al-fātiḥa* with respect to how all things are rooted in mercy. No less important is the fact that in the *Asfār*, the passage in question is ascribed to Ibn ʿArabī, to whom it indeed belongs.[46] Yet in the *Tafsīr Sūrat al-fātiḥa*, the same text now becomes Ṣadrā's. It is perfectly naturalized into his treatment of the two feet of the All-Merciful, and, without explicitly citing Ibn ʿArabī, he explicates "his" important point. In the end, God's walking staff will be cast aside, and all things will end in repose and tranquility:

> The feet will not be contracted except from the root from which they became manifest, namely the All-Merciful. So they only give mercy, for by virtue of wisdom, the end returns to the beginning, except that between the beginning and end there is a path. If this were not the case, there would be no beginning and end to it. The journey is where one can expect to find [*maẓinna*] fatigue, misfortune, and toil. This is the cause of the emergence of the wretchedness that has become manifest in the cosmos in terms of this world, the next world, and the isthmus [*barzakh*]. At the end of the sojourn, the walking staff [*ʿaṣā al-tasāyur*] will be cast aside and repose [*rāḥa*] in the abodes of permanence and perdition will reign.[47]

Ṣadrā freely borrows material from the *Futūḥāt* again, this time in slightly paraphrased fashion.[48] Ibn ʿArabī/Ṣadrā anticipate a possible objection to the question of how residence in Hell can entail repose and comfort for its dwellers. They acknowledge that, although from one perspective it is correct to say that Hell is not a place of comfort, one who does so has not given the matter "complete consideration" (*al-naẓar al-tāmm*).[49] Then the example of two types of wayfarers is given. One of these wayfarers lives an opulent and easy life. Such a person is like the one who arrives at the Garden. The other type of wayfarer travels by foot and has paltry provisions along the way. When he reaches his home, he is tired and miserable for a while. Then, when his fatigue wears off, he finds repose. The latter wayfarer is like the person in Hell. He is chastised for a while, and then, by virtue of God's all-embracing mercy, is given repose.[50] These people will be ranked in Hell according to the level of punishment owed to them. Once the punishment expires, that is, once they are purged of the dross of their sins (just as the wayfarer suffers fatigue until he is restored to full health), they will be felicitious.[51]

Intellectual and Scriptural Fidelity

Now that we have sufficiently surveyed most of the details concerning Ṣadrā soteriology, it would be fitting to briefly take stock of the different arguments against an eternal Hell that we have already encountered thus far, either explicitly or implicitly.[52] Several Qur'ānic verses (i.e., Q 2:39, 13:5, 43:74, etc.) state that a party of individuals will reside in Hell forever. Yet what does it mean, exactly, to reside in Hell *forever*? Does this mean that those in Hell forever will suffer forever? If so, one may justifiably ask how a human being should suffer eternally for actions which were purely finite in their nature. And since God is not wronged in any way by His servants' wrong actions, why make them suffer for eternity? Moreover, if we assume, as has traditionally been the case, that punishment in Hell is a form of cleansing for its inhabitants, then surely there must come a point when they will become purified, at which time suffering in Hell would seem superfluous.

We may also approach the question of eternal suffering in Hell with reference to the human "situation" itself: if human beings did not will to come into existence, does not placing some of them in Hell eternally violate God's responsibility toward His creatures?[53] Ultimately, we can seek an answer to this problem with reference to God's mercy: since God is the All-Merciful, surely an eternal state of suffering for any human being would contradict this fundamental principle.

What is at stake here for thinkers like Ṣadrā and Ibn ʿArabī is not only that an eternal state of punishment in Hell raises serious intellectual problems if one also upholds belief in a God who is forgiving, infinitely merciful, and loving. Just as important for them is that a belief in eternal punishment in Hell squarely contradicts scripture (defined here as both the Qurʾān and Ḥadīth). As Ibn ʿArabī notes, although the Qurʾān speaks of people abiding in the Fire forever (*khālidīna fīhā abadan*), it does not state that they will be punished in it forever.[54] And even when the Qurʾān speaks of "the punishment of eternity" (*ʿadhāb al-khuld*) at Q 10:52 and 32:14, the case is not unequivocal. Ibn Qayyim observes with reference to the expression *ʿadhāb al-khuld* that the *kh.l.d.* Arabic root "may connote an extended yet ultimately limited period of time."[55]

Another important scriptural reference which the notion of eternal suffering in Hell would negate—and one upon which, as we have seen, Ibn ʿArabī and Mullā Ṣadrā base their argument—is the *ḥadīth qudsī* which says that God's mercy outstrips His wrath.[56] Thus, the most faithful reading of scripture would be to maintain that although there will be people in Hell forever (as stated in the Qurʾān), they will not be punished therein eternally (as not stated in the Qurʾān). This is to say that by virtue of the all-pervasiveness of mercy and its essentiality as articulated in scripture, human beings will eventually be enveloped in mercy, despite the fact that the structure of the cosmic order in terms of the distribution of the divine names metaphysically demands that some ultimately end up in Hell and others in Heaven.[57]

Revealing and Concealing

Ṣadrā's *Tafsīr Sūrat al-baqara*, although incomplete, is most likely his last *tafsīr* composition. Based on internal references in the *Tafsīr Sūrat al-fātiḥa*, we know that that book is fairly late. And, since the *Tafsīr Sūrat al-baqara* explicitly refers to the *Tafsīr Sūrat al-fātiḥa* on two separate occasions, we have no good reason to doubt that it was written after this last complete *tafsīr* work.[58] It is therefore interesting to note that Ṣadrā also discusses the issue of eternal chastisement in Hell in the *Tafsīr Sūrat al-baqara*. But here he closely follows the points made in the *Tafsīr Āyat al-kursī*,[59] and does not take up the same line of interpretation we find in the *Tafsīr Sūrat al-fātiḥa*.

As with the *Tafsīr Āyat al-kursī*, Ṣadrā has a theological bone to pick in the *Tafsīr Sūrat al-baqara*, but this time with the Muʿtazilites and the Ashʿarites. In the context of his discussion of why it is that most theologians (or, as he would have it, "those who want to limit the Qur'ān's realities") believe that chastisement in Hell must be eternal, he tells us that what really motivates them is the subtle fear that the pleasures of heavenly rewards would be liable to seizure if it were possible that Hell's punishments could seize.[60] With respect to the Mu'tazilites in particular, elsewhere in the same *tafsīr* he discusses their views, both scriptural and intellectual, for why punishment in Hell should be eternal.[61] Again drawing on the *ḥadīth qudsī* of God's mercy outstripping His wrath,[62] as well as the *ḥadīth qudsī* which speaks of the intercession of the "Most Merciful of the merciful"[63] (which was so fundamental to his argument in the *Tafsīr Sūrat al-fātiḥa*), Ṣadrā dismisses the Mu'tazilites' arguments in somewhat cynical fashion.

Unlike the *Tafsīr Sūrat al-fātiḥa,* in the *Tafsīr Sūrat al-baqara* Ṣadrā does not explicitly argue for his soteriology. And, again unlike the former text, in the latter, he devotes some time to summarizing the different views of people who believe in eternal chastisement and those who do not. He first gives the views of the people who believe in an eternal state of chastisement in Hell.[64] While he observes later on that there are no clear-cut textual proofs to believe that Hell's chastisements are eternal, and noting the dubious nature of language in the transmitted sciences,[65] he then cites the views of those who believe that Hell's chastisements will eventually come to an end.[66] He notes that amongst this group of individuals there are some people who have taken the problem in a totally different direction, and which has even shocked some of the philosophers and gnostics. Here he has in mind Ibn 'Arabī, Qūnawī, and the main commentators upon the *Fuṣūṣ,* such as Qayṣarī. While he does not have trouble citing several texts from Ibn 'Arabī's *Fuṣūṣ* and *Futūḥāt* in this regard,[67] and also reproduces some of Qayṣarī's points, which he also cited in his *Tafsīr Āyat al-kursī,*[68] Ṣadrā does not give us a passage from Qūnawī, and this is because Qūnawī probably does not treat the issue head-on in his writings.[69]

It is clear from the *Tafsīr Sūrat al-baqara* that Ṣadrā does not present us with anything new on the question of eternal suffering in Hell which cannot be gleaned from his earlier *tafsīr* works, including the *Tafsīr Sūrat al-fātiḥa*. What does give occasion to surprise is what we read in Ṣadrā's *al-Ḥikma al-'arshiyya* ("The Wisdom of the Throne"), commonly referred to as the *'Arshiyya*. In this text, we encounter a strange passage in which Ṣadrā takes a position on the question of the pleasurable nature of Hell which flatly contradicts all of his statements from the *Tafsīr Āyat al-kursī* to the *Tafsīr Sūrat al-baqara*. To cite him, "[I]t would appear that Hell is not an abode of comfort. Rather, it is only a place of pain, suffering, and endless torment."[70]

We can be fairly sure that the *ʿArshiyya* was written after the *Asfār* since it mentions this book on a number of occasions and reproduces much of its material in condensed form. In the *ʿArshiyya* Ṣadrā also makes mention of his *Taʿlīqāt ʿalā Sharḥ Ḥikmat al-ishrāq* ("Glosses upon the 'Commentary on the Philosophy of Illumination' "),[71] which in turn mentions the *Tafsīr Sūrat al-fātiḥa*.[72] If we were to assume that the *ʿArshiyya* was in fact written after the *Taʿlīqāt* and the *Tafsīr Sūrat al-fātiḥa*—and there seems to be no good reason not to do so—we would appear to have a contradiction between Ṣadrā's position concerning the pleasurable nature of Hell as explicated in the *Asfār* and the *Tafsīr Sūrat al-fātiḥa* and as it appears in the *ʿArshiyya*. This passage is cited by Khwājawī as proof that Ṣadrā did in fact uphold the view that Hell was a place of actual and perpetual anguish,[73] which would be in keeping with Khwājawī's insistence on Ṣadrā's understanding of eternal punishment in Hell for at least some individuals.[74]

Naṣīrī accepts Khwājawī's argument that in the *ʿArshiyya* Ṣadrā ultimately recanted his position on the pleasurable nature of Hell.[75] He even attempts to offer an explanation for the clear contradiction. He politely suggests that if Ṣadrā would occasionally make an error in his *tafsīr* or non-*tafsīr* works, he would correct these mistakes in other works.[76] But the only way such a convenient formula would work with respect to Ṣadrā's treatment of soteriology is if we ignore his statements on the issue in which he explicitly defends the position throughout his corpus,[77] while also managing to overlook the ultimate implications of his metaphysics. In other words, accepting Naṣīrī's argument is tantamount to saying that Ṣadrā openly supported the idea of Hell's pleasurable nature throughout his career and in several of his major writings (one of which was his magnum opus, the *Asfār*), only to change his mind in one sweeping statement (with no follow up) in the *ʿArshiyya*. Surely there must be another, more reasonable explanation. And indeed there is.

The operation does not seem difficult when we consider the circumstances under which Ṣadrā wrote the *ʿArshiyya*. The *ʿArshiyya*, unlike the *Asfār* and *Tafsīr Sūrat al-fātiḥa*, for example, is a much less technical book, and hence more accessible to nonspecialists. As has been noted by Michel Chodkiewicz, prudence at times forced Ṣadrā to conceal his borrowings from Ibn ʿArabī.[78] This is undoubtedly because Sufism, especially the more theoretical type, was not always viewed favorably by the Safavid *ʿulamāʾ*.[79] Thus, Ṣadrā's distancing himself from his true position concerning the nature of Hell in the *ʿArshiyya* was a cautionary move in order to forestall condemnation by the *ʿulamāʾ*, and perhaps even his own son, Mīrzā Ibrāhīm Shīrāzī (d.

1070/1659).[80] This point is confirmed by James Morris, who notes that "Sadra's suppression here in the *ʿArshiyya* of all but the faintest allusion to his agreement with Ibn Arabi is in keeping with one level of intention of his work."[81] This "level of intention," Morris tells us, was dictated by Ṣadrā's awareness of his social and political context, which necessitated that he conceal his more extreme interpretations from *ʿulamāʾ* hostile to anything against what they considered the acceptable norm.[82]

Chastisement's Sweetness

Returning to the *Tafsīr Sūrat al-fātiḥa,* it should be clear that, in this text, Ṣadrā treats the question of the nature of eternal residency in Hell in a much more explicit manner than he does in the *Asfār* or any of his other *tafsīr* writings. Reproduced below is Ṣadrā's final citation from the *Futūḥāt.* This passage, more than any other, demonstrates his stance on the question of eternal suffering and serves as an effective summary of his arguments in the *Asfār* and the earlier parts of the *Tafsīr Sūrat al-fātiḥa.* Indeed, it demonstrates the logical outcome of Ṣadrā's ontology when expressed in the language of scripture. Ibn ʿArabī/Ṣadrā tell us that the last batch of people in Hell who are there by virtue of God's solicitude (*ʿināya*) will be trapped in Hell and surrounded by its flames. Like the nonbelievers mentioned in Q 60:13 who despair over "the people of the graves" (*aṣḥāb al-qubūr*) (i.e., in their thinking that death is the end of all things and that the people of the graves will not be brought back to life), the people enclosed by Hell's fires will also despair. It is at that moment that God's mercy will overcome them and provide for them a constitution which will allow them to experience joy in the Fire. Their chastisement (*ʿadhāb*) will therefore become sweetness (*ʿadhb*):

> They will find the chastisement [*ʿadhāb*] sweet [*yastaʿdhibūna*], so pains will cease and the chastisement [*ʿadhāb*] will become sweetness [*ʿadhb*]. . . .[83] God willing, the inhabitant of every abode will taste sweetness. So understand! Do you not see the truth of what we have said? Because of the deficiency and nonexistence of fullness that is in it, the Fire will not cease to be painful until the Compeller [*al-jabbār*] places His foot in it, as has been related in the tradition.[84] This is one of the two aforementioned feet on the Footstool. The other [foot] is the one whose resting place will be the

> Garden: *Give glad tidings to those who believe, that they have a foot of firmness with their Lord* [Q 10:2]. The name "Lord" will be with them, and the name "Compeller" will be with the others because the Fire is the abode of majesty, domination, and awe, whereas the Garden is the abode of beauty, intimacy, and the subtle divine alighting place [*manzil al-ilāhī al-laṭīf*].[85] The two of them are face to face with the two grips mentioned in the Sacred tradition: "One for the people of the Fire, and I don't care; the other for the people of the Garden, and I don't care." He does not care because the end for both is to the all-embracing mercy.[86]

We have by this point seen a number of instances in both the *Asfār* and the *Tafsīr Sūrat al-fātiḥa* in which Ṣadrā freely borrows material from Ibn ʿArabī's *Futūḥāt*. In all cases in which Ṣadrā cites Ibn ʿArabī in the *Asfār*, he does so explicitly. At the same time, both Ibn ʿArabī's *Fuṣūṣ* and *Futūḥāt* are cited explicitly in the *Tafsīr Sūrat al-fātiḥa*.[87] It would seem that when Ibn ʿArabī is acknowledged as a direct source for one of Ṣadrā's statements, it is because the latter is trying to demonstrate how a problematic theological question had been dealt with by his most illustrious predecessor—someone for whom he had unqualified admiration. This is a rare exception, given how critical Ṣadrā is of almost all of his predecessors, from Avicenna[88] to his own teacher Mīr Dāmād (d. 1041/1631).[89]

Interestingly, a number of Ibn ʿArabī's statements from the *Futūḥāt* explicitly cited by Ṣadrā in the *Asfār* appear, as we have seen above, as Ṣadrā's own words in the *Tafsīr Sūrat al-fātiḥa*. This would lend support to our argument that the latter text, by virtue of having been written several years after the *Asfār*, gave Ṣadrā the perfect chance to present a much more coherent soteriological argument than he did in the *Asfār*. Thus, when in the *Tafsīr Sūrat al-fātiḥa* Ṣadrā reworks Ibn ʿArabī's statements into his writings and does not acknowledge his source or seems to do so in a somewhat vague manner, it might be because he is trying to be as direct as possible in making his point, a point which doubtless came from the pen of Ibn ʿArabī,[90] but which Ṣadrā was then able to integrate into his perspective as his "own" point.[91] Hence, despite the fact that Ṣadrā lifts these passages from Ibn ʿArabī almost verbatim, we have every reason to assume that the soteriology articulated in these passages is his soteriology as well.

Why Ṣadrā would resort to a scriptural mode of expression concerning the final return of all creatures as opposed to his more philosophical arguments found in the *Asfār* is in keeping with the overall goal of his work on the Qurʾān, namely to clothe within the garb of scriptural symbols the philosophical truths which he had verified for himself. At the heart of this personal experience undergone by Ṣadrā was his profound encounter with being. Since mercy is to religious language what being is to philosophical language, when tackling the problem of soteriology, which for Ṣadrā is naturally discussed within the universe of the Islamic revelation, it was all the more fitting that he would choose to express himself most clearly within the context and terminological "confines" of his commentary upon the Qurʾān's most widely known and recited chapter.

Conclusion

For all of our knowledge of Mullā Ṣadrā's life and philosophical teachings, a number of aspects of his religious thought remain terra incognita. His work on the Qur'ān is a good place to start. Not only were Ṣadrā's compositions on the Qur'ān and its sciences voluminous, but he made sure that his writings on scripture would give a more concrete form to the abstract ideas contained in his philosophical books. For Ṣadrā, the Qur'ān and being are, from one perspective, two sides of the same coin. This fundamental insight allows his work on the Qur'ān to demonstrate the manner in which his philosophical teachings can be modulated into religious language.

This explains why, in his function as a scriptural exegete, Ṣadrā does not simply read the Qur'ān as a philosopher. Just as he ably articulates his experience of being in his philosophical writings, so too does he convey his experience of the Qur'ān in his works on scripture. This phenomenon is illustrated very well in the *Mafātīḥ al-ghayb*, Ṣadrā's most important theoretical work on scripture. The *Mafātīḥ* is unique in that Ṣadrā viewed it as occupying a special place amongst his writings on the Qur'ān. It articulates the basic esoteric perspective which informs all of his writings on the Qur'ān by demonstrating the intimate link shared between the book of being and the becoming of the human soul. Although this work is a rather late addition to the Ṣadrian oeuvre, we know that several parts of it were written earlier on in his career, as portions of Miftāḥ 1 are expanded versions of sections from the *Asfār*. This indicates that Ṣadrā's understanding of the nature of scripture had already taken shape even before he had completed his independent *tafsīr* works, which in part accounts for the consistent doctrinal perspective we find amongst these *tafsīr*s. At the same time, in Miftāḥ 1 of the *Mafātīḥ*, Ṣadrā's presentation of the theoretical underpinnings of his Qur'ānic hermeneutics is most consistently presented, and there is an added dimension of depth not to be found in the corresponding sections of the *Asfār*. This explains why Ṣadrā understood the *Mafātīḥ* to have occupied a special place amongst his writings on the Qur'ān.

The central importance of the *Mafātīḥ* in general, and Miftāḥ 1 in particular is, therefore, not in its being an introduction to Ṣadrā's individual *tafsīr*s, but, rather, in its ability to summarize the general hermeneutical perspective which informs these *tafsīr*s. The hermeneutical perspective argued for in Miftāḥ 1 takes Ṣadrā's ontology for granted. Like being, the Qur'ān is also revealed in "modes" and grades. And, since being is the prototype of man, so too is the Qur'ān the prototype of man. The levels of being therefore find their perfect parallel in the levels of the human soul, just as the levels of the Qur'ān, and, hence, its types of readers, find their perfect parallel in the levels of the human soul.

If the *Mafātīḥ* is Ṣadrā's most important work on the Qur'ān in terms of theory, the *Tafsīr Sūrat al-fātiḥa,* which is his last complete *tafsīr,* is his most important work on the Qur'ān in terms of practice. As a commentator upon the Fātiḥa, which occupies central importance in Muslim daily life, Ṣadrā is impelled by it verses to reflect upon and provide solutions to some of the core issues which lie at the heart of human existence itself: what is the nature of gratitude, mercy, compassion, praise for God, belief, and unbelief? To aid his meditations on the Fātiḥa, Ṣadrā incorporates into his unique philosophical perspective the teachings of a number of his predecessors who tackled similar issues. At the same time, while the *Tafsīr Sūrat al-fātiḥa* presents us with a handy exposition of Ṣadrā's key doctrines (albeit in "mythic" form), some of the positions taken in his earlier books undergo modifications in the context of his commentary on the Fātiḥa's verses.

A close reading of the *Tafsīr Sūrat al-fātiḥa*'s teachings in metaphysics reveals that Ṣadrā, taking his lead from Q 1:1, is able to successfully recast his sophisticated ontology of the fundamentality of being into a theological and scripture-based framework. This allows him to then go on to address two questions which are central to his scriptural hermeneutics: (1) what is the nature of the cosmos? and (2) what is the nature of man? By presenting his ontology in less philosophical language (and relying, instead, upon the language Ibn ʿArabī and some of his "followers"), Ṣadrā demonstrates how these two questions are to be answered in the context of his commentary upon the Fātiḥa. The cosmology of praise attendant upon Ṣadrā's ontology thus enables his theoretical discussions from the *Mafātīḥ* to come to life. Here we see how God's self-praise results in the emergence of the cosmos, and how the cosmos, as the "stuff" of God's self-praise, is nothing other than a seamless expression of modes or instantiations of praise. Since being is graded and multilevel, the more one manifests of praise, the more he manifests of being.

Ṣadrā seems to want to connect his cosmology of praise with his answer to his second question: if all things are modes of praise in the cosmos, then human beings are themselves modes of God's praise. As a manifestation of the Muhammadan Reality, the Perfect Man is the most perfect mode of praise for God amongst all of His creatures since he has ascended the scale of being and reached the highest possible rung on the ladder of praise. Since the Perfect Man is the highest mode of praise for God and the Fātiḥa contains all that is in the Qur᾿ān, and, hence, in existence, the Perfect Man and the Fātiḥa share a special relationship. It is, therefore, only the Perfect Man who can interpret the Fātiḥa, since, in reading it, he offers a reading of himself.

In the *Tafsīr Sūrat al-fātiḥa*, Ṣadrā demonstrates his heaviest reliance upon the teachings of Ibn ʿArabī in addressing two additional questions: (1) what is the nature of idol worship? and (2) what is the ultimate fate of all human beings? In tackling the first problem, Ṣadrā articulates a version of the position—well-known to Islamic thought by his time—concerning the "God created in beliefs." He relates this idea to his theoretical scriptural hermeneutics: since the Qur᾿ān and being are two sides of the same coin from one perspective, those who remain on the surface of being, who have a particular idolized conception of the nature of reality, will likewise remain on the surface of the Qur᾿ān. It is only when man penetrates being, that is, shatters his intellectual constructs concerning the nature of reality (and, hence, God) that he may penetrate the ocean of the Qur᾿ān. Such a profound view of things is reserved for the Perfect Man, who, by virtue of not falling into the trap of "metaphysical idolatry," sees the cosmos for what it truly is: a theatre for the manifestation of God. The station of praise in which the Perfect Man stands allows him to understand the nature of existence in its entirety. And, since the Qur᾿ān and being can be said to have the same reality, the Perfect Man can likewise understand the nature of the Qur᾿ān in its entirety.

Ṣadrā also reminds us that knowing the nature of existence is tantamount to knowing God's mercy, since mercy and being are the same reality. Understanding God's mercy demands a vision of the cosmic order in which all things proceed from mercy and return to mercy. Since all things issue from God and are nothing but modes of God's being, they can also be said to issue from mercy and be nothing but modes of God's mercy. Likewise, since all modes of being must return to their Source of being, so too must all modes of mercy return to their Source of mercy. Hence, the end for all creatures is mercy. Yet beyond this point Ṣadrā also attempts to address another important problem which appears to be demanded by the content of the Fātiḥa itself, namely the fact that there *are* differences in grades of individuals.

In attempting to address the question of how one can believe in universal salvation while also taking into account the obvious disparity in types of human beings, Ṣadrā articulates a picture of the afterlife in which the form of salvation received by human beings is shaped by the differing paths which they had chosen during their time on earth. The result is a highly individualized presentation of the nature of human beings' return to their Source of mercy: the route that each soul takes as it ascends the scale of being/mercy is entirely unique to it, just as the route taken by each soul in descending the scale of being/mercy is entirely unique to it. Yet Ṣadrā does not want to negate God's wrath. Some people, in returning to the abode of mercy, must come through the door of wrath. But, despite the fact that human beings will return to God in very different states—some in beautiful robes of honor and others in tattered garments of humiliation—in the end, it is God's mercy that shall have the final say.

Appendix 1

Some Key Texts from the *Mafātīḥ al-Ghayb*

Translated here, with my own descriptive headings, are some of the most important passages concerning the nature of the Qur'ān which are to be found in Ṣadrā's *Mafātīḥ al-ghayb*, almost all of which have appeared in Chapter 1 in the context of my explication of Ṣadrā's scriptural hermeneutics.

God's Firm Rope
***Mafātīḥ*, 89**

The Qur'ān is God's firm rope [*ḥabl Allāh al-matīn*] which was sent down from Heaven in order to save those shackled in the cradle of satans and the abyss of those who have descended. It is one of God's lights [*nūr min anwār Allāh*]: it contains guidance for wayfarers, and through it one can ascend from the lowest of worlds to the highest way stations [*manāzil*] of the ʿIlliyyīn and the most exalted levels of those seated upon *the seat of truth* [Q 54:55] and certainty. So read it, O impoverished one, and advance!

How to Read the Qur'ān
***Mafātīḥ*, 78-9**

O intelligent, discerning one! If you want to investigate the science of the Qur'ān, the wisdom of God and the principles of faith—that is, faith in God, His angels, books, messengers, and the Final Day—then you need to return to the guardians [*ḥafaẓa*] of the secrets of the Qur'ān and its meanings, seek out its folk and those who bear it, and ask the "people of remembrance" about its contents. As He—exalted is His name—says, *Ask the people of remembrance if you do not know* [Q 16:43], just as, with the rest of the arts and sciences, you would seek out their folk.

The Nature of *Ta'wīl*
Mafātīḥ, 79

As for *ta'wīl, it does not spare nor leave anything out* [*lā tubqī wa-lā tadhar*] [Q 74:28], for it comes—thanks be to God!—as a discourse [*kalām*] in which there is no crookedness, nor does doubt or confusion assail it.

The Qur'ān's Levels of Descent
Mafātīḥ, 98

Although the Qur'ān is one reality, it has many levels in its descent [*nuzūl*] and many names in accordance with these levels. So in every world and configuration it is called by a name which corresponds to its specific station and particular rank.

The Weight of the Word
Mafātīḥ, 98-9

The Qur'ān was revealed to people [*khalq*] with thousands of veils in order for those with weak intellects and blind eyes to comprehend. If, given its greatness, the Throne [*'arsh*] of the *bā'* of the *basmala* were to descend to the earth [*farsh*], the earth would perish and become annihilated. There is an indication to this meaning in His saying, *Were we to cause this Qur'ān to descend upon a mountain, you would see it humbled and split apart out of fear of God* [Q 59:21].

The Perfect Words
Mafātīḥ, 94

The highest level of the Word is the Word itself in terms of its principial purpose [*maqṣūd awwalī*], there being no other purpose after it because of the nobility of its existence, the perfection of its being, and because of its being the final goal [*ghāya*] of whatever is beneath it. This is like God's originating the World of the Command through the Command *"Be!"* [Q

2:117], and nothing else. These are God's Perfect Words [*al-kalimāt al-tāmmāt*] which are never exhausted, nor do they perish.

The Articulation of the Word
Mafātīḥ, 93-4

The cosmos [*ʿālam*] does not become manifest except through the Word. Rather, the cosmos is the Word itself, its parts being commensurate to its twenty-eight stations [*maqāmāt*] and ranks [*manāzil*] within the Breath of the All-Merciful [*nafas al-raḥmān*], just as words and vocal letters [*al-ḥurūf al-ṣawtiyya*] subsist within the self of the human speaker commensurate to his points of stopping and articulation [*manāzil wa-makhārij*]. The speaker's aim in speaking is, firstly, to produce the entities of letters and existentiate them from the points of articulation. This is the very essence of making-known [*iʿlām*].

The Individuation of the Word
Mafātīḥ, 103

Just as when the Command becomes an act, as in His saying *"Be!," and it is* [Q 2:117], when the Word becomes individuated [*tashakhkhaṣa*] and descends, it becomes a book. The scroll [*ṣaḥīfa*] of the being of the created world is the book of God [*kitāb Allāh*], and its signs [*āyāt*] are the entities of the existent things [*aʿyān al-mawjūdāt*]: *In the alternation of night and day, and in what God created in the heavens and on earth, are signs for a people who are God-wary* [Q 10:6].

Dimensions of the Qurʾān, Dimensions of Man
Mafātīḥ, 105

Know that the Qurʾān, like man, is divided into a manifest [*ʿalan*] and hidden dimension [*sirr*], each of which has an outer [*ẓahr*] and inner [*baṭn*] aspect. Its inner aspect has another inner aspect known only to God: *and none knows its interpretation but God* [Q 3:7]. It has also been related in the *ḥadīth*, "The Qurʾān has an outer and inner aspect." Its inner aspect consists of up to seven inner dimensions [*abṭun*] which are like the levels of man's inner dimensions, such as the soul [*nafs*], heart [*qalb*], intellect [*ʿaql*], spirit [*rūḥ*], innermost mystery [*sirr*], and the hidden and most hidden [*al-khafī wa-l-akhfāʾ*].

The Husk and the Kernel
Mafātīḥ, 117

The Qurʾān has degrees and ranks, just as man has levels and stations. The lowest level of the Qurʾān is like the lowest level of man: the Qurʾān's lowest level is what is contained in the book's binding and covering [*jild wa-aghlāf*], just as the lowest rank of man is what is in the outer covering and skin [*al-ihāb wa-l-bashara*]. The husk [*qishr*] of man attains nothing but the blackness of the Qurʾān and its sensory form. The man of the outward husk only perceives husk-like meanings [*al-maʿānī al-qishriyya*]. As for the spirit of the Qurʾān, its kernel [*lubb*], and its secret, none but *the possessors of deep understanding* [*ulū al-albāb*] [12:111] perceive it. They do not attain this through knowledge acquired by way of learning and thinking. Rather, [they attain this] through God-given [*ladunī*] knowledge.

Unity in Multiplicity
Mafātīḥ, 90-1

Because the people of this world are in the station where forms are gathered and meanings separated [*al-jamʿiyya al-ṣūriyya wa-l-tafarruqāt al-maʿnawiyya*], they witness various letters as unified and letters which are of one species as numerous individual parts. Thus, when they look at the letters *He loves them and they love Him* [*yuḥibbuhum wa-yuḥibbūnahu*] [Q 5:54], they see them as a unified species which is divided in its parts. However, those who have divested themselves of this world—for whom the veil has been lifted and the clouds of doubt and blindness have dispersed from the face of their insight—[they] see these letters through inner sight in this way: *H-e-l-o-v-e-s-t-h-e-m* [*yāʾ-ḥāʾ-bāʾ-hāʾ-mīm*]. Then, when they ascend from this station to a higher station, they see them as tiny dots [*niqāṭ*].

Appendix 2

Key Texts from the *Tafsīr Sūrat al-Fātiḥa*

Translated here, with my own descriptive headings, are the most important passages to be found in Ṣadrā's *Tafsīr Sūrat al-fātiḥa*, a number of which have already appeared in Chapters 3–5 and Chapter 7. I have sought to present these translated texts (a) in the order in which they unfold within the *tafsīr*, and (b) in isolation from the detailed textual, historical, and theoretical issues considered in the previous chapters, thereby allowing Ṣadrā's key teachings in the *Tafsīr Sūrat al-fātiḥa* to stand on their own.

Introduction

The Call of an Exegete
***Tafsīr*, 1:1**

Now is the time to penetrate the loci of witnessing [*mashāhid*] of the Qurʾān's signs, after laying out the keys to the doors of paradise, making clear the lamps of the lights of guidance and gnosis, and firmly planting the foundations of wisdom and faith.

The Mother of the Qurʾān
***Tafsīr*, 1:1**

It is called the Mother of the Qurʾān [*umm al-Qurʾān*] because of its containing [*iḥtiwāʾ*] all of the meanings which are in the Qurʾān.

The Nature of the Qur'ān
Tafsīr, 1:2

Each of its *sūra*s is an ocean full of jewels of meaning and exposition. Rather, [they are] celestial spheres filled with the stars of the realities and essences. Every one of its verses is a shell within which are hidden precious pearls, all of which are valuable for man's soul.

The Special Nature of the Fātiḥa
Tafsīr, 1:2

The light of guidance and the life of faith proceed from His lights [*lumʿān*], especially this *sūra* which, despite its concision, contains all of the verses of the Qur'ān and the sum total of the secrets of the Origin, Return, and the states of creatures on the Final Day before the All-Merciful. So listen with the ear of your heart to the recitation of God's verses, and let the lights of the miracle of the Messenger of God penetrate your insides.

*

I seek refuge in God from Satan the accursed

On the *istiʿādha* Formula
Tafsīr, 1:7

The better and more illustrious one is, and the higher and more perfect his rank, his devil is stronger, more seductive, more astray, and has subtler ruses, more intricate and hidden ways, is further off the course of the straight path, more averse to the right–guiding practices, and more blind to seeing the Real. Since the status of reciting the revelation and listening to its verses is the most illustrious status, the command has been instituted to seek refuge in God from the devil, who is distant and banished from oneness. This is why he is qualified by the exaggerative form of being accursed [in the *istiʿādha* formula].

God's Words
Tafsīr, 9–10

His Speech [*qawl*] and Word [*kalima*] are not of the genus of sounds and letters, just as His Essence and attributes are not of the genus of bodies and modalities. Nor are they of the genus of substances and accidents. Rather, His Word [*qawl wa-kalām*] and Command [*amr*]—as has been stated in the *Mafātīḥ*—is pure intellective disembodied being. So His Words are holy existents [and] spiritual matters which are the intermediaries between God and the creatures, and through which is realized His knowledge, power, and the penetration of His will and desire amongst the existent things.

The Perfect Words
Tafsīr, 10–1

The proof that, by the "Words of God," the absolute, intellective divine existences are what is intended, is that the Words are described as "Perfect."... So God, glorified and exalted is His Word, is above completion and is the End of ends, since through Him is the completion of every thing, the life of every living one, the light of everything that is illumined, and the medicine and cure of every sickness and ailment.

There is a fine point here: the origination of bodies—their substances, dark and other accidents, natures, and natural effects—is only gradational [*tadrījī*], [proceeding] bit by bit. [This is] similar to motion, which is the gradual exiting from potentiality into actuality. As for innovated things, their existentiation and exiting [potentiality and going] into actuality only obtains in one instant: *And Our Command is nothing but one, like the blink of an eye* [Q 56:5]. When the Command is like this, its origination from God resembles the origination of letters [comprising a word] which only come to exist in one instant, that is, at that very indivisible moment. Because of this likeness, their completion is their very beginning. That which comes about through the carrying out of His determination is called the "Word," and is described as "Perfect."

The Emergence of Evil
Tafsīr, 1:16

The first of existent things to issue from Him is the world of His Command and decree, in which there is fundamentally no evil... except, by God, what becomes hidden under the radiance of the First Light. This is the murkiness which necessitates contingent quiddities, which arise from the diminution of their existential ipseities from the divine Ipseity.

*

In the Name of God, the All-Merciful, the Compassionate (Q 1:1)

The Different Approaches to the Qurʾān
***Tafsīr*, 1:28–9**

Know, O one concerned with understanding the meanings of the book!—God guide you to the right way—that here there are investigations into written expressions [*lafẓ*]. Some of these are related to the imprints of the letters and their written appearances, and forms of words and their sonal qualities, for [all of] which God put in place a people—such as scribes, reciters, and memorizers—and rendered the utmost of their endeavors to be knowledge of the proper recitation and beautiful writing of these expressions. Some of these are related to knowing the states of [their] structure, derivation, the states of inflection, and the building of words. And some of these are related to knowing the primary senses of the individual and composite terms. All of these [forms of investigation] fall short of the furthest goal and the loftiest station [*al-maqṣad al-aqṣā wa-l-manzil al-asnā*]. A party of each of these [investigators] has reached the boundary of the end and risen therein to the utmost expanse [of these investigations into written expressions]. God has set them up to acquire these partial sciences [*al-ʿulūm al-juzʾiyya*]—which are relied upon for understanding the realities of the Qurʾān—so that their rank may be the rank of servants and instruments for that which, in reality, is the result and end, and which leads to the perfection of the human species.

Know that speech consists of expressions and allusions, just as the existence of man is composed of an unseen and visible dimension [*ghayb wa-shahāda*]. Expressions are for the people of observance [*riʿāya*], and allusions are for the people of solicitude [*ʿināya*]. Expressions are like the enshrouded dead person, whereas allusions are like the subtle, recognizing, knowing [faculty] which is man's reality. Expressions come from the World of the Visible [*ʿālam al-shahāda*], whereas allusions come from the World of the Unseen [*ʿālam al-ghayb*]. Expressions are the shadows of the unseen, just as man's individuation [*tashakhkhuṣ*] is the shadow of his reality.

As for the people of outward expressions and writing [*ahl al-ʿibāra wa-l-kitāba*], they have wasted their lives away in acquiring words and foundations, and their intellects have drowned in trying to grasp expositions and meanings. As for the people of the Qurʾān and the Word [*ahl al-Qurʾān wa-l-kalām*]—and they are the people of God [*ahl Allāh*] who have been singled out for the divine love, lordly attraction, and Prophetic proximity—God has facilitated the way for them and accepted from them few works for the journey. That is because of the purity of their intentions and their hearts.

The Religion of the Folk of God
***Tafsīr*, 1:30**

Every party has a position [*madhhab*] and an opinion [*raʾy*] in accordance with what they think draws them near to God and [increases their] servanthood to Him. Because of the differences in their positions [*mashārib wa-madhāhib*], they pursue it and aspire toward it, *rejoicing in what is with them* [Q 30:32] and mocking what someone else comes with, even if *he is on a clear evidence from his Lord* [Q 11:17]. People take positions concerning what they love. But the position of the folk of God is something else: their religion is the *sincere religion* [Q 39:3]. Rather, they have no position other than God, and no religion other than Him: *Is sincere religion not for God?* [Q 39:3].

Those who love out of caprice take diverse positions.
As for me, I have a single position, and dwell in it alone.

In reality, they are *the servants of the All-Merciful* [Q 25:63], while the others are the servants of their positions and opinions, and students of their egos and caprice. This is because servitude and obedience toward the Lord is a branch of knowledge and seeking proximity to Him, since seeking the unknown is impossible. Thus, whoever is not a knower of God or of His Dominion [*malakūt*], how can he love and seek Him and endeavor to become proximate to, and intimate with, Him?

However, the Real, out of the perfection of His compassion [*raʾfa*] and mercy [*raḥma*] toward His servants, the all-encompassing nature [*shumūl*] of His benevolence [*ʿāṭifa*], the unfolding [*inbisāṭ*] of the light of His being toward the contingent things, and the self-disclosure [*tajallī*] of the [manifest] face of His Essence to the existent things, made for each of them a likeness [*mithāl*] which they could imitate, a refuge [*mathāba*] toward which they could strive, a path which they could traverse, a direction toward which they could aspire, a *qibla* with which they would be satisfied, and a law in accordance with which they could act. He says, *For everyone there is a direction to turn, so vie for the good. Wherever you are, God will bring you all together* [Q 2:148]; *For each of you We have made a law and a way* [Q 5:48]; *Each party rejoicing in what is with them* [Q 30:32].

The Word of God is one of the flashes of His Essence. Just as there are differences of opinion [*ikhtilāf wa-tafāwut*] in peoples' positions and beliefs concerning God—i.e., between the one who declares God bodily [*mujassim*] and the one who declares Him dissimilar [*munazzih*], the philosopher [*mutafalsif*] and denier of God's attributes [*muʿaṭṭil*], the one who ascribes partners to God [*mushrik*] and the one who declares Him one [*muwaḥḥid*]—so too are there differences of opinion between them in understanding [the Qurʾān]. This is one of the proofs of the Qurʾān's perfection, for it is a deep ocean in whose current most people drown, and from which none are saved except a few.

How Supplication Produces Effects
***Tafsīr*, 1:33**

According to the verifiers amongst the scholars, it has been affirmed that the effecter [*muʾaththir*] of the substances of existents is none other than the Originator—exalted is His name!—or, with His permission, one of His angels brought near. So, in terms of bringing into or out of being, bodily accidents do not produce effects [*taʾthīr*] in substantial things. The best of invocations and supplications merely bring about effects from the side of their meanings and the soul's being connected—when it invokes—to their active principles. Thus, the world of *the wise remembrance* [Q 3:58] is the well-spring of success-giving to matters of concern and the beginning-point of answers to supplications, not the clashing of letters and sounds and the movement of lips with words and expressions.

That the Name is not Accidental
***Tafsīr*, 1:33**

It appears as if the gnostics' customary usage corresponds to the customary usage of the Qurʾān and Ḥadīth. For the name in His saying, *Glorify the name of your Lord, the Most High* [Q 87:1] and *Blessed is the name of your Lord, Possessor of Majesty and Generosity* [Q 55:78], is far from having been intended to be a letter or sound and what is connected to them, for they belong to the accidents of bodies. And what is like this is the most vile of things. . . . So, according to them, God's name is a meaning sanctified beyond the blemish of temporal origination and renewal [*waṣmat al-ḥudūth wa-l-tajaddud*], [and] is exalted above the deficiency of becoming [*takawwun*] and change [*taghayyur*]. For this reason, seeking assistance and blessings [*istiʿāna wa-tabarruk*] fall upon His name.

On the Divine Names
***Tafsīr*, 1:34–6**

According to the great ones amongst the gnostics, the name "God" [*ism Allāh*] is an expression of the All-Gathering Divine Level [*martabat al-ulūhiyya al-jāmiʿa*] for all of the tasks [*shuʾūn*], standpoints [*iʿtibārāt*], descriptions, and perfections, within which all of the names and attributes—these being nothing but the flashes of His light and the tasks of His Essence—are ranked. This Level marks the first instance of multiplicity to come about in existence, and is an isthmus between the Presence of Exclusive Oneness [*al-ḥaḍra al-aḥadiyya*] and the loci of creation and the engendered Command [*al-maẓāhir al-amriyya wa-l-khalqiyya*]. In itself, this name brings together every contrary quality and opposing name, as you have already come to know. With each quality, the Essence takes on a [specific] name—the names articulated in speech being the "names of the names" [*asmāʾ al-asmāʾ*]—and the multiplicity in them is in accordance with the multiplicity of the [names'] characteristics and attributes. This multiplicity is nothing but the standpoints of His unseen levels and His divine tasks, which are "the keys to the unseen" [*mafātīḥ al-ghayb*] whose shadows and reflections fall upon existent things.

All that is in the world of contingency is a form of one of the names of God and a locus of one of the tasks. So God's names are intelligible meanings in the Unseen Being of the Real [*ghayb al-wujūd al-ḥaqq*], meaning that the Essence of Exclusive Oneness [*al-dhāt al-aḥadiyya*] is that which the intellect has no way of conceiving, since were It to "exist" or occur to the intellect in order for the intellect to grasp It, these meanings would be divested from It, and the intellect would [be unable to] qualify It with itself. Thus, given Its unity and simplicity, the Essence of Exclusive Oneness allows for the predication of these meanings to It without there being an added quality [to It], as has already been discussed.

Like all of the universal concepts, these meanings are, in themselves, neither existent nor nonexistent, neither general nor specific, and neither universal nor particular. They are not like the existential ipseities which are existent in themselves and individuated in their ipseities, since these latter are like rays and connections to the Being of the Real: when they come to one's mind, something bound to God's Essence—which is existent through His being and necessary through His necessity—is thought of. They are unlike the universal meanings because they may become universal in the mind, but particular externally; and they may be existent in the intellect, but nonexistent in reality. Yet they do have properties and effects in actual existence. Rather, the properties of existence are applied to them accidentally, and, from the pre-eternal necessity and oneness, the properties become illuminated through His light and tinged with His colour.

One of the People of God said: "The Real Existent is God exclusively with respect to His Essence [*dhāt*] and entity [*ʿayn*], not with respect to His names. For the names have two denotations: one of them [denotes] God as such [*ʿaynuhu*], that is, the very entity of the Named [*ʿayn al-musammā*]. The other is what denotes Him, namely that through which one name is differentiated from another and what is distinguished in the intellect. So that through which every name is the other name itself, and that through which it is other than it, has become clear to you. That through which one name is identical [with the other names] is the Real, and that through which one name is other than [the other names] is the imagined Real. . . . So glory to the One who has no denotation other than Himself, and whose being is not affirmed except by Himself!"

The Withness of the Essence
Tafsīr, 1:36

The withness [*maʿiyya*] between God's Essence and His most beautiful names is not like the withness between the essential and the accidental, especially because of what is [implied in the relationship] between substance and accident. Nor is it like the withness of essences amongst contingent quiddities, for the Real does not have a universal quiddity. Rather, His reality is nothing but holy, simple, and pure being which has neither name nor description. An allusion cannot be made to It except by way of pure gnosis [*ṣirf al-ʿirfān*], and It does not have an essential definition. Nor can It be demonstratively proven except by way of the light of witnessing [*nūr al-ʿiyān*], since He is the proof [*burhān*] for every thing, and the witness [*shāhid*] in every entity [*ʿayn*].

The Nonexistence of the Entities
Tafsīr, 1:36

So all of the intelligible entities and universal natures are, in reality, nothing but imprints and signs denoting the modes [*anḥāʾ*] of contingent existents which are drops of the ocean of necessary reality, rays of the sun of the Absolute Being [*al-wujūd al-muṭlaq*], and loci of manifestation [*maẓāhir*] of His names, attributes, beauty, and majesty. As for these very entities and quiddities which in a specific sense are secluded from the existents, they are fundamentally nonexistent, both to the eye and intellect. Rather, they are only names, as He says, *These are merely names that you and your fathers have given to them. God has not revealed an authority concerning them* [Q 53:23].

The Indefinable Essence
Tafsīr, 1:37

God's Essence has no definition, just as there is no proof for It. As for what is understood by the expression "God," does it have a definition or not? The Real is the First because the meaning predicated of Him is a sum total which gathers the meanings of all the attributes of perfection. Thus, every meaning of God's names forms a part of this name, when the name is differentiated.

The Inaccessibility of the Name
Tafsīr, 1:39

The concepts [*mafhūmāt*] of all the divine names and their existential loci [*maẓāhir*], which are parts of the cosmos—both outwardly and inwardly—despite their multiplicity,

[form] a real definition [*ḥadd ḥaqīqī*] in signifying God's name [*ism Allāh*]. It follows that all the meanings of the realities of the cosmos are a definition of God's name, just as all the meanings of the divine names define Him, except that it is possible for the human intellect to encompass [*iḥāṭa*] all the definitions of defined things in their particulars, as opposed to the meanings of the particulars of His definition, because these meanings cannot be confined [*ghayr maḥṣūra*].

On Ibn ʿArabī's Reference to "the Real"
Tafsīr, 1:39–40

What was intended by "the Real" in Ibn ʿArabī's saying "The Real is defined by every essential definition" was that which is meant by [*mufād*] the word "God" [*Allāh*] from the standpoint of its universal meaning and intellectual concept, not from the standpoint of the reality of its meaning, which is the Essence of Exclusive Oneness [*al-dhāt al-aḥadiyya*] and the Unseen of the unseens [*ghayb al-ghuyūb*], since It has neither essential definition, nor name, nor description, and intellectual perception does not have a way to It. The people of unveiling and witnessing cannot attain a flash of Its light except after the passing away of their selfhood, and the crumbling of the mountain [cf. Q 7:143] of their existence.

Idols of Belief
Tafsīr, 1:40–2

Know O friend of God [*walī*]!—God illumine your heart with faith—that most people do not worship God insofar as He is God. They merely worship the objects of their beliefs in accordance with what they have formed for themselves as objects of worship. In reality, their gods are those imaginary idols which they form [*yataṣawwarūna*] and carve [*yanḥitūna*] with the power [*quwwa*] of their intellectual or imaginary beliefs. This is what one of the knowers of the People of the Household—namely Muḥammad b. ʿAlī al-Bāqir [i.e., the fifth Imam, d. 114/732]—alluded to [when he said], "Whatever distinction you make using your imagination in coming up with the most precise of meanings is something created like you, and returns to you."

That is, a believer amongst the veiled ones—those who create the divinity in the forms of the object of their belief and nothing else—only worships a god on account of what he creates within himself and forms [*taṣawwara*] using his imagination. In reality, his God is created for himself and sculpted with the hand of his controlling power [*bi-yad quwwatihi al-mutaṣarrifa*]. So there is no difference between those idols which are taken as gods [externally] and his God, owing to the fact that they are all created for the self, whether they be external or internal to it.

External idols are also only worshipped because of their worshipper's belief in their divinity. The mental forms are the objects of their worship essentially, and the external forms are their objects of worship accidentally. Thus, the objects of worship of every idol worshipper are nothing but the forms of his beliefs and the caprices [*ahwāʾ*] of his soul, as has been alluded to in His saying, *Have you seen the one who takes his caprice for his god?* [Q 65:23].

Just as worshippers of bodily idols worship what their hands have created, so too do those who have partial beliefs concerning God worship what the hands of their intellects have gathered. His words have proven true against them and their objects of worship: "*Woe to you and what you worship apart from God!*" [Q 21:67]. Likewise are His words, *You and what you worship apart from God will be rocks for Hell* [Q 21:98]. Because of his deficiency in understanding the meaning [of this verse], Ibn Zabʿarī objected to the Messenger of God, stating that the angels and the Messiah are also worshipped. But he and those who had his rank did not know that the object of worship of the one who worships the angels and the Messiah is itself one of the acts of Satan.

As for the perfect ones amongst the gnostics, they are the ones who worship the Absolute, the Real—who is given the name "God"—without the delimitation of a particular name or a specified quality. The Real who is described by every name discloses Himself to them and they never deny Him in any of the self-disclosures of His names, acts, and traces, unlike the delimited and veiled one who worships God according to a specific wording: *if good befalls him, he reposes in it; if affliction befalls him, he turns away on his face* [Q 22:11]. That is because of the predominance of the properties of some of the homesteads [*mawāṭin*] and the veiling of his vision by some of the loci of manifestation [*maẓāhir*] over others.

From this veiling, differences amongst people in matters of belief come about. Thus, some of them anathematize others, and some curse others, while every one of them affirms for the Real what the other denies, thinking that what they opine and believe is the highest form of exaltation of God! But they err and display bad etiquette toward God, while they think that they have attained the highest rank in knowledge and etiquette!

So also is the case with many of the people of declaring God's incomparability—because of the predominance of the properties of disengagement upon them, they are veiled like the angels [who are veiled] by the light of declaring God holy, while they are opposed to those who declare God's similarity, who, like animals, are veiled by the darknesses of declaring God bodily.

As for the Perfect Man, he knows the Real in every object of witnessing [*mashāhid*] and religious rite [*mashāʿir*], and he worships Him in every homestead and locus of manifestation. So he is the servant of God [*ʿabd Allāh*] who worships Him in all of His names and attributes. On account of this, the most perfect of human individuals—Muhammad, God bless him and his family—was given this name. Just as the divine name [Allah] brings together all the names—which are unified because of the Exclusive Unity of All-Gatheredness—so too does its path bring together the paths of all the names, even if each of these paths are specified by a name which sustains its locus, and each locus is worshipped and its straight path particular to it is traversed from that perspective. There is no path that brings together the paths of all of the loci of manifestation except the one upon which the locus of the Gathering Prophetic Seal travels—which, being the path of declaring God's oneness and upon which were all of the prophets and friends of God [*awliyāʾ*]—is travelled by the elect of the Prophet's community, which is the best of communities.

The Subsistence of Mercy
Tafsīr, 1:42

It is just as He says, *And do not follow the paths* [subul], *for they will divert you from His path* [sabīlihi] [Q 6:153], that is, the path which is for you contains felicity and salvation, for if this were not the case, then all paths would lead to Him, since God is the end-point of every purpose and the Final Goal [*ghāya*] of every endeavor. However, not everyone who returns to

Him will attain felicity and salvation from dispersion and chastisement. For the path to felicity is one: *Say: "This is my path* [sabīlī]. *Upon insight I call to God myself and those who follow me"* [Q 12:108]. As for the other paths, all of their goals is God [*Allāh*] firstly. Then the All-Merciful [*al-raḥmān*] will take over for Him [*yatawallāhu al-raḥmān*] at the end, and the property of the All-Merciful will subsist amongst them for eternity. This is a strange affair! I have not found anyone upon the face of the earth who knows it as it truly should be known.

The Names "God" and "He"
***Tafsīr*, 1:42–3**

Know that the relationship of the name "He" [*huwa*] to the name "God" [*Allāh*] is like the relationship of existence to quiddity in a contingent thing, except that the Necessary has no quiddity other than existence [*anniyya*]. It has already been discussed that the concept of the name "God" is one of the things that has a true essential definition, but that intellects are unable to encompass [*iḥāṭa*] all of the meanings that enter into its essential definition. For the form of a definition is only known when the forms of the essential definitions of all the existents are known. If this is not the case, then the form of the essential definition cannot be known [*wa-idh laysa fa-laysa*]. As for the name "He," It has no definition and no allusion can be made to It. So It is the most exalted station and the highest rank. For this reason, the perfect arrived ones have been singled out [*yukhtaṣṣu*] with perpetually being [*mudāwama*] in this noble invocation. A fine point in this is that when the servant invokes God with some of His attributes, he is not drowned in knowledge of God, because when he says "O All-Merciful," he is invoking His mercy, and his nature inclines to seeking it. . . . But when he says "O He!," while knowing that He is a pure ipseity which is uncontaminated by generality, specificity, multiplicity, plurality, finitude, and definition, this [then] is the invocation which does not denote anything at all except Perfect Existence [*al-anniyya al-tāmma*], which is uncontaminated by a meaning dissimilar to It. At that time, the light of Its invocation will settle in the servant's heart. This light cannot be defiled by the darkness generated by invoking other than God, for this is where there is perfect light and complete unveiling.

The End for All is Mercy
***Tafsīr*, 1:70–2**

Know that God's mercy embraces all things with respect to existence and quiddity. So the existence of wrath, in terms of the entity of wrath [*ʿayn al-ghaḍab*], is also from God's mercy. For this reason, His mercy outstrips His wrath, since being is that very mercy which encompasses [*shāmila*] everything, as He says, *And My mercy embraces all things* [Q 7:156]. Amongst the totality of entities and quiddities—all of which the existential mercy [*al-raḥma al-wujūdiyya*] reaches—are the entities of wrath and vengeance. Through mercy, God gives existence to the entity of wrath, so its root is good, as is what results from it, such as pain, sickness, tribulation, trial, and the like. . . .

Whoever closely examines the concomitants of wrath [*lawāzim al-ghaḍab*], such as sickness, pain, poverty, ignorance, death, and others, will find all of them to be nonexistent in themselves [*bi-mā hiya*] or nonexistent matters considered to be amongst the evil things. With respect to them being existents, they are all good, pouring forth from the well-spring of the mercy that is all-embracing and the existence that pervades all things. Because of this, the intellect will judge that the attribute of mercy is essential to God and that the attribute of wrath is accidental, which arises out of the causes either because the contingent existents lack perfection in accordance with the ranks of their distance from the Real, the Self–Subsisting, or because of the incapacity of matter to receive existence in the most perfect manner. On account of this, it is unveiled that "the end for all is mercy." As has been related in the tradition, God says, "The angels have interceded, the prophets have interceded, and the believers have interceded—there remains none but the Most Merciful of the merciful."

In *The Meccan Openings*, Shaykh al-ʿArabī says: "Know that God intercedes with respect to His names. His name 'the Most Merciful of the merciful' intercedes for His names 'the Compeller' and 'Terrible in Chastisement' in order that He may withdraw His chastisement from these parties. Thus, the one who did no good whatsoever will exit the Fire. God has called attention to this station: *The day We muster the God-wary* [muttaqīn] *to the All-Merciful in droves* [Q 19:85]. The 'God-wary' person merely sits with that divine name on account of which fear [*khawf*] falls into the hearts of servants. God's intimate is called 'wary of Him' [*muttaqī minhu*]. God will lift him from this name to that name which gives him safety from that which he was fearful. For this reason, the Prophet said concerning the intercession, 'the Most Merciful of the merciful remains.' This relationship relates to intercession to the Real from the Real with respect to His names."

In his treatise entitled *The Divine Flashes*, Shaykh al-ʿIrāqī relates that Abū Yazīd al-Basṭāmī heard the verse, *The day We muster the God-wary to the All-Merciful in droves*. So he let out a cry and said, "How will He muster to Him those who are with him?" The other one [i.e., Ibn ʿArabī] came and said, "From the name 'the Compeller' to the name 'The All-Merciful,' and from the name 'the Overbearing' to [the name] 'the Compassionate.' "

*

Praise is for God (Q 1:2)

The Cosmology of Praise
***Tafsīr*, 1:74–5**

As for the customary usage of the unveilers, "praise" is a kind of speech [*nawʿ min al-kalām*]. It has already been said that "speech" [*kalām*] is other than that which is specified by the tongue. This is why God praises Himself by means of that which He is worthy and deserving, just as the Prophet said, "I cannot enumerate Your praises. You are as You have praised Yourself." Likewise, everything praises and glorifies Him, as He says, *There is nothing except that it glorifies His praises; but you do not understand their glorification* [Q 18:44]. So the reality of praise, according to the verifying gnostics, is the act of making God's attributes of perfection manifest [*iẓhār al-ṣifāt al-kamāliyya*]. This could either be through words [*qawl*]—as is well-known amongst the masses—or it could be in act [*bi-l-fiʿl*], which is like God's praise for Himself and the praise of all things for Him. . . .

God's praise for Himself—which is the most exalted level of praise—is His existentiation [*ījād*] of every existing thing. . . . His existentiation of every existent is "praise" in the infinitive sense, similar to the way speaking denotes beauty [of voice] through speech. The existent itself is "praise" in the sense of actualizing the infinitive. In this sense, it is valid to call every existent thing "praise." And just as every existent is a "praise," so too is it a praiser [*ḥāmid*] because of its being composed of an intellectual constituent and a rational substance. . . . This is why this intellectual denotation has been expressed in the Qurʾān as "speech" [*nuṭq*]: *"God, the one who causes all things to speak, has caused us to speak"* [Q 41:22]. Likewise, every existent, with respect to the totality of its arrangement, is a single praise and a single praiser.

[This is] in accordance with what has been affirmed, namely that the sum total [*al-jamīʿ*] is like one large man with one reality, one form, and one intellect. This is the First Intellect, which is the form and reality of the world, and is the complete Muhammadan Reality [*al-ḥaqīqa al-Muḥammadiyya al-tamāmiyya*]. So the most exalted and most tremendous level of praise is the level of the Muhammadan Seal, which subsists through the existence of the Seal [*al-martaba al-khatmiyya al-Muḥammadiyya al-qāʾima bi-wujūd al-khātam*] on account of the Prophet's arrival at the promised praiseworthy station in His saying, *Perhaps your Lord will raise you to a praiseworthy station* [Q 17:79]. So his hallowed essence is the utmost level of praise through which God praises Himself. This is why the Prophet has been singled out with the banner of praise [*liwāʾ al-ḥamd*], and was called "praiser" [*ḥammād*], "most praiseworthy" [*aḥmad*], and "praised" [*maḥmūd*]. . . .

The Specification of Praise
Tafsīr, 1:76–7

All levels of existents (with respect to spirit, body, intellect, and sense perception) in every tongue (with respect to speech, act, and state) praise God, glorify Him, and magnify Him in this world and the next world in accordance with their primordial disposition [sic: *fiṭra aṣlī*] as required by their essential drive [*al-dāʿiya al-dhātiyya*]. There is no doubt that every innate act [*fiʿl gharīzī*] has an essential end and original calling [*ghāya dhātiyya wa-bāʿith aṣlī*]. It has been established that His Essence is the Final Goal of final goals [*ghāyat al-ghāyāt*] and the End for [all] objects of desire. For this reason, it is possible that His saying, *Praise is for God* [*al-ḥamdu li-llāh*] [Q 1:2] is an allusion to the Origin of existence and its End. Likewise, the [first] *lām* in for God [*li-llāh*] is [an allusion] to the Final Goal, or to the specification [of praise]. The reality of existence (or all its individual parts) is "for" God [*li-llāh*]. Since they are "for" Him, He is also "for" them. As the Prophet says, "Whoever is for God, God is for him." God's Essence is the Final Cause of all things and the Final Goal of the perfection of every form of existence, either without an intermediary, as is the case with the

Muhammadan Reality, which is the form of the world's arrangement and its root and origin; or through the medium of His most holy effusion and His hallowed existence, as is the case with the rest of the existents. In this lies the secret of intercession and the banner of praise.

*

Lord of the worlds (Q 1:2)

Man is a Macrocosm
Tafsīr, 1:79

In Bayḍāwī's *tafsīr*, [he says the following]: "It is said that by it [i.e., the word *ʿālamīn* in Q 1:2] He means 'people,' for every one of them is a 'world' insofar as he contains, in a manner similar to the macrocosm, the substances and accidents through which the Artisan is known, just as He is known through what He created in the macrocosm. This is why gazing upon the two is equal. God says, *And within yourselves—do you not see?*" [Q 51:21].

I say that the existence of every individual person (or most of them), as a locus of gazing, is composed in a manner similar to the macrocosm, whether it be most or all of it. Most people do not go beyond the confines of animality to the station of the intellect. So man's comprising some of the things in a manner similar [to the macrocosm] is not peculiar to him.

By "the worlds" [*ʿālamīn*], He could mean the "scholars" [*ʿulamāʾ min al-insān*]. With respect to the usage common [*ʿurf*] amongst the lexicographers, this is clear. With respect to what is customary usage [*mutaʿāraf*] amongst people, it is because every knower (with a *kasra*) [*ʿālim*] is a world (with a *fatḥa*) [*ʿālam*]. With respect to the point of view that man contains something of all that is in the macrocosm [*al-ʿālam al-kabīr*], it is because his perfect configuration [*nashʾatuhu al-kāmila*] is the locus of manifestation of all the divine names and attributes and is the gathering place of all of the existential realities, as is known to those who assiduously pursue the signs in the horizons and within their selves [cf. Q 41:53]. So man is a prototype for all of what is in the cosmos. From this perspective, he is a small world [*ʿālam ṣaghīr*], which is why he is called the "microcosm" [*al-ʿālam al-ṣaghīr*], for it is as if he is a book that has condensed and abridged the entire cosmos [*kitāb mukhtaṣar muntakhab min jamīʿ al-ʿālam*], [which] *"does not leave anything out, neither insignificant nor great, except that it takes account of it"* [Q 18:49], just as the Qur'ān, despite its concision, contains all of the heavenly books.

*

The All-Merciful, the Compassionate (Q 1:3)

Why Q 1:3 Repeats Part of Q 1:1
Tafsīr, 1:82

Mention of this verse occurs a second time for purposes of rhetoric and affirmation. Or, it is because, in the first instance, [God's] divinity was mentioned [before it, that is, in Q 1:1], thus leading to the remembrance of those blessings through which servanthood is actualized; whereas here, [God's] praise is mentioned [before it, that is, in Q 1:2], thus leading to the remembrance of that through which praise and gratitude for blessings are actualized. So there is no repetition in this verse.

*

Master of the Day of Judgment (Q 1:4)

The Causer of Causes on the Final Day
Tafsīr, 1:86

Potencies and preparednesses do not exist in the afterlife since everything in potentiality will become actualized there. For actuality is concomitant with the actualizer unbound to a receptacle. And God is the Causer [*musabbib*] of every existent cause and the existentiator of every actualizer of existence. Thus, His power overpowers all others powers, and through His light every light and luminosity is disclosed. He will be Master of all things on the day in which the surface of the earth and the heavens are unfolded. There, things will be appointed their own times and attached to the [actualized] existence of their receptacles and preparednesses. Just as He says, *To whom does the kingdom belong today? To God, the One, the Overbearing* [40:16].

*

You alone do we worship, and from
You alone do we seek aid (Q 1:5)

The Nature of Worship and Seeking God's Aid
Tafsīr, 1:91

Man is composed of a body (like a steed) and a spirit (like a rider), as God created him for the journey to the next life, and the goal of his journey is to meet God. This is why he has been created, and upon it he is innately disposed and naturally inclines, for it is the spirit's purpose. The body's purpose is to acquire benefits, obtain good things, and free itself from evils and vices. This is the meaning of "servitude" [*ʿibāda*] and "service" [*khidma*].

There is no doubt that the best of states for the body comes about through works which draw the spirit closer to God, reverencing He who is worshipped and serving Him. This is the first of the levels of felicity for man, and is what is meant by His words, *we seek aid* (Q 1:5).

The best of states for the spirit are for it to be tied to the Real, attached to Him and cut off from other than Him, and disengaged from the world and what it contains. For when man persists in acquiring this rank and in continuously disengaging himself [*dhāt*] and freeing it from material attachments and worldly coverings, a time will come when something of the lights of holiness and the flashes of the unseen will be manifest to him. When his essence is illumined by the light of gnosis and servanthood, he will know that the originator of his love for the World of the Dominion [*ʿālam al-malakūt*] and the one prodding his essence to pursue nearness to God is not, and cannot be, other than God, the Revolver of hearts [*muqallib al-qulūb*] and Proder of souls. Man cannot rely upon himself to perform these acts of worship and scale these ranks. Nor would the performance [of these acts of worship] make it possible for him to acquire something of the perfections of knowledge and practice, except with God's success-giving, solicitude, and protection. And this is the meaning of His saying, *and from You alone do we seek aid* (Q 1:5).

*

Guide us upon the straight path (Q 1:6)

The Path of the Perfect Man
Tafsīr, 1:108

Just as these special qualities [*khaṣāʾiṣ*] and miracles—such as being created upon the form of the All-Merciful, having been breathed into with His Spirit, ennobled with the miracle of being taught the names, entrusted to the land of the body and the sea of spirits, kneaded in the clay of the soul and intellect by the two hands, specified [*makhṣūṣ*] with being God's representative in the great and small worlds, prostrated to by God's angels in the bodily and spiritual constitutions—are only for the Real Spiritual Man [*al-insān al-maʿnawī al-ḥaqīqī*], not these resemblances and likenesses in formal numbers, so too is arrival to Him through the ascent of the spirit and the inner journey on the straight path of God specified [*yukhtaṣṣu*] for him and not others. If this were not so, then every walking animal and others would be traversing his path which He has specified [*yakhuṣṣuhu*], heading towards the direction [cf. Q 2:144] of the Real.

The Motion of Natural Disposition
Tafsīr, 1:111

Know that the path [*ṣirāṭ*] is not a path except through one's traversing it. An allusion has been made to the fact that every creature is heading towards the direction of the Real, towards the Causer of causes [*musabbib al-asbāb*] in an innate manner of turning [*tawajjuh gharīzī*] and a motion of natural disposition [*ḥaraka jibilliyya*]. In this motion of natural disposition, diversion and fleeing from what God has fixed for each of them cannot be conceived with respect to them. God takes them by their forelock, as He says, *"There is not a creature except that He takes it by its forelock. Verily my Lord is upon a straight path"* [Q 11:56].

Substantial Motion
Tafsīr, 1:112–3

As for essential motion [*ḥaraka dhātiyya*], it is substantial motion [*ḥaraka jawhariyya*]. As with all types of motion, it has an agent, receptacle, traversed distance, beginning, and end, except that motion in substance differs from the others in one manner: the distance traversed in this motion is the moving body [*mutaḥarrik*] itself, both in reality and existence. The agent of this essential human motion is God, and its receptacle, that is, its object, is the human soul with respect to the power of the receptivity of its soul [*quwwatihā al-istiʿdādiyya al-nafsāniyya*] and its passive hylic intellect.

Why Peoples' Natures Differ
Tafsīr, 1:118–21

It is because of their disparities in purity and murkiness, power and weakness, and nobility and lowliness; it is also in accordance with bodily causes and worldly states—such as material preparednesses and the continuous chain of accidents ending in high matters—which occur to them. And [it is because] of the preeternal decree. . . .

In sum, the disparity in creation in terms of perfection and imperfection and felicity and wretchedness is either by way of substantial essential matters, or by way of accidental matters acquired by means of religious devotions and actions. So the difference is in accordance with essential matters by way of pure divine solicitude, which calls for beauty of order and excellence of arrangement [in the cosmos].

The Path is the Soul
Tafsīr, 1:122

Know that were you to traverse the path and were God to firmly place your feet upon it such that He causes you to arrive to Paradise, [it would be] the form of guidance which you created for your soul in the abode of this world by virtue of God's guiding you by way of actions related to the heart and body. In this abode, it is not witnessed as a sensory form. On the Day of Resurrection, and according to the view of the people of insight who have been overcome by witnessing the constitution of the afterlife, it is spread out for you as a sensory bridge [*jisr maḥsūs*] extended over the surface of Hell, its start being in [this] place, and its end being at the door of Paradise. Whoever witnesses it will know that it is of his design and building, and that it is an extended bridge in this world over the surface of his Hell in the fire of his nature, within which is the shadow of his reality.

*

The path of those whom You have blessed (Q 1:7)

God's Writing
Tafsīr, 1:135

All of the cosmos is His writing. Indeed, the writing of authors derives from His writing which He caused to be written through the medium of the hearts of His servants. So there is nothing astonishing about an author. Rather, there is astonishment over the one who subjected him.

*

Not of those who incur wrath, nor of those who stray (Q 1:7)

God's Hands and Feet
Tafsīr, 1:149–50

God—hallowed is His Essence and exalted are His attributes above being composed of parts and limbs—has two holy hands, both of which are right [*yamīn Allāh*]. These exalted acts are face to face with the two contrary attributes, such as the attributes of mercy and wrath, and good–pleasure and anger. Each of the contrary attributes has a grip [*qabḍa*], as is indicated in His saying, *The entire earth will be in His grip on the Day of Resurrection, and the heavens will be folded in His right hand* [Q 39:67]. It has been related in a tradition that the Messenger of God said, "God will fold the heavens on the Day of Resurrection. Then He will take them [i.e., the people] by His right hand and will say, 'I am the King. Where are the haughty ones? Where are the proud ones?' Then he will fold the earth in His right hand." And in a [different] narration, [the Prophet said], "He will take them by His other hand, and then will say, 'Where are the haughty ones? Where are the proud ones?' "

In His establishing Himself upon the Throne, He also has two feet which were let down onto the Footstool. The one which designates the foot of firmness gives fixity [*thubūt*] to the people of the Gardens in their Gardens, while the other one, which designates the foot of compulsion [*jabarūt*], gives fixity to the people of Hell in Hell. These matters are amongst the divine levels and their concomitants amongst the general matters, which are accidental to contingent existents because of the inability of their rank in perceiving the divine levels.

Know that the ruling property [*ḥukm*] of the divine wrath is the perfection of the level of the grip of the left hand [*qabḍat al-shimāl*], for although both of His hands are holy, blessed, and right, the ruling property of each of them—leftness [*shimāliyya*] and rightness [*yamīniyya*]—is in opposition to the other from their respective standpoints. For this reason, He says, *The entire earth will be in His grip on the Day of Resurrection, and the heavens will be folded in His right hand*. He will render the earth "gripped" and the heavens "folded." So understand! The hand to which all of the felicitous belong contains mercy and Gardens, while the other contains chastisement and Fires.

The Preponderance of Mercy
***Tafsīr*, 1:151–2**

The general mercy will necessitate the all-encompassing bestowal upon everything. There is no doubt that the affair will take place in this way. So the Word will prove true and blessings will be general. Wrath's ruling property will become manifest, and then mercy will overcome [it]. Nothing of the contingents will be without mercy, each of them [receiving it] in accordance with their states and the rank of their way stations.

Just as His mercy encompasses and embraces all things, so too does His wrath, except that the side of mercy is preponderant because of its being essential, while wrath is accidental because of the inability of contingents in their contingency to receive the complete light. There is an allusion to this in the saying of the Commander of the Faithful [i.e., ʿAlī]: "Glory to the one whose mercy embraces His friends in the intensity of His vengeance, and whose vengeance is intensified towards His enemies in the embrace of His mercy."

None Worships Anyone but Him
***Tafsīr*, 1:153**

In a narration it has been related that God is beautiful and He loves beauty. He is the artisan of the cosmos and brings it into existence in His form [*shākila*], as He says, *[Say:] "everyone acts according to their form"* [Q 17:84]. . . . So the entire cosmos is of the utmost beauty because it is a mirror for the Real. This is why the knowers become enraptured by it and the verifiers realize love for it. For He is the object of gaze in every eye, the beloved in every form of love, the object of worship in every act of worship, and the Final Goal in both the unseen and the seen. The entire cosmos prays to Him, praises Him, and glorifies Him.

The Transmutations of God
***Tafsīr*, 1:154**

The last form into which He will transmute Himself for His servants will be the ruling property of contentment [*riḍāʾ*]. So the Real will transmute Himself into the form of bliss. . . . He will be gracious towards, and forgive on His own behalf, those who angered Him by removing whatever there was in

Him of annoyance, distress, and wrath. Then He will apply this to those who are objects of wrath [*maghḍūb*]. Whoever understands this will be safe from His wrath, but will not "feel safe from God's deception" [cf. Q 7:99], and whoever does not understand will come to know, and will understand that the end is to Him.

The End of the Sojourn
Tafsīr, 1:154–5

When God created the Throne, He made it the locus of the establishment of existential mercy and the Unity of the Word of existentiation, which is the saying *"Be!"* [Q 2:117]. And He created the Footstool, and the Word was divided into two matters—Command and creation—so that He could create a pair of everything. . . . The two feet were let down onto the Footstool until the Word of the Spirit became divided in the Footstool, for the Footstool is the second in form and shape after the Throne. From the Footstool, two shapes came about in the body of the natural world. So the two feet were let down onto the Footstool, and each foot alighted in a place. One place was called the "Garden" and the other "Hell." There is no place to which the two feet can travel beyond these two places. And they will not be contracted except from the root from which they became manifest, namely the All-Merciful. So they only give mercy, for by virtue of wisdom [*ḥikma*], the end [*nihāya*] returns to the beginning [*bidāya*], except that between the beginning and end there is a path. If this were not the case, there would be no beginning and end to it. The journey is where one can expect to find [*maẓinna*] fatigue, misfortune, and toil. This is the cause of the emergence of the wretchedness that has become manifest in the cosmos in terms of this world, the next world, and the isthmus [*barzakh*]. At the end of the sojourn, the walking staff [*ʿaṣā al–tasāyur*] will be cast aside and repose [*rāḥa*] in the abodes of permanence and perdition will reign.

The Likeness of Two Travelers
Tafsīr, 1:155

To the one who says that the matter is not such that one will find repose should he dwell in a place called "the Fire," it could be said to him: you are correct, but complete reflection [*al-naẓar al-tāmm*] has escaped you! This is because travelers are of two types: one is in a state of comfort on his journey because of his being beloved, served—all of his needs being provided for him on a platter which is supported by the necks of men—and protected from change in climate. His likeness in arriving to his home is like the people of the Garden in the Garden. [The other] traveler treads on the path with his feet, has paltry provisions, and diminished supplies. When he arrives home, fatigue and hardship remain with him for a while, until they depart him. Then he finds repose. This is like the one who is punished and wretched in the Fire (which is his home), and then the mercy which encompasses all things becomes widespread. Between these two types of travelers there is a traveler who does not have the comforts of the person of the Garden, nor the chastisement [*ʿadhāb*] of the person of the Fire. So he is between repose and fatigue. [He belongs to] a party which will be taken out of the Fire through *the intercession of the interceders* [Q 74:48] and the removal of the Most Merciful of the merciful [*arḥam al-rāḥimīn*]. And this party will be in ranks in accordance with the fatigue that remains with them. In the Fire, the fatigue will be removed bit-by-bit [*shay'an fa-shay'an*]. When their time is up, they will be taken to the place of repose [*maḥall al-rāḥa*], which is the Garden.

Chastisement's Sweetness
Tafsīr, 1:156

The last of those who remain are those who did no good whatsoever, neither by way of having faith nor by way of displaying excellent character traits. It is just that they were preceded by solicitude [*ʿināya*], [which demands] that they should be amongst the people of this abode. . . . Then the doors will be locked, and the Fire will surround [them] and there will be despair over getting out. At that time, mercy will spread amongst the Fire's inhabitants because they had despaired getting out of it, *just as the nonbelievers despair over the people of the graves* [Q 60:13]. He had given them a constitution which is agreeable to one who inhabitants this abode. So when they despair, they will rejoice—their bliss will be the measure [of their despair], this being the first bliss that they will find and their state in the Fire, as we have mentioned. . . . Thus they will find the chastisement [*ʿadhāb*] sweet [*yastaʿdhibūna*], so pains will cease and the chastisement [*ʿadhāb*] will become sweetness [*ʿadhb*]. . . . God willing, the inhabitant of every abode will taste sweetness. So understand! Do you not see the truth of what we have said? Because of the deficiency and nonexistence of fullness that is in it, the Fire will not cease to be painful until the Compeller places His foot in it, as has been related in the tradition. This is one of the two aforementioned feet on the Footstool. The other [foot] is the one whose resting place will be the Garden: *Give glad tidings to those who believe, that they have a foot of firmness with their Lord* [Q 10:2]. The name "Lord" will be with them, and the name "Compeller" will be with the others because the Fire is the abode of majesty, domination, and awe, whereas the Garden is the abode of beauty, intimacy, and the subtle divine alighting place [*manzil al-ilāhī al-laṭīf*]. The two of them are face to face with the two grips mentioned in the Sacred tradition: "One for the people of the Fire, and I don't care; the other for the people of the Garden, and I don't care." He does not care because the end for both is to the all-embracing mercy.

*

On the Merits of the Fātiḥa

The Fātiḥa and the Perfect Man
***Tafsīr*, 1:163–4**

By my life, it is like the form of the All-Gatheredness of the world, which is created upon the form of the All-Merciful [and] denotes, in its appearance, structure, and its comprising the loci of the attributes of beauty—such as the angels and their lights—and the attributes of majesty—such as bodies and their faculties—the existence of the one *to whom belong creation, and the Command* [7:54].

The relationship of the *Sūrat al-fātiḥa* to the entire Qurʾān is like the relationship of man—who is the small world—to the world, which is the great man. And just as the Perfect Man is a succinct book [*kitāb wajīz*] and an abridged transcription [*nuskha muntakhab*] within whom is found all that is in the All-Gathering great book [*al-kitāb al-kabīr al-jāmiʿ*] . . . so too is the "opener of the book" [*fātiḥat al-kitāb*], within which, despite its brevity and concision, is found the sum total [*majāmiʿ*] of the aims of the Qurʾān and their secrets and lights. This All-Gatheredness [*jāmiʿiyya*] is not for the other Qur'ānic *sūras*, just as none of the forms of the world's parts have what man has with respect to [his bringing together] the form of the Divine Gatheredness [*al-ṣūra al-jamʿiyya al-ilāhiyya*]. As it is said:

> God does not find it objectionable
> that He gather the cosmos in one individual.

As has been indicated, the realized gnostic [*al-ʿārif al-muḥaqqiq*] understands from this one *sūra* all of the sciences and universal forms of knowledge spread throughout the verses and *sūras* of the Qur'ān. So whoever does not understand this *sūra* so as to derive from it the support of the secrets of the divine sciences and lordly forms of knowledge, such as the states of the Origin and the Return and the science of the soul and what is below and above it—which is the key to all the rest of the sciences—is not a lordly knower and is not guided in his interpretation [*tafsīr*]. If this *sūra* did not, as we said, contain the secrets of the Origin and the Return and the science of man's wayfaring to his Lord, the reports about its superiority would not have been related. Indeed, it is equal to the entire Qur'ān, since, in reality, a thing does not have rank and excellence except on account of its containing divine matters and their states, as has already been mentioned.

The Return of All things to God
***Tafsīr*, 1:166**

His saying *Master of the Day of Judgment* [Q 1:4] is an allusion to the reality of the Return [in general], and the return of everything to Him [in particular], because He is the Final Goal of final goals [*ghāyat al-ghāyāt*].

The Path is the Qur'ān
***Tafsīr*, 1:166–7**

It [i.e., the word *ṣirāṭ* in Q 1:6] is an allusion to the Majestic Qur'ān, which is the noblest of heavenly books which [themselves] are the spiritual Tablets [*al-alwāḥ al-nafsiyya*] that have been revealed to the previous prophets. [The reason the Qur'ān has been revealed to the Prophet is] because his intellectual, spiritual substance (this being the substance of prophecy) is, from one perspective, a divine Word, and, from [another] perspective, *a clarifying book* [Q 5:15] in which there are verses of wisdom and gnosis. . . . In himself, the Prophet is "the Path of God, the Exalted, the Praiseworthy" [cf. Q 14:1], since the servant's arrival to God is not possible except after arriving at knowledge of the Prophet's essence. Likewise [is the case with] the one who represents him, as the detached Qur'ānic letters indicate: "ʿAlī is the path of truth to which we cling [*ʿAlī ṣirāṭ ḥaqq numsikuhu*]."

A Tradition on the Distinction of the Fātiḥa
Tafsīr, 1:168

The Prophet said, "By the one in whose hand is my soul, God did not reveal its like in the Torah, Gospels, Psalms, or [anywhere else in] the Qur'ān. It is the mother of the book [cf. Q 43:4] and the doubled seven [allusion to Q 15:87]. It is divided between God and His servant, and for His servant is what he asks."

The Fātiḥa as all that Man Needs
Tafsīr, 1:170

One of the merits of this *sūra* is that it brings together [*jāmiʿa*] all that man needs with respect to knowledge of the Origin, the middle, and the Return.

The Path is the Soul Revisited
Tafsīr, 1:175

With respect to its containing the science of the Return, which is the science of the states of the human soul that is perfect in knowledge and action [and] free from the disease of ignorance and the deficiency of sin, His saying *the Path of those whom You have blessed* . . . [Q 1:7] is an allusion to the science of the soul. And it is "the Path of God, the Exalted, the Praiseworthy" [cf. Q 14:1], and God's gate. . . . Through the acting and knowing perfect soul that is guided by God's Light, people are driven to God, and, from this gate, all created things enter the path of return to the Creator, for being is in the form of a circle whose second part [i.e., the arc of descent] joins with the first part [i.e., the arc of ascent].

Appendix 3

Passages from the *Futūḥāt* Reworked into the *Tafsīr Sūrat al-Fātiḥa*

Presented here are the passages from Ibn ʿArabī's *Futūḥāt* which Ṣadrā assimilated into his *Tafsīr Sūrat al-fātiḥa* without citing his source. I have juxtaposed the relevant sections with one another in order to demonstrate the carry-over of ideas from one text to the other. The *Futūḥāt* passage in section I is taken from Ibn ʿArabī, "Towards God's Signs," trans. William Chittick in Ibn ʿArabī, *The Meccan Revelations*, 1:182. A part of the *Futūḥāt* passage in section IV is reproduced from Chittick, "Ibn al-ʿArabī's Hermeneutics of Mercy," 166. In both cases, I have modified these translations in order to maintain terminological/ conceptual consistency amongst the texts presented.

I

Futūḥāt, 3:449 (Beirut)

It is reported in the *Ṣaḥīḥ* [of Muslim] that the Messenger of God said, "God is beautiful and He loves beauty." It is He who made the world and brought it into existence upon His own form [*ṣūra*]. So the whole world is beautiful in the extreme; there is no ugliness in it. . . . That is why the knowers become enraptured by it and the verifiers realize love for it. And that is why we have said concerning it in some of our explanations of it that it is God's mirror. So the knowers see nothing in it but God's form. . . . For He is the one revealed in every face, the one sought after in every sign, the object of gaze in every eye, the object of worship in every act of worship, and the Final Goal in both the unseen and the seen. . . . So the whole cosmos prays to Him, prostrates itself before Him, and glorifies His praise.

Tafsīr, 1:153–4

In a narration it has been related that God is beautiful and He loves beauty. He is the artisan of the cosmos and brings it into existence in His form [*shākila*], as He says, [*Say:*] *"everyone acts according to their form"* [Q 17:84]. . . . So the entire cosmos is of the utmost beauty because it is a mirror for the Real. This is why the knowers become enraptured by it and the verifiers realize love for it. For He is the object of gaze in every eye, the beloved in every form of love, the object of worship in every act of worship, and the Final Goal in both the unseen and the seen. The entire cosmos prays to Him, praises Him, and glorifies Him.

II

Futūḥāt, 3:462 (Beirut)

When God made the Throne the locus for the oneness of the Word, which is the [name] the All-Merciful and none other than it, and [when] He created the Footstool, he divided the Word into two affairs in order to create two pairs from everything so that one of the two pairs would be qualified by highness and the other by lowness (one being active and the other passive). . . . The two feet were let down onto the Footstool when the Word of the All-Merciful became divided in the Footstool, for from the Footstool itself the division of the Word became manifest. This is because amongst the forms of bodies which become manifest in the primary substance the Footstool is second after the all-encompassing Throne, while they are both forms in the universal natural body. So the two feet were let down onto the Footstool, and each foot alighted in a place which was not the place in which the other alighted. This was the end of their alighting. One place was called the "Garden" and the other "Hell." There is no place to which the two feet can travel beyond these two places. These two feet will not be contracted except from the root from which they became manifest, namely the All-Merciful. So they only give mercy, for by vir-

Tafsīr, 1:154–5

When God created the Throne, He made it the locus of the establishment of existential mercy and the Unity of the Word of existentiation, which is the saying *"Be!"* [Q 2:117]. And He created the Footstool, and the Word was divided into two affairs—Command and creation—so that He could create a pair from everything. . . . The two feet were let down onto the Footstool until the Word of the Spirit became divided in the Footstool, for the Footstool is the second in form and shape after the Throne. From the Footstool, two shapes came about in the body of the natural world. So the two feet were let down onto the Footstool, and each foot alighted in a place. One place was called the "Garden" and the other "Hell." There is no place to which the two feet can travel beyond these two places. And they will not be contracted except from the root from which they became manifest, namely the All-Merciful. So they only give mercy, for by virtue of wisdom [*ḥikma*], the end [*nihāya*] returns to the beginning [*bidāya*], except that between the beginning and end there is a path. If this were not the case, there would be no beginning and end to it. The journey is where one can expect to find fatigue, misfortune, and toil.

tue of God's decision [*ḥukm*], the end [*nihāya*] returns to the beginning [*bidāya*], except that between the beginning and end there is a path. . . . If it were not for this path, there would be no beginning and goal [*ghāya*]. A journey is what occurs between the beginning and the goal, and is where one can expect to find fatigue and misfortune. This is the cause of the emergence of the wretchedness that has become manifest in the cosmos in terms of this world, the next world, and the isthmus. At the end of the sojourn, the walking staff will be cast aside and repose in the abodes of permanence and perdition will reign.

This is the cause of the emergence of the wretchedness that has become manifest in the cosmos in terms of this world, the next world, and the isthmus. At the end of the sojourn, the walking staff will be cast aside and repose in the abodes of permanence and perdition will reign.

III

***Futūḥāt*, 3:462 (Beirut)**

If you were to say that the matter is not such that repose is to be found should one dwell in a place called "the Fire," we would say [the following]: you are correct, but reflection [*naẓar*] has escaped you! This is because travelers are of two types: one traveler's journey is as if he did not move anywhere because of the state of comfort he was in by virtue of his being served—all of his needs being provided for him on a platter which is supported by the necks of men—and protected from change in climate. In arriving to his home he is like the people of the Garden in the Garden. [The other] traveler treads on the path with his feet, has paltry provisions, and diminished supplies. When he arrives home, fatigue and hardship remain with him for a while, until they depart him. Then he finds repose. This is like the one who is punished and wretched in the Fire (which is his home), and then the mercy which encompasses all things becomes widespread. Between these two types of travelers there is a traveler who does not have the comforts of the person of the Garden, nor the discomforts [*shaẓaf*] of the person of the Fire. So he is between repose and fatigue. [He belongs to] a party which will be taken out of the Fire through

***Tafsīr*, 1:155**

To the one who says that the matter is not such that one will find repose should he dwell in a place called "the Fire," it could be said to him: you are correct, but complete reflection [*al-naẓar al-tāmm*] has escaped you! This is because travelers are of two types: one is in a state of comfort on his journey because of his being beloved, served—all of his needs being provided for him on a platter which is supported by the necks of men—and protected from change in climate. His likeness in arriving home is like the people of the Garden in the Garden. [The other] traveler treads on the path with his feet, has paltry provisions, and diminished supplies. When he arrives home, fatigue and hardship remain with him for a while, until they depart him. Then he finds repose. This is like the one who is punished and wretched in the Fire (which is his home), and then the mercy which encompasses all things becomes widespread. Between these two types of travelers there is a traveler who does not have the comforts of the person of the Garden, nor the chastisement [*ʿadhāb*] of the person of the Fire. So he is between repose and fatigue. [He belongs to] a party which will be taken out of the Fire *through the intercession of the interceders the intercession of the interceders* [Q. 74:48] and the removal of the Most Merciful of the merciful. And this party will be in ranks. This is why amongst them there will be those who are ahead and those who lag behind, in accordance with the fatigue that remains with them. In the Fire, the fatigue will be removed bit-by-bit [*shayʾan baʿd shayʾ*]. When [the one in the fire's] time is up, he will be taken to the place of repose, which is the Garden.

[Q. 74:48] and the removal of the Most Merciful of the merciful. And this party will be in ranks in accordance with the fatigue that remains with them. In the Fire, the fatigue will be removed bit-by-bit [*shayʾan fa-shayʾan*]. When their time is up, they will be taken to the place of repose, which is the Garden.

IV

***Futūḥāt*, 3:463 (Beirut)**

Those remaining will be the ones whom the Most Merciful of the merciful will cause to come out. They are the ones who did no good whatsoever, neither by way of having faith nor by way of displaying excellent character traits. It is just that they were preceded by solicitude, [which demands] that they should be amongst the people of this abode. . . . Then the doors will be locked, and the Fire will surround [them] and there will be despair over getting out. At that time, mercy will spread amongst the Fire's inhabitants, because they had despaired getting out of it. They had feared leaving [i.e., despaired leaving] the Fire when they saw that the Most Merciful of the merciful was taking people out, whereas God had given them a constitution which is agreeable to one who inhabits this abode. . . . So when they despair, they will rejoice—their bliss will be the measure [of their despair], this being the first bliss that they will find and their state in the Fire, as we have mentioned. . . . Thus they will find the chastisement [*ʿadhāb*] sweet [*yastaʿdhibūna*], so pains will cease, though the chastisement [*ʿadhāb*] remains. This is why it is called sweetness [*ʿadhb*]—the final issue is that those who abide within it find it sweet. . . . So understand! The inhabitant of every abode

***Tafsīr*, 1:156**

The last of those who remain are those who did no good whatsoever, neither by way of having faith nor by way of displaying excellent character traits. It is just that they were preceded by solicitude, [which demands] that they should be amongst the people of this abode. . . . Then the doors will be locked, and the Fire will surround [them] and there will be despair over getting out. At that time, mercy will spread amongst the Fire's inhabitants, because they had despaired getting out of it, *just as the nonbelievers despair over the people of the graves* [Q 60:13]. He had given them a constitution which is agreeable to one who inhabitants this abode. So when they despair, they will rejoice—their bliss will be the measure [of their despair], this being the first bliss that they will find and their state in the Fire, as we have mentioned. . . . Thus they will find the chastisement [*ʿadhāb*] sweet [*yastaʿdhibūna*], so pains will cease and the chastisement [*ʿadhāb*] will become sweetness [*ʿadhb*]. . . . God willing, the inhabitant of every abode will taste sweetness. So understand! Do you not see the truth of what we have said? Because of the deficiency and nonexistence of fullness that is in it, the Fire will not cease to be painful until the Compeller places His foot in it, as will be felicitous, God willing! Have you not looked at the truth of what we have said, namely that the Fire will continue to be painful because of what is in it by way of the deficiency and nonexistence of fullness, until the Compeller places His foot in it? This is one of the two aforementioned feet on the Footstool. The other foot is the one whose resting places will be the Garden: *Give glad tidings to those who believe, that they have a foot of firmness with their Lord* [Q 10:2]. The name "Lord" will be with them, and the name "Compeller" will be with the others because the Fire is the abode of majesty, domination, and awe, whereas the Garden is the abode of beauty, intimacy, and the subtle divine descent [*tanazzul al-ilāhī al-laṭīf*]. The foot of firmness is one of the two feet on the Footstool, and both feet are God's two "grips." One is for the Fire, and He does not care. The other is for the Garden, and He does not care. Because their end is to mercy—that is why He does not care.

has been related in the tradition. This is one of the two aforementioned feet on the Footstool. The other [foot] is the one whose resting place will be the Garden: *Give glad tidings to those who believe, that they have a foot of firmness with their Lord* [Q 10:2]. The name "Lord" will be with them, and the name "Compeller" will be with the others because the Fire is the abode of majesty, domination, and awe, whereas the Garden is the abode of beauty, intimacy, and the subtle divine alighting place [*manzil al-ilāhī al-laṭīf*]. The two of them are face to face with the two grips mentioned in the Sacred tradition: "One for the people of the Fire, and I don't care; the other for the people of the Garden, and I don't care." He does not care because the end for both is to the all-embracing mercy.

Notes

Introduction

1. Horten's first study on Ṣadrā, *Die Gottesbeweise bei Schirázi (1640†)* (Bonn: Friedrich Cohen, 1912), is a translation and commentary of texts from Ṣadrā's oeuvre dealing with proofs for God's existence. The second work, *Das philosophische System von Schirázi (1640†)* (Strasbourg: Trübner, 1913), represents a problematic attempt to explain Ṣadrā's main ideas by summarizing his central teachings, particularly ontology and physics. For a listing and brief discussion of Horten's many contributions to the study of earlier and later Islamic thought, see Gustav Pfannmüller, *Handbuch der Islam-Literatur* (Berlin: De Gruyter, 1923), 353–6. It should be noted that before Horten's studies, Muhammad Iqbal's *The Development of Metaphysics in Persia* (London: Luzac, 1908) discussed some of later Islamic philosophy's key figures, but in summary fashion.

2. Tim Winter, "Introduction," in *The Cambridge Companion to Classical Islamic Theology*, ed. Tim Winter (Cambridge: Cambridge University Press, 2008), 1–2, attributes these older Western attitudes toward Islamic thought to Eurocentrism. To be sure, this antiquated approach to Islamic intellectual history was Eurocentric since Islam's intellectual history was simply an ingredient to the way Western/European scholars understood the development of their own intellectual history. Thus, the value and significance of Islamic thought was gauged through a Western/European lens. At the same time, many Muslims writing on Islamic thought from the later part of the nineteenth century to the middle of the twentieth century, influenced as they were by the works of Orientalists in their representations of Islamic civilization, tended to view their own religion's intellectual legacy through the eyes of their colonial masters. As Seyyed Hossein Nasr argues (*Islamic Life and Thought* [Albany: State University of New York Press, 1981], chap. 12), colonialism determined what version of "Islamic" philosophy was circulated in the Muslim world, as views of Western philosophy prevailed amongst Muslims in accordance with the brand of philosophy taught to them by their colonizers. Thus, in Egypt, because of the presence of the French, philosophy came to be identified with various forms of Marxism; and in India, where the British ruled, philosophy

was of the logical positivist type. This phenomenon, in turn, had a devastating effect upon how Islamic philosophy was understood by those Muslims in the east who studied Islamic thought in early post-colonial times (Iqbal being one of them). See also Oliver Leaman, "Orientalism and Islamic Philosophy," in *History of Islamic Philosophy*, ed. Seyyed Hossein Nasr and Oliver Leaman (New York: Routledge, 1996), 2:1143–8; Muhsin Mahdi, "Orientalism and the Study of Islamic Philosophy," *JIS* 1, no. 1 (1990): 73–98. Cf. Dimitri Gutas, "The Study of Arabic Philosophy in the Twentieth Century: An Essay on the Historiography of Arabic Philosophy," *BJMES* 29, no. 1 (2002): 5–25.

3. See Heidegger, "Qu'est-ce que la métaphysique?," trans. Henry Corbin, *Bifur* 8 (1931): 5–27.

4. Corbin's seminal study on Avicenna was originally published in 1952 under the title *Avicenne et le récit visionnaire*, and was eventually translated as *Avicenna and the Visionary Recital*, trans. Willard Trask (Irving: Spring Publications, 1980). Corbin's critical edition of Suhrawardī's Arabic works, entitled *Opera metaphysica et mystica*, was published in Istanbul in 1945 and 1946. The edition was reissued as the first two volumes of Shihāb al-Dīn Suhrawardī, *Majmūʿa-yi muṣannafāt-i Shaykh-i Ishrāq*, ed. Henry Corbin (vols. 1–2) and Seyyed Hossein Nasr (vol. 3) (reprint, Tehran: Imperial Iranian Academy of Philosophy, 1976–7).

5. For the school of Isfahan and beyond, see Corbin, *En islam iranien* (Paris: Gallimard, 1971–2), 4:9–201; Corbin, *La philosophie iranienne islamique aux XVIIe et XVIIIe siècles* (Paris: Buchet/Chastel, 1981); Nasr, *Islamic Philosophy from Its Origins to the Present: Philosophy in the Land of Prophecy* (Albany: State University of New York Press, 2006), chap. 11; Nasr, *The Islamic Intellectual Tradition in Persia*, ed. Mehdi Aminrazavi (Richmond: Curzon, 1996), chaps. 21–3; Nasr, "The Place of the School of Iṣfahān in Islamic Philosophy and Sufism," In *The Heritage of Sufism*, ed. Leonard Lewisohn (vols. 1–3) and David Morgan (vol. 3) (Oxford: Oneworld, 1999), 3:3–15. Prior to the rise of the school of Isfahan, Shiraz was the center of philosophical and theological activity for roughly a century and a half. An account of this period and its main figures can be found in Reza Pourjavady, *Philosophy in Early Safavid Iran: Najm al-Dīn Maḥmūd al-Nayrīzī and His Writings* (Leiden: Brill, 2011), chap. 1.

6. Many details concerning Ṣadrā's life and times have been reconsidered in Sajjad Rizvi, *Mullā Ṣadrā Shīrāzī: His Life and Works and the Sources for Safavid Philosophy* (Oxford: Oxford University Press, 2007), chap. 1.

7. Some of the more useful recent studies include Reza Akbarian, *The Fundamental Principles of Mulla Sadra's Transcendent Philosophy* (London: Xlibris, 2009); Ibrahim Kalin, *Knowledge in Later Islamic Philosophy: Mullā Ṣadrā on Existence, Intellect and Intuition* (New York: Oxford University Press, 2010); Rizvi, *Mullā Ṣadrā and Metaphysics: Modulation of Being* (London: Routledge, 2009). A handy general introduction to Ṣadrā's thought can be found in Sayeh Meisami, *Mulla Sadra* (Oxford: Oneworld, forthcoming).

8. We will not be concerned with Ṣadrā's Ḥadīth commentaries here. A listing of the scholarship on this aspect of his thought is available in Mohammed Rustom, "Approaching Mullā Ṣadrā as Scriptural Exegete: A

Survey of Scholarship on His Qur'ānic Works," *CIS* 4, no. 1 (2008): 77n13, to which can be added the excellent study by Maria Dakake, "Hierarchies of Knowing in Mullā Ṣadrā's Commentary on *al-Kāfī*," *JIP* 6 (2010): 5–44. Incidentally, it is interesting to note that the earliest Safavid biographical sources—whether conscientiously or not—tended to recycle the image of Ṣadrā as a famous philosopher who was in some sense concerned with "scripture," but only in terms of Ḥadīth. See the entry on Ṣadrā in Ibn Maʿṣūm Shīrāzī, *Sulāfat al-ʿaṣr fī maḥāsin al-shuʿarāʾ bi-kull miṣr* (Cairo: Maktabat al-Wafd, 1906), 499, which was then reproduced in Mīrzā ʿAbd Allāh Afandī, *Riyāḍ al-ʿulamāʾ wa-ḥiyāḍ al-fuḍalāʾ*, ed. Sayyid Aḥmad Ḥusaynī (Qum: Maṭbaʿat al-Khayyām, 1981), 5:15; Muḥammad b. al-Ḥasan al-Ḥurr al-ʿĀmilī, *Amal al-āmil*, ed. Sayyid Aḥmad Ḥusaynī (Baghdad: Maktabat al-Andalus, 1965), 2:233.

9. Although Ṣadrā never compiled these works under one cover, they are available in a seven-volume edition: *Tafsīr al-Qurʾān al-karīm*, ed. Muḥammad Khwājawī (Qum: Intishārāt-i Bīdār, 1987–90). Indeed, he had the intention of eventually writing a complete *tafsīr* upon the Qur'ān (he makes this point at ibid., 6:6), of which these aforementioned commentaries would have formed a part. Nonetheless, one biographer from the Qajar period speaks of having "a sizeable volume of his grand Qur'ān commentary [*mujallad-i ḍakhīmī az tafsīr-i kabīr-i ū*]" in his possession. See Muḥammad Bāqir Khwānsarī, *Rawḍāt al-jannāt fī aḥwāl al-ʿulamāʾ wa-l-sādāt* (Tehran: Kitābfurūshī-yi Islāmī, 1976–81), 4:241. For a thoroughly annotated listing of Ṣadrā's Qur'ānic works (including works of doubtful authenticity), see Rustom, "The Nature and Significance of Mullā Ṣadrā's Qur'ānic Writings," *JIP* 6 (2010): 109–30.

10. Robert Wisnovsky challenges the widely held dogma that the philosophical commentaries in post-Avicennan Islamic thought represent a "stagnation" of philosophical thinking in Islam. He argues that such a view is symptomatic of an ill-informed dichotomy between "philosophy" and "theology" in later Islamic thought. The exegetical nature of later Islamic theological texts itself represents further developments in philosophical and theological thinking. Thus, theological and philosophical commentaries in post-Avicennan Islamic thought actually function as philosophical texts in their own right. See Wisnovsky, "The Nature and Scope of Arabic Philosophical Commentary in Post-Classical (ca. 1100–1900 AD) Islamic Intellectual History: Some Preliminary Observations," in *Philosophy, Science and Exegesis in Greek, Arabic and Latin Commentaries*, ed. Peter Adamson, Han Baltussen, and M. W. F. Stone (London: Institute of Classical Studies, 2004), 2:149–91. If this is true for commentaries upon philosophical texts then, mutatis mutandis, it also holds true for the philosophical commentaries written upon Ṣadrā's Qur'ānic writings. It can also be noted that the phenomenon discussed by Wisnovsky is not unique to the development of Islamic thought. As Pierre Hadot argues, from early antiquity to the end of the "middle ages," exegesis and philosophy came part and parcel with the development of philosophy proper. See Pierre Hadot, *Philosophy as a Way of Life: Spiritual Exercises from Socrates to Foucault*, ed. Arnold Davidson, trans. Michael Chase (Malden, MA: Blackwell, 1995), 71–7.

11. For Sabziwārī, Nūrī, and other related figures, see Nasr, *Islamic Philosophy from Its Origins to the Present*, chap. 13. Sabziwārī wrote a commentary on Ṣadrā's *Mafātīḥ al-ghayb*. This commentary was, in turn, translated into Persian in the late Qajar period by the courtier Ḥusām al-Dīn Shīrāzī. See Kalin, "An Annotated Bibliography of the Works of Mullā Ṣadrā with a Brief Account of His Life," *ISt* 42, no. 1 (2003): 35–41; Rizvi, *Ṣadr al-Dīn Shīrāzī*, 78. We cannot rule out the possibility that the manuscript discovered by Mehdi Mohaghegh, which contains a Persian translation of parts of Ṣadrā's *Mafātīḥ*, is by this same figure. See Mohaghegh, *Bīst guftār* (Tehran: Naqsh-i Jahān, 1971), 137. But it is really Nūrī's writings which are most noteworthy as commentaries upon Ṣadrā's Qur'ānic works, as he is the author of a series of detailed and lengthy glosses (*ta'līqāt*) upon nearly half of Ṣadrā's writings in the Qur'ānic sciences. These glosses are particularly helpful for shedding light on difficult phrases and concepts which appear in these texts.

12. Knysh, "Multiple Areas of Influence," in *The Cambridge Companion to the Qur'ān*, ed. Jane McAuliffe (Cambridge: Cambridge University Press, 2006), 224–5. A detailed history of philosophical Qur'ānic exegesis is yet to be written. For starters, see the relevant but significantly underrepresented section in Muḥammad Ḥusayn al-Dhahabī's *al-Tafsīr wa-l-mufassirūn* (Cairo: Dār al-Kutub al-Ḥadītha, 1961–2), 2:399–414. A helpful characterization of this work can be found in Walid Saleh, "Preliminary Remarks on the Historiography of *tafsīr* in Arabic: A History of the Book Approach," *JQS* 12 (2010): 7–10. For a general survey of the manner in which Muslim philosophers and theologians have approached the Qur'ān, see Muṣṭafā Muḥaqqiq Dāmād, "The Quran and Schools of Islamic Theology and Philosophy," trans. Seyyed Hossein Nasr in *The HarperCollins Study Quran*, ed. Seyyed Hossein Nasr et al. (San Francisco: HarperOne: forthcoming), chap. 7. See also the helpful comments in Nasr, "The Qur'ān and Ḥadīth as Source and Inspiration of Islamic Philosophy," in *History of Islamic Philosophy*, 1:27–39.

13. So much so is this the case that we would have to reevaluate earlier, brash characterizations of certain Muslim figures. Take, for example, the famous philosopher and scientist Abū Bakr al-Rāzī (d. 313/925 or ca. 323/935), who has often been misrepresented as outrightly rejecting prophecy and, a fortiori, the Qur'ān. We now know that he was in fact quite faithful to the Qur'ān, and even offered some interpretations of its verses. See the discussion in Peter Adamson, *Abū Bakr al-Rāzī* (Oxford: Oneworld, forthcoming), chap. 6. Also, when we turn to the work of Fārābī, we notice that citations from the Qur'ān are infrequent if not nonexistent. However, this is not to say that key Qur'ānic themes and concepts do not underlie Fārābī's worldview. Telling in this regard are the observations in Ian Richard Netton, *Allāh Transcendent: Studies in the Structure and Semiotics of Islamic Philosophy, Theology, and Cosmology* (London: Routledge, 1989), 102–3, 127, despite the author's insistence on the "un-Qur'anic substrate of the universe of Alfarabism" (p. 125). See also Majid Fakhry, *Al-Fārābī, Founder of Islamic Neoplatonism: His Life, Works and Influence* (Oxford: Oneworld, 2002), 101–17, for some "Islamic" (and hence Qur'ānic) terms and concepts which inform Fārābī's political philosophy. But cf. Jacques

Langhade, *Du Coran a la philosophie: la langue arabe et la formation du vocabulaire philosophique de Farabi* (Damascus: Institut Français de Damas, 1994), 284ff.

14. See Adamson, *Al-Kindī* (New York: Oxford University Press, 2007), 41–4; Jules Janssens, "Al-Kindī: The Founder of Philosophical Exegesis of the Qur'ān," *JQS* 9, no. 2 (2007): 1–21.

15. Examples of their approach to the Qur'ān can be found in Carmela Baffioni, "Metaphors of Light and the 'Verse of Light' in the Brethren of Purity," in *In the Age of al-Farābī: Arabic Philosophy in the Fourth/Tenth Century*, ed. Peter Adamson (London: The Warburg Institute of Advanced Study, 2008), 163–177; Yves Marquet, *La philosophie des Iḫwān al-Ṣafā'*, 2nd ed. (Milan: Archè; Paris: Société d'études de l'histoire de l'alchimie, 1999), 194, 210ff. and passim. For the most comprehensive study of the Ikhwān's use of the Qur'ān, see Omar Ali-de-Unzaga, "The Use of the Qur'ān in the Epistles of the Pure Brethren (*Rasā'il Ikhwān al-Ṣafā'*)" (PhD diss., University of Cambridge, 2004).

16. See Muhammad Abdul Haq, "Ibn Sīnā's Interpretation of the Qur'ān," *IQ* 32, no. 1 (1988): 46–56; Daniel De Smet and Meryem Sebti, "Avicenna's Philosophical Approach to the Qur'an in the Light of His *Tafsīr Sūrat al-Ikhlāṣ*," *JQS* 11, no. 2 (2009): 134–148; Dimitri Gutas, *Avicenna and the Aristotelian Tradition: Introduction to Reading Avicenna's Philosophical Works* (Leiden: Brill, 1988), 72, 75, 77, 164–5; Janssens, "Avicenna and the Qur'ān: A Survey of His Qur'ānic Commentaries," *MIDEO* 25–26 (2004): 177–192. For an older study of Avicenna's work on the Qur'ān, accompanied by the relevant texts in Arabic, see Ḥasan ʿĀṣī, *al-Tafsīr al-Qur'ānī wa-l-lugha al-ṣūfiyya fī falsafat Ibn Sīnā* (Beirut: al-Mu'assasa al-Jāmiʿa li-l-Dirāsa wa-l-Nashr wa-l-Tawzīʿ, 1983).

17. For the use of the Qur'ān in Averroës' work, one can consult Majid Fakhry, "Philosophy and Scripture in the Theology of Averroes," *MS* 30 (1968): 78–89, as well as Fakhry, "Philosophy and the Qur'ān," in *EQ*; Avital Wohlman, *Al-Ghazali, Averroës and the Interpretation of the Qur'an: Common Sense and Philosophy in Islam*, trans. David Burrell (London: Routledge, 2010), chaps. 4–5.

18. A Particularly useful anthology of Suhrawardī's comments upon select verses of the Qur'ān is now available: *Āyat-i ishrāq: Tafsīr wa-ta'wīl-i āyāt-i Qur'ān-i karīm dar āthār-i Suhrawardī*, ed. Sīmā Nūrbakhsh (Tehran: Mihr Niyūshā, 2008).

19. For Rāzī's *tafsīr*, one can consult, inter alia, Michel Lagarde, *Les secrets de l'invisible: essai sur le Grand commentaire de Faḫr al-Dîn al-Râzî (1149–1209)* (Beirut: Albouraq, 2008).

20. A discussion of the manner in which Ṣadrā's work in general functions as a helpful resource for the history of Islamic thought can be found in Nasr, *Islamic Life and Thought*, chap. 15.

21. For an insightful treatment of how Ṣadrā's work on the Qur'ān has been perceived in modern scholarship, see ʿAlī Naṣīrī, *Maktab-i tafsīrī-yi Ṣadr al-muta'allihīn* (Tehran: SIPRIn, 2007), 87–106. I came to know of this work while my survey of scholarship on Ṣadrā's Qur'ānic writings ("Approaching Mullā Ṣadrā") was in press, and thus did not have an opportunity to discuss

it there. Broadly speaking, this is a fairly useful study of Ṣadrā's work on the Qur'ān, especially since the author provides a large number of citations and passages in translation from Ṣadrā's vast oeuvre on the Qur'ān. Another merit of this work is that it takes into account some of the studies on Ṣadrā's work on the Qur'ān which have appeared in Iran over the past several decades. However, since Naṣīrī's scope is far too wide, he often skirts over (or does not mention) a variety of key issues that pertain to Ṣadrā's work as a scriptural exegete. A telling example is his treatment of Ṣadrā's soteriology (see Chapters 6–7 of this study). We are thus left with a number of leads on aspects of Ṣadrā's work on the Qur'ān, such as his theoretical scriptural hermeneutics (pp. 136–66), but without a satisfactory historical, textual, and analytical framework which can demonstrate how Ṣadrā's philosophy in general relates to his work on the Qur'ān in particular.

22. For more on this point, see Marḍiya Akhlāqī, "Sirisht-i maʿnā'ī wa-zabān-i waḥy az dīdgāh-i Ṣadr al-muta'allihīn," *KHNṢ* 52 (2008): 70–86; ʿAlī-Riḍā Dihqānpūr, "Ruykard-i ḥikmat-i Ṣadrā'ī ba-tafsīr-i Qur'ān," *KHNṢ* 56 (2009): 54–68; Nasr, *Ṣadr al-Dīn Shīrāzī and His Transcendent Theosophy*, 2nd ed. (Tehran: Institute for Humanities and Cultural Studies, 1997), 71.

23. Cf. the observations in Gholamreza Aavani and Nāṣir Muḥammadī, "Zabān-i Qur'ān wa-zabān-i tamthīl az dīdgāh-i Ṣadr al-muta'allihīn," *KHNṢ* 54 (2008): 4–17.

24. Two tentative chronologies of the composition of Ṣadrā's Qur'ānic works (one with respect to his Qur'ānic writings only and the other with respect to his entire oeuvre) are available in the appendix in Rustom, "Nature and Significance."

25. A good example of this kind of approach is evidenced in Majīd Falāḥpūr, *Mabānī-yi uṣūl wa-rawish-i tafsīrī-yi Mullā Ṣadrā* (Tehran: SIPRIn, 2010); Muḥammad Taqī Karāmatī, *Ta'thīr-i mabānī-yi falsafī dar tafsīr-i Ṣadr al-muta'allihīn* (Tehran: SIPRIn, 2006); and Naṣīrī, *Maktab-i tafsīrī*. Although Christian Jambet does not attempt to do this in his phenomenal study of Ṣadrā's philosophy, he does not distinguish between Ṣadrā's Qur'ānic writings and his other philosophical works in his engagement with the main outlines of Ṣadrā's thought. See Jambet, *The Act of Being: The Philosophy of Revelation in Mullā Sadrā*, trans. Jeff Fort (New York: Zone Books, 2006). Rustom, "Approaching Mullā Ṣadrā," 87–9, offers a critical appraisal of this approach with respect to Ṣadrā's Qur'ānic writings.

26. Needless to say, it is beyond the scope of the present study to attempt to trace the influence of Ṣadrā's Qur'ānic writings, whether partly or in whole, upon the later *tafsīr* tradition. Suffice it to say that, shortly after his death, we know that passing references are made to some of his Qur'ānic works in an anonymous Persian commentary on the Fātiḥa. For an edition of this work, see Jalāl al-Dīn Āshtiyānī (ed.), *Tafsīr Fātiḥat al-kitāb* (Mashhad: Chāpkhāna-yi Dānishgāh-i Mashhad, 1978).

27. Annemarie Schimmel aptly describes the Fātiḥa as "the true centre." See Schimmel, *Deciphering the Signs of God: A Phenomenological Approach to Islam* (Edinburgh: Edinburgh University Press, 1994), 143 (her treatment of

the Fātiḥa, which extends to p. 144 and beyond, is telling in this regard). For the attention the Fātiḥa has received in Muslim daily life, as well as in Islam's rich exegetical traditions, see William Graham, "Fātiḥa," in *EQ*. Cf. Mahmoud Ayoub, "The Prayer of Islam: A Presentation of Sūrat al-Fātiḥa in Muslim Exegesis," *JAAR* 47S (1979): 635–47.

28. For texts from Ṣadrā's *Tafsīr Sūrat al-fātiḥa* in which he discusses the merits of the Fātiḥa, see Appendix 2 s.v. "On the Merits of the Fātiḥa."

29. This saying is found, inter alia, in Ghazālī, *Iḥyā' ʿulūm al-dīn* (Beirut: Dār al-Jayl, 1997), 1:383. See also Ṣadrā, *Sih aṣl*, ed. Seyyed Hossein Nasr (Tehran: University of Tehran Press, 1961), 82–3. A translation of this work can be found in *The Three Principles of Mullā Ṣadrā: Divine Gnosis, Self-Realisation and the Dangers of Pseudo-Knowledge in Islam*, trans. Colin Turner (London: Routledge forthcoming). For the metaphysical and ethical teachings of ʿAlī, see the study by Reza Shah-Kazemi, *Justice and Remembrance: Introducing the Spirituality of Imam ʿAlī* (London: I. B. Tauris in association with The Institute of Ismaili Studies, 2006).

30. Ṣadrā, *Mafātīḥ al-ghayb*, ed. Muḥammad Khwājawī (reprint, Beirut: Mu'assasat al-Tārīkh al-ʿArabī, 2002).

31. For this work's dates, see Rustom, "Nature and Significance," 129–30.

32. There is an excursus in the text in which Ṣadrā argues for the fundamentality of being, but this section of the work has no bearing on Ṣadrā's actual arguments as they unfold within the scripture-based framework of the *Tafsīr Sūrat al-fātiḥa* (I discuss this section of the *tafsīr* in Chapter 2). It can also be noted that the other famous Ṣadrian thesis, which serves as a complement to the notion of *tashkīk*, namely that of "substantial motion" (*al-ḥaraka al-jawhariyya*), figures in the *Tafsīr Sūrat al-fātiḥa* in the context of Ṣadrā's treatment of soteriology (although he uses a different term to express the idea). See Chapter 7.

33. Chittick, "Translator's Introduction," in Ṣadrā, *The Elixir of the Gnostics*, ed. and trans. William Chittick (Provo: Brigham Young University Press, 2003), xxi.

34. See Jambet, *Act of Being*, 403. Jambet employs this phrase with specific reference to what can be called the Ibn ʿArabization of Ṣadrā's ideas.

35. Some English translations of commentaries on the Fātiḥa—either in part or whole—can be found in Ayoub, *The Qur'an and Its Interpreters* (Albany: State University of New York Press, 1984–92), vol. 1; Jaʿfar al-Ṣādiq, *Spiritual Gems: The Mystical Qur'ān Commentary Ascribed by the Sufis to Imām Jaʿfar al-Ṣādiq (d. 148/765)*, trans. Farhana Mayer (Louisville: Fons Vitae, 2011), 3–9; Muḥammad b. ʿAbd al-Karīm al-Shahrastānī, *Keys to the Arcana: Shahrastānī's Esoteric Commentary on the Qur'ān*, trans. Toby Mayer (Oxford: Oxford University Press in association with The Institute of Ismaili Studies, 2009), 133–88. There are a number of *tafsīr*s of the Fātiḥa written in the English language, amongst which are two important Sufi commentaries: Nasr, *The Garden of Truth: The Vision and Promise of Sufism, Islam's Mystical Tradition* (New York: HarperOne, 2007), 13–20; Reza Shah-Kazemi, *Spiritual Quest: Reflections*

on Qur'ānic Prayer According to the Teachings of Imam ʿAlī (London: I. B. Tauris in association with The Institute of Ismaili Studies, 2011), 15–40. It can also be noted here that Fons Vitae, in association with the Royal Aal al-Bayt Institute for Islamic Thought, has, to date, published complete translations of several major classical Arabic *tafsīrs* (both Sufi and non-Sufi), each of which contain commentaries upon the Fātiḥa.

Chapter 1

1. See Badakhchani's introduction to Ṭūsī, *Shi'i Interpretations of Islam: Three Treatises on Islamic Theology and Eschatology*, ed. and trans. S. J. Badakhchani (London: I. B. Tauris in association with The Institute of Ismaili Studies, 2010), 18. Cf. Ḥasanzādah Āmulī's notes in Ṭūsī, *Āghāz wa-anjām*, ed. Ḥasanzādah Āmulī (Tehran: Wizārat-i Farhang wa-Irshād-i Islāmī, 1987), 75–232 (pp. 78–80 in particular). A translation of *Āghāz wa-anjām* can be found in Ṭūsī, *Shi'i Interpretations of Islam*, 45–88.

2. See the observations in Landolt's introduction to Ṭūsī, *The Paradise of Submission: A Medieval Treatise on Ismaili Thought*, ed. and trans. S. J. Badakhchani (London: I. B. Tauris in association with The Institute of Ismaili Studies, 2005), 11. For the phenomenon of Ṣadrā reworking other authors' texts into his writings, see Chapters 2, 5, and 7, as well as Chittick, "Translator's Introduction," xvii–xx, xxxii–v.

3. See Rustom, "Nature and Significance."

4. Rizvi, "'Au-delà du miroir' or Beyond Discourse and Intuition: Pedagogy and Epistemology in the Philosophy of Mullā Ṣadrā Šīrāzī [ca. 1571–1635]," in *Miroir et savoir: la transmission d'un thème platonicien des Alexandrins à la philosophie arabo-musulmane*, ed. Daniel De Smet and Meryem Sebti (Louvain: Peeters, 2008), 254. For editions of the *Asrār* and the *Mutashābihāt* respectively, see *Asrār al-āyāt wa-anwār al-bayyināt*, ed. Sayyid Muḥammad Mūsawī (Tehran: Intishārāt-i Ḥikmat, 2006); *Mutashābihāt al-Qur'ān* in Ṣadrā, *Sih risāla-yi falsafī*, ed. Jalāl al-Dīn Āshtiyānī, 2nd ed. (Tehran: Markazī-yi Intishārāt-i Daftar-i Tablīghāt-i Islāmī, 2000), 257–84. A translation of the *Mutashābihāt* is available as an appendix in David Dakake, "Defining Ambiguity: Early and Classical Commentary on the *Mutashābih* Verses of the Qur'ān" (PhD diss., Temple University, in progress). Rustom, "Nature and Significance," 124–6, discusses the structure and content of the *Asrār* and the *Mutashābihāt*.

5. Rizvi's dates for these and other works by Ṣadrā are given in his *Mullā Ṣadrā Shīrāzī*, chap. 2. For a tentative chronology of the order of composition of Ṣadrā's writings on the Qur'ān and its sciences, see the appendix in Rustom, "Nature and Significance"

6. I list here the volume and page numbers from the *Asfār* and their corresponding, expanded sections in the *Mafātīḥ*: *Asfār*, 7:44–6 → *Mafātīḥ*, 85; *Asfār*, 7:50–4 → *Mafātīḥ*, 88; *Asfār*, 7:2–4 → *Mafātīḥ*, 93; *Asfār*, 7:32–4 → *Mafātīḥ*, 97–8; *Asfār*, 7:30–2 → *Mafātīḥ*, 98–9; *Asfār*, 7:10–8 (cf. *Asfār*, 7:10–3 with *Elixir*

of the Gnostics, 27) → *Mafātīḥ*, 100–5; *Asfār*, 7:19–28 → *Mafātīḥ*, 106–13; *Asfār*, 7:34–6 → *Mafātīḥ*, 113; *Asfār*, 7:36–40 → *Mafātīḥ*, 115. References in this study to the *Asfār* are to the standard and widely-available 1981 edition: *al-Ḥikma al-mutaʿāliya fī l-asfār al-ʿaqliyya al-arbaʿa*, ed. Riḍā Luṭfī, Ibrāhīm Amīnī, and Fatḥ Allāh Ummīd (Beirut: Dār Iḥyāʾ al-Turāth al-ʿArabī, 1981). I have also identified two other passages in Miftāḥ 1 that are lifted from Ṣadrā's *Tafsīr Sūrat al-sajda*, a work written well before the *Mafātīḥ*: *Tafsīr*, 6:17–8 → *Mafātīḥ* 90–1; *Tafsīr*, 6:22–3 → *Mafātīḥ* 98.

7. See Rizvi, *Mullā Ṣadrā Shīrāzī*, 54, for the *Asfār*'s dates of composition.

8. A number of scholars have noted the theoretical importance of the *Mafātīḥ* in general. See, for example, Nasr, *Ṣadr al-Dīn Shīrāzī*, 127; Latimah Peerwani, "Qurʾānic Hermeneutics: The Views of Ṣadr al-Dīn Shīrāzī," *PBSMS* (1991): 468–77. Cf. Muḥsin Bīdārfar, "Taqdīm," in Ṣadrā, *Tafsīr*, 1:109; Muḥammad Khwājawī, *Lawāmiʿ al-ʿārifīn fī sharḥ aḥwāl Ṣadr al-mutaʾallihīn* (Tehran: Āriyan Press, 1987), 123.

9. Ṣadrā, *Mafātīḥ*, 77.

10. Ibid.

11. For these works, see Rustom, "Nature and Significance," 112–23.

12. Ṣadrā, *Mafātīḥ*, 76–7.

13. Ibid.

14. Ibid.

15. Ibid.

16. In the context of Sufi Qurʾānic exegesis, *ḥadd* can either refer to the lawful and unlawful (and hence "legal") dimensions of a specific Qurʾānic verse, or to the utmost limit of one's understanding of a verse. See Gerhard Böwering, *The Classical Vision of Existence in Islam: The Qurʾānic Hermeneutics of the Ṣūfī Sahl al-Tustarī (d. 283/896)* (Berlin: de Gruyter, 1979), 139–41; Kristin Sands, *Ṣūfī Commentaries on the Qurʾān in Classical Islam* (London: Routledge, 2006), 8–12.

17. Ṣadrā, *Mafātīḥ*, 79. Notice Ṣadrā's use of this famous saying concerning the "senses" of scripture. Cf. Corbin, *En islam iranien*, 1:212ff. A survey of the reception of this tradition and its interpretation by both Sufi and non-Sufi authors can be found in Böwering, *Classical Vision of Existence*, 139–41; Sands, *Ṣūfī Commentaries*, 8–13. See also Ṣadrā, *Mafātīḥ*, 147–8, where he inveighs against those who only know the outward purport of scripture. Sands, *Ṣūfī Commentaries*, 47–50, contains a helpful discussion concerning the prohibition of interpreting the Qurʾān using one's own opinion.

18. For ʿAbd al-Razzāq Kāshānī's (d. 736/1335) use of this verse and the above-cited tradition in the introduction to his Sufi *tafsīr*, see Mahmoud Ayoub, *The Qur'an and Its Interpreters*, 1:5. For a study of Kāshānī's *tafsīr*, see Pierre Lory, *Les commentaires ésotériques du Coran d'après 'Abd al-Razzâq al-Qâshânî* (Paris: Les Deux Océans, 1980). Cf. Peter Heath's explanation of this statement in his "Creative Hermeneutics: A Comparative Analysis of Three Islamic Approaches," *Arabica* 36, no. 2 (1989): 210.

19. Ṣadrā, *Mafātīḥ*, 79.

20. Ibid., 78–9.

21. Ibid. Cf. Ṣadrā, *Sharḥ Uṣūl al-kāfī*, ed. Muḥammad Khwājawī (Tehran: Muʾassasa-yi Muṭālaʿāt wa-Taḥqīqāt-i Farhangī, 1987), 1:166.

22. Ṣadrā, *Mafātīḥ*, 81.

23. Ibid.

24. Ibid. 127–135.

25. Ibid., 147–52.

26. Ibid., 152–76.

27. For a summary of Ghazālī's guidelines, see Sands, *Ṣūfī Commentaries*, 32–4 (Sands follows Richard Gramlich in identifying Makkī as Ghazālī's main source here; see ibid., 32; 152n15). For these guidelines in Ṣadrā, see *Mafātīḥ*, 136–143, 145–7 (he mentions Ghazālī as his source on p. 147). The section reworked from Ibn ʿArabī (*Futūḥāt*, 3:127–8 [Beirut]) corresponds to *Mafātīḥ*, 143–5. Ṣadrā's listing is partially translated and summarized in Peerwani, "Translator's Introduction," in Ṣadrā, *On The Hermeneutics of the Light Verse of the Qurʾān*, trans. Latimah Peerwani (London: ICAS Press, 2004), 23–8. Peerwani does not count numbers 1 and 10, thus enumerating only eight points. A more recent discussion of these points can be found in Janis Ešots, "Speech, Book, and Healing Knowledge: The Qurʾanic Hermeneutics of Mullā Ṣadrā," in *Esoteric Approaches to the Interpretation of the Qurʾān* (working title), ed. Annabel Keeler and Sajjad Rizvi (Oxford: Oxford University Press in association with The Institute of Ismaili Studies, forthcoming).

28. Peerwani, "Translator's Introduction," 9–22, provides an interesting attempt to reconstruct, from Ṣadrā's oeuvre, his general "rules" for interpreting scripture. Apart from failing to distinguish between the principles and preconditions required for reading scripture, her approach is misleading since Ṣadrā's hermeneutics cannot easily be summarized by a set of formal rules. If there is such a set of rules, Ṣadrā certainly does not adhere to them in any of his *tafsīr*s. For a critical appraisal of Peerwani's earlier and later views on this issue, see Rustom, "Approaching Mullā Ṣadrā," 80–1.

29. See Ṣadrā, *Kitāb al-Mashāʿir*, ed. and trans. Henry Corbin as *Le livre des pénétrations métaphysiques* (Tehran: Département d'iranologie de l'Institut franco-iranien, 1964), 6–12 (from here onward, I will refer to "*Mashāʿir*" when citing the Arabic text, and "*Le livre des pénétrations métaphysiques*" when citing the French translation.) The *Mashāʿir*, one of Ṣadrā's most mature philosophical compositions, offers the fundamentals of his ontology in remarkably lucid fashion. For more on this text and its manuscripts, see Rizvi, *Mullā Ṣadrā Shīrāzī*, 66–8. Particularly helpful discussions of the basic distinction between the concept and reality of existence can be found in Cécile Bonmariage, *Le Réel et les réalités: Mullā Ṣadrā Shīrāzī et la structure de la réalité* (Paris: Vrin, 2008), 28–30; Toshihiko Izutsu, *The Concept and Reality of Existence* (Tokyo: The Keio Institute of Cultural and Linguistic Studies, 1971), 68–85; Kalin, *Knowledge in Later Islamic Philosophy*, 89–96; Nasr, *Islamic Philosophy from Its Origins to the Present*, 73–4.

30. See Aristotle, *Topics*, 103b14–15, in Aristotle, *The Complete Works of Aristotle: The Revised Oxford Translation*, ed. Jonathan Barnes (Princeton, NJ: Princeton University Press, 1984), 1:170.

31. Following Izutsu, *Sufism and Taoism: A Comparative Study of Key Philosophical Concepts*, 2nd ed. (Berkeley: University of California Press, 1984), 30, and the glossary in Shihāb al-Dīn Suhrawardī, *The Philosophy of Illumination*, ed. and trans. John Walbridge and Hossein Ziai (Provo: Brigham Young University Press, 1999), 197, I render *ḥadd* as "essential definition" as opposed to simply "definition," which is denoted by the general and more widely-applicable Arabic term *taʿrīf*. Needless to say, the terms for definitions employed by Ṣadrā here became standard in Islamic philosophy from Avicenna onward. For the evolution of definitions in early Islamic philosophy, see Kiki Kennedy-Day, *Books of Definition in Islamic Philosophy: The Limits of Words* (London: RouledgeCurzon, 2003), pt. 1.

32. Translated from the Arabic text of the *Kitāb al-ḥudūd* published in Kennedy-Day, *Books of Definition*, 163. Cf. Kennedy-Day's translation of this passage on p. 102.

33. Walbridge and Ziai describe an essential definition as a "definition that conveys the quiddity of the species by naming the proximate genus and the differentia." See Suhrawardī, *Philosophy of Illumination*, 197.

34. It is important to distinguish between two types of quiddity: there is (1) quiddity in the most specific sense (*al-māhiyya bi-maʿnā al-akhaṣṣ*), and (2) quiddity in the most general sense (*al-māhiyya bi-maʿnā al-aʿamm*). The first type of quiddity is simply the answer to the question, "what is it?," whereas the second type is a thing's essence proper, that is, that by virtue of which it is what it is. Being does have a quiddity in the most specific sense, since if we were to ask what being is, we can answer "being." But being does not have a quiddity in the most general sense since it escapes all definition, and that because it does not have a genus or differentia. See Izutsu, *Concept and Reality of Existence*, 75n34, 101; Kalin, *Knowledge in Later Islamic Philosophy*, 182n24; Nasr, *Islamic Philosophy from Its Origins to the Present*, 66.

35. In later Islamic thought, the important philosophical term *anniyya* becomes a synonym for *wujūd*. See Chittick, *The Heart of Islamic Philosophy: The Quest for Self-Knowledge in the Writings of Afḍal al-Dīn Kāshānī* (New York: Oxford University Press, 2001), 317n18; Ṣadrā, *Asfār*, 6:48–57. Cf. Bonmariage, *Le Réel et les réalités*, 37. For a survey of the opinions of historians of Islamic philosophy concerning the term's provenance, and a thorough discussion which suggests its possible Syriac origins, see Richard Frank, "The Origin of the Arabic Philosophical Term *ʾanīya*." *CB* 6 (1956): 181–201. More recent discussions of *anniyya* are in Adamson, *The Arabic Plotinus: A Philosophical Study of the 'Theology of Aristotle'* (London: Duckworth, 2002), 124ff.; Gerhard Endress and Dimitri Gutas (ed.), *A Greek and Arabic Lexicon* (Leiden: Brill, 1992–), 1:427–37; Toby Mayer, "Anniyya," in *EI*³.

36. That is, the reality of being is the most manifest of things in its mode of presence since it is "present" where it "is," which is everywhere; and it is the most manifest of things in its mode of disclosure since it is "disclosed" wherever it may "be," which is everywhere.

37. Lit., "the freest of all things with respect to definition," or "the most independent of all things in terms of definition."

38. "Entification" and "individuation" refer to the concretization of being, that is, the various modes in which it becomes instantiated in concreto. The term entification will re-appear in Ṣadrā's commentary upon Q 1:1, for which, see Chapter 3.

39. Ṣadrā, *Mashāʿir*, 6 (cf. Rizvi, *Mulla Sadra and Metaphysics*, 41). See also Ṣadrā, *Asfār*, 1:83.

40. *Mafhūmuhu min aʿrafi-l-ashyāʾi / wa-kunhuhu fī ghāyati-l-khafāʾi*. For the text, see Mullā Hādī Sabziwārī, *Sharḥ-i Manẓūma*, ed. Mehdi Mohaghegh and Toshihiko Izutsu (Tehran: McGill University Institute of Islamic Studies, 1969), 4. For alternative translations of this verse, see Nasr, *Islamic Philosophy from Its Origins to the Present*, 297n29; Sabziwārī, *The Metaphysics of Sabzavārī*, trans. Mehdi Mohaghegh and Toshihiko Izutsu (Delmar: Caravan, 1977), 31.

41. Talk of the self-evidentiality of the reality of being should not be confused with the self-evidentiary nature of the concept of being. The former, as Izutsu puts it, "forever escapes direct conceptualization" (*Concept and Reality of Existence*, 78). But the latter can be conceived and its structure analyzed.

42. Ṣadrā, *Mashāʿir*, 6.

43. Ibid.

44. When we look at any particular thing—whether it exists extramentally or not—we can say that it "is" being. We cannot, strictly speaking, say that particular things "have" being, for they are nothing but instantiations of being. Or, as Plato would put it, they "participate in existence." To say that B has A is to say that the two are distinct. But if A itself is the ground for B and without which B would be nonexistent, it would be absurd to say that B "has" A. Rather, it would be more fitting to say that B "is" A, but in a limited sense.

45. Izutsu, *Concept and Reality of Existence*, 68–9.

46. Ibid., 76.

47. Although Izutsu notes that these two orders of the concept of being are linked by quiddities, he is more concerned with analyzing the structure of the notion of being proper, which is why he posits these two orders. To be sure, Izutsu himself says that philosophers in the school of Mullā Ṣadrā often do not make this two-tiered distinction of the notion of being explicitly, instead using the term *mafhūm* to denote both senses of notion. See Izutsu, *Concept and Reality of Existence*, 76–7.

48. See the remarks in Sabziwārī, *Sharḥ-i Manẓūma*, 42; Sabziwārī, *Metaphysics of Sabzavārī*, 31–2. A basic Ṣadrian principle is that the "less" there "is" of being, the "more" there "is" of quiddity, and the "more" there "is" of being, the "less" there "is" of quiddity. See Bonmariage, *Le Réel et les réalités*, 66ff; Jambet, *Act of Being*, chap. 4; Fazlur Rahman, *The Philosophy of Mullā Ṣadrā* (Albany: State University of New York Press, 1975), 35ff.

49. Cf. Ṣadrā, *Asfār*, 1:38–9: "Since the reality of each thing is the specificity [*khūṣūṣiyya*] of its existence which is established for it, being is more prior than that thing. Indeed, it is more prior than everything because it possesses reality, just as whiteness is more prior in its being white than

what is not white and to which whiteness is accidental. So being in itself is existent, while all things other than being are not, in themselves, existent. Rather, existence is accidental to them."

50. See Ṣadrā, *Mashāʿir*, 6–7.

51. See Ṣadrā, *Asfār*, 1:56ff., 427–46. For expositions of Ṣadrā's concept of the gradation of being, see Bonmariage, *Le Réel et les réalités*, pt. 1; Jambet, *Act of Being*, chap. 4; Rizvi, *Mullā Ṣadrā and Metaphysics*, chaps. 2–5.

52. See Annabel Keeler, "Mullā Ṣadrā's Commentary on *Sūrat al-Sajda*," in *Islam-West Philosophical Dialogue: The Papers Presented at the World Congress on Mullā Ṣadrā (May, 1999, Tehran)* (Tehran: SIPRIn, 2001–5), 10:343–6. Cf. Rizvi, *Mullā Ṣadrā and Metaphysics*, 70.

53. Ṣadrā, *Mafātīḥ*, 86.

54. Ibid.

55. See Q 10:57, 17:82, 41:44.

56. ʿAllāma Muḥammad Bāqir Majlisī, *Biḥār al-anwār* (Qum, 1956–72), 92:176.

57. Najm al-Dīn Rāzī, *Mirṣād al-ʿibād*, ed. Muḥammad Amīn Riyāḥī (Tehran: Bungāh-i Tarjama wa-Nashr-i Kitāb, 1973), 268. Cf. Ešots, "Speech, Book, and Healing Knowledge."

58. Ṣadrā, *Mafātīḥ*, 85. For the healing nature of the Qurʾān, see *Tafsīr*, 6:8. Cf. *Tafsīr*, 1:2, 6:10. See also Dihqan Mangabadi, "Mullā Ṣadrā's Method of Qurʾān Commentary," in *Islam-West Philosophical Dialogue*, 10:436; Hasan Sa'idi, "Illumination, Unveiling and Intuition in Mullā Ṣadrā's Qurʾānic Commentary," in *Islam-West Philosophical Dialogue*, 10:521–2.

59. Depending on the context, the Qurʾānic term *nashʾa* (Q 56:62), which denotes the makeup of a particular thing, can either refer to the configuration of a place or world (as it is used in this passage), or a human being's constitution. For discussions of this term, see Ṣadrā, *Elixir of the Gnostics*, 98n31; *The Wisdom of the Throne*, trans. James Morris (Princeton, NJ: Princeton University Press, 1981), 250n302.

60. Ṣadrā, *Tafsīr*, 7:9. Cf. ibid., 1:2.

61. See Corbin, *Avicenna and the Visionary Recital*, 16–28.

62. A clear allusion to Q 3:103, which speaks of "God's rope" (*ḥabl Allāh*).

63. Mentioned in Q 83:18–9, this term in early Qurʾānic exegesis was understood to refer to an exalted station in Paradise, whereas later commentators took it to mean the "inscribed book" (*kitāb marqūm*) (mentioned in Q 83:20), which contains a record of the deeds of the righteous. In this context, Ṣadrā clearly favors the earlier interpretations. See Frederik Leemhuis, "ʿIlliyyūn," in *EQ*. Cf. Ṣadrā, *Elixir of the Gnostics*, 98n34. See also Daniel De Smet, "'Illiyyûn et Sijjîn," in *DC*.

64. Ṣadrā, *Mafātīḥ*, 89.

65. Bīdārfar, "Taqdīm," 1:57. See also Fāṭima Ārānī, "Taṭābuq-i madārij-i Qurʾān wa-maʿārij-i insān az manẓar-i Ṣadr-i mutaʾallihīn," *KHNṢ* 32 (2002): 48–9.

66. Peerwani, "Translator's Introduction," 15.

67. Lit. "its reality has many levels in descent."

68. Reading *asmāʾ* for *asmāʿ*.

69. Ṣadrā, *Mafātīḥ*, 98, taken from *Tafsīr*, 6:22–3.

70. Cf. Nāṣir-i Khusraw, *Knowledge and Liberation: A Treatise on Philosophical Theology*, ed. and trans. Faquir Hunzai (London: I. B. Tauris in association with The Institute of Ismaili Studies, 1998), 84.

71. Cf. Ṣadrā, *Elixir of the Gnostics*, 95n10.

72. Ṣadrā, *Asrār*, 76. A page earlier, Ṣadrā makes the following remark: "[In] His saying, *If the sea were ink for the Words of my Lord, the sea would be exhausted before the Words of my Lord would be exhausted, even if we were to come with its like in assistance* [Q 18:109], the 'Words' are an allusion to the luminous essences through which the effusion of being [*fayḍ al-wujūd*] reaches bodies and corporeal entities; the 'sea' is an allusion to the prime matter of bodies which are characterized by reception and renewal. The renewal of the effusion occurs in accordance with the succession of the bodies' passivities and preparednesses."

73. For a discussion of the function of the reverberation of the Word in the cosmos, see Rustom, "Story-Telling as Philosophical Pedagogy: The Case of Suhrawardī," in Sebastian Günther (ed.), *Knowledge and Education in Classical Islam* (Leiden: Brill, forthcoming).

74. That the Word and the Command are, from one perspective, the same reality, is confirmed by Ṣadrā at *Asrār*, 75–6: "From the perspective of various standpoints, the names are many and the Named one. Insofar as the making-known [*iʿlām*] of realities from God occurs through them, they are called 'Words.' Insofar as the existence of engendered things [*wujūd al-kāʾināt*] is necessitated by them—each at its appropriate moment—they are called God's 'Command' [*amr Allāh*] and 'Irrevocable Decree' [*qaḍāʾuhu al-ḥatmī*]. Insofar as the life of existing things is through them, they are called God's 'Spirit' [*rūḥ*]: *Say: 'The Spirit is from the Command* [amr] *of my Lord'* [Q 17:85]. In its essence, the names are one: *Our Command* [amrunā] *is nothing but one* [Q 54:50]. But they are numerous by virtue of the numerous types of effects: *And He revealed in each heaven its Command* [amrahā] [Q 41:12]. Or, from the perspective of their directions of their effusions upon the things or their attachments to them, they become 'many' through their abundance, just as being is one reality which becomes numerous through the abundance of quiddities—not because the quiddities exercise effects upon being, but because of the unification of quiddity with being." See also Corbin's remarks in Ṣadrā, *Le livre des pénétrations métaphysiques*, 196–8n86. At *Tafsīr*, 1:190–1, Ṣadrā makes a similar point with respect to the fragmentation of letters, that is, they are one but take on different designations (*alqāb*) because of the diversity of ranks and loci of manifestation (*maẓāhir*). He also relates this phenomenon to the many names taken on by God, who is, however, One in Himself. For Ṣadrā's discussion of this point in the context of his *Tafsīr Sūrat al-fātiḥa*, see Chapter 3.

75. Ṣadrā, *Mafātīḥ*, 93–4.

76. See the point in Chittick, *The Sufi Path of Knowledge: Ibn al-ʿArabī's Metaphysics of Imagination* (Albany: State University of New York Press, 1989), 127, and the corresponding note on p. 398n8.

77. For Ibn ʿArabī's treatment of the Breath of the All-Merciful, see ibid., 127–34.

78. Ṣadrā seems to take the former term from Ṣadr al-Dīn Qūnawī, *al-Tafsīr al-Ṣūfī li-l-Qurʾān (Iʿjāz al-bayān fī taʾwīl umm al-Qurʾān)*, ed. ʿAbd al-Qādir Aḥmad ʿAṭāʾ (Cairo: Dār al-Kutub al-Ḥadītha, 1969), 193. Cf. Daniel De Smet, Daniel, "Le Souffle du Miséricordieux (*Nafas ar-Rahmán*): un élément pseudo-empédoclée dans la métaphysique de Mullá Sadrá aš-Širázi," *DSTFM* 10 (1999): 467–86.

79. Ṣadrā, *Mafātīḥ*, 100–1. See also ibid., 93–4, which is reproduced in slightly different form in the *Tafsīr Sūrat al-baqara* (see *Tafsīr*, 1:188), a work that was written after the *Mafātīḥ*. For its structure and content, see Rustom, "Nature and Significance," 111–2.

80. To speak of God's "mind" is to say that the realities of things fixed in His knowledge are contained in the Preserved Tablet (*al-lawḥ al-maḥfūẓ*) or the Angelic Intellects. See Ṣadrā, *Mafātīḥ*, 104.

81. One of the implications of the cosmos being nothing other than an articulation of the Breath of the All-Merciful is that all things in existence are instantiations of mercy, as they came about as a result of mercy. This will have important implications for Ṣadrā's soteriology in the *Tafsīr Sūrat al-fātiḥa*. See Chapter 7.

82. As will be seen in Chapter 4, this is a term which will play a significant role in Ṣadrā's *Tafsīr Sūrat al-fātiḥa*.

83. Cf. Ṣadrā, *Mafātīḥ*, 104, which does not bring in the notion of the Breath here, and which speaks of God's hidden knowledge and not His Self-knowledge as such (although, metaphysically speaking, they amount to the same thing). See also Rahman, *Philosophy of Mullā Ṣadrā*, 184–8, who starts off in the right direction, but misses several crucial points as his brief treatment of Ṣadrā's understanding of revelation developments.

84. Ṣadrā, *Mafātīḥ*, 94. Cf. ibid., 103–6, where Ṣadrā describes the manner in which the Word is formed intellectually and then verbally.

85. Cf. Nāṣir-i Khusraw, *Knowledge and Liberation*, 84.

86. Ṣadrā, *Mafātīḥ*, 94. The most common version of the supplication is, "I seek refuge in God's Perfect Words from the evil that He created." See Tirmidhī, Daʿwāt 151. Although it lies outside of the scope of this study to unpack the meaning of the last part of this supplication, "from the evil that He created" (see also Q 113:2), it should suffice to say that, in the Islamic intellectual tradition, one way this phrase has been understood is not that God has "created" evil, but that evil issues from *what* He has created (see also the related discussion in Appendix 2 s.v. "The Emergence of Evil" [*Tafsīr*, 1:16]). Philosophically speaking, we can also say that "evil," that is, the privation of good or perfection, is inherent to material things because, as temporal and hence imperfect entities, they are in need of change in order to attain their

own perfection. See the useful discussion in Jon McGinnis, *Avicenna* (New York: Oxford University Press, 2010), 221–6.

87. Ṣadrā, *Mafātīḥ*. 94–5.

88. Ibid., 95–6. A treatment of the engendering (*takwīnī*) and prescriptive (*tashrīʿī*) Commands can be found in Chittick, *Imaginal Worlds: Ibn al-'Arabī and the Problem of Religious Diversity* (Albany: State University of New York Press, 1994), 141–4.

89. Cf. Ṣadrā's observations cited in Appendix 2 s.v. "God's Words" (*Tafsīr*, 1:9–10). See also Ṣadrā, *Mashāʿir*, 57.

90. Yet from another perspective, we can say that the Perfect Words are identifiable with the World of the Command itself. See Ṣadrā, *Sharḥ*, 2:617. I will not attempt to delve into these intricate details here, since, in the present context, they will only obscure the point at hand.

91. "Shadows" also because the Perfect Words themselves are luminous substances (Ṣadrā, *Sharḥ*, 4:146), which is why Ṣadrā, from one perspective, also identifies them with the Imams.

92. For this point in Ibn ʿArabī, see Denis Gril, "Commentaries on the *Fātiḥa* and Experience of Being According to Ibn ʿArabī," trans. Josip Rainer, *JMIAS* 20 (1996): 33–52 (particularly p. 40 onward).

93. Cf. Ṣadrā, *Mashāʿir*, 57–8.

94. Ṣadrā, *Mafātīḥ*, 103.

95. Cf. Izutsu's observation: "What makes revelation such a particular non-natural kind of linguistic behaviour is that here the speaker is God and the hearer is a man, that is to say, the phenomenon of word occurs here between the supernatural order of being and the natural order of being, so that there is in fact no ontological balance or equilibrium of rank and level between speaker and hearer" ("Revelation as a Linguistic Concept in Islam," *SMT* 5 [1962]: 127).

96. Ṣadrā, *Tafsīr*, 7:9. Cf. ibid., 1:2.

97. For a discussion of this verse, see Sands, *Ṣūfī Commentaries*, chap. 2.

98. Ṣadrā, *Mafātīḥ*, 115. This passage is also translated in Shigeru Kamada, "Mullā Ṣadrā Between Mystical Philosophy and Qurʾān Interpretation through His Commentary on the 'Chapter of the Earthquake'," *IJAS* 2, no. 2 (2005): 280. See also Ešots, "Speech, Book, and Healing Knowledge." Cf. Peerwani, "Translator's Introduction," 15. Although Ṣadrā does not provide us with a citation, he derives the notion of the seven *abṭun* of the Qurʾān—either directly or indirectly—from an earlier source. See, in particular, Jamal Elias, *The Throne Carrier of God: The Life and Thought of ʿAlāʾ ad-Dawla as-Simnānī* (Albany: State University of New York Press, 1995), 79–99.

99. Ṣadrā, *Mafātīḥ*, 87.

100. Ibid., 88.

101. Ibid., 92. See also Ṣadrā, *Tafsīr*, 4:164, for the necessity of esoteric interpretation. Cf. Muhammad Khamenei, *The Qur'anic Hermeneutics of Mulla Sadra* (Tehran: SIPRIn, 2006), 49–64.

102. Cf. Ṣadrā, *Tafsīr*, 6:30–1, where he emphasizes the need to remain close to the conventions of the Arabic language. For the passage in context, see Sa'idi, "Illumination, Unveiling and Intuition in Mullā Ṣadrā's Qurʾānic

Commentary," 10:525. For further appeals to clarity when there is no need to be "esoteric," see the passage in ibid., 10:528 (translating Ṣadrā, *Tafsīr*, 4:150–1). Ṣadrā seems to closely follow Ibn ʿArabī on this point, for which, see Michel Chodkiewicz, *An Ocean Without Shore: Ibn 'Arabî, the Book, and the Law*, trans. David Streight (Albany: State University of New York Press, 1993), chap. 1.

103. It is unclear who Ṣadrā intends by this appellation in this context. In another work, he employs the term in what is likely an allusion to Ghazālī. See Morris' note in Ṣadrā, *Wisdom of the Throne*, 183–4n174. Although Ghazālī was a much older contemporary of Zamakhsharī, he could not have been the critic of the *Kashshāf* mentioned in the passage, since the work was written after Ghazālī's death. For the *Kashshāf*'s dates, see Andrew Lane, *A Traditional Muʿtazilite Qurʾān Commentary: The Kashshāf of Jār Allāh al-Zamakhsharī (d. 538/1144)* (Leiden: Brill, 2006), 48ff. An updated account of Ghazālī's life and times can be found in Frank Griffel, *Al-Ghazālī's Philosophical Theology* (New York: Oxford University Press, 2009), chap. 1.

104. Ṣadrā, *Sih aṣl*, 84. Cf. Corbin's introduction to Ṣadrā, *Le livre des pénétrations métaphysiques*, 24; Peerwani, "Translator's Introduction," 29.

105. Cf. Ṣadrā, *Tafsīr*, 7:109.

106. The word *lubb* (pl. *albāb*) signifies the innermost aspect or quintessence of a thing, as well as the heart or intellect. I translate it here as "kernel" in order to demonstrate its concrete juxtaposition with the term *qishr* or "husk."

107. A phrase that occurs in the Qurʾān on sixteen occasions. An alternate translation of this expression, in keeping with my rendering of *lubb* as "kernel" in the same passage, would be "possessors of the kernels."

108. Ṣadrā, *Mafātīḥ*, 117. Note here the Qurʾānic provenance of *ʿilm ladunī* (i.e., Q 18:65). See also *Tafsīr*, 1:206, for a fine characterization of the different types of knowers with reference to the language of shells, outer layers, etc. Cf. the related passage in Ṣadrā, *Sharḥ*, 1:43, translated in Dakake, "Hierarchies of Knowing," 38–9.

109. See Corbin, *En islam iranien*, 1:212–3.

110. For a fine discussion of this point, see Kalin, *Knowledge in Later Islamic Philosophy*, 227–45. See also the pertinent passage in Ṣadrā's *Sih aṣl*, 14, translated in Rustom, "Philosophical Sufism," in *The Routledge Companion to Islamic Philosophy*, ed. Richard Taylor and Luis Xavier López-Farjeat (New York: Routledge, forthcoming).

111. Paul Ballanfat offers a preliminary attempt at understanding Ṣadrā's treatment of the heart in his article, "Considérations sur la conception du coeur chez Mullâ Sadrâ," *KN* 5 (1999): 33–46, 67–84. For this phenomenon in the context of a rich comparative analysis of two major medieval mystics, one Christian and the other Muslim, see Robert Dobie, *Logos and Revelation: Ibn 'Arabi, Meister Eckhart, and Mystical Hermeneutics* (Washington: The Catholic University of America Press, 2010), 19ff.

112. For Ṣadrā's treatment of the book of the soul and the book of God, see *Elixir of the Gnostics*, 26–8.

113. Ṣadrā, *Mafātīḥ*, 90.

114. At *Tafsīr*, 1:215–8, Ṣadrā summarizes Avicenna's discussion of this topic as found in his *al-Risāla al-nayrūziyya fī maʿānī al-ḥurūf al-hijāʾiyya*, in

Avicenna, *Tis' rasā'il* (Constantinople: Maṭba'at al-Jawā'ib, 1880), 92–7. For Avicenna, the detached letters are the names of essential realities. See Lory, *La science des lettres en islam* (Paris: Dervy, 2004), chap. 4, although Avicenna does not relate them to the Perfect Words, which seems to be Ṣadrā's unique contribution here. For Ibn 'Arabī's treatment of the detached letters, see Ibn 'Arabī, "The Science of Letters," trans. Denis Gril in Ibn 'Arabī, *The Meccan Revelations*, ed. Michel Chodkiewicz (New York: Pir Press, 2002–4), 2:161–75.

115. Ṣadra, *Mafātīḥ*, 90–1, reworked from 'Ayn al-Quḍāt Hamadānī, *Nāmahā*, ed. 'Alī Naqī Munzawī (vols. 1–3) and 'Afīf 'Usayrān (vols. 1–2) (Tehran: Intishārāt-i Asāṭīr, 1998), 2:98–9, also cited in Ṣadrā, *Tafsīr*, 6:17–8. Cf. Abū l-Qāsim Ḥusayn-Dūst, "Ḥurūf-i munqaṭi'a-yi Qur'ān dar ḥikmat-i muta'āliya-yi Mullā Ṣadrā," *KHNṢ* 36 (2004): 58–63. See Rustom, "Approaching Mullā Ṣadrā," 85, for a critical appraisal of this study.

Chapter 2

1. See Nasr, *Islamic Life and Thought*, chap. 15.

2. Kalin, *Knowledge in Later Islamic Philosophy*, xiii.

3. The most significant instance is Ṣadrā's incorporating into his *Elixir of the Gnostics* a thoroughly revised version of the *Jāwidān-nāma* ("The Book of the Everlasting") by Afḍal al-Dīn Kāshānī (d. ca. 610/1213–4) (commonly referred to as Bābā Afḍal). See Chittick, "Translator's Introduction," xxxii–v, for a full discussion of this phenomenon. A translation of "The Book of the Everlasting," along with translations of many of Bābā Afḍal's other philosophical treatises and quatrains, can be found in Chittick, *Heart of Islamic Philosophy*.

4. This is also the case with some of Ṣadrā's other writings. See the observations in Chittick, "Translator's Introduction," xxxv.

5. For a recent study of Ṣadrā's *Sharḥ Uṣūl al-kāfī*, see Dakake, "Hierarchies of Knowing."

6. For a commentary on the famous *ḥadīth* of the hidden treasure commonly attributed to him, see Armin Eschraghi, "'I Was a Hidden Treasure': Some Notes on a Commentary Ascribed to Mullā Ṣadrā Shīrāzī: Sharh ḥadīth: 'Kuntu kanzan makhfīyyan (sic)'," in *Islamic Thought in the Middle Ages: Studies in Text, Transmission and Translation, in Honour of Hans Daiber*, eds. Wim Raven and Anna Akasoy, 91–100 (Leiden: Brill, 2008); 'Alī Aṣghar Ja'farī, "Sharḥ-i ḥadīth 'kuntu kanzan makhfiyyan'," *KHNṢ* 32 (2002): 61–3. For Ṣadrā's commentary on the *ḥadīth*, "People are asleep—when they die, they shall awaken," which he later reincorporated into his *Tafsīr Sūrat yāsīn*, see Rustom, "Psychology, Eschatology, and Imagination in Mullā Ṣadrā Shīrāzī's Commentary on the *Ḥadīth* of Awakening," *IS* 5, no. 1 (2007): 9–22.

7. See Rizvi, *Mulla Ṣadrā Shīrāzī*, 10.

8. For a general overview of Ṣadrā's use of Ḥadīths in his *tafsīr* writings, see Naṣīrī, *Maktab-i tafsīrī*, 167–86.

9. For this genre of traditions, see William Graham, *Divine Word and Prophetic Word in Early Islam* (The Hague: Mouton, 1977).

10. See Ṣadrā, *Tafsīr*, 1:26, 177, 183.

11. Ibid., 1:71, 81, 93, 96, 151, 155, 156, 157–8, 162.

12. Ibid., 1:9 reproduces a *ḥadīth qudsī* from Kulaynī's *Kāfī*. Ṣadrā refers to the collection as "one of the divine books."

13. Ṣadrā, *Tafsīr*, 1:47, 70, 105, 159, 180.

14. The designator obviously derives from the pregnant term *walāya*, which, in Shīʿī contexts, primarily signifies the sanctity and spiritual authority of the Imams. For the development of *walāya* in its early Shīʿī doctrinal context, and the manner in which it came to inform the communal categories and boundaries amongst the Shīʿī faithful, see Dakake, *The Charismatic Community: Shiʿite Identity in Early Islam* (Albany: State University of New York Press, 2007).

15. Ṣadrā, *Tafsīr*, 1:40, 168 (two).

16. Ibid., 1:9; 12 (two); 15; 24; 25 (two); 31; 33; 44; 72 (cf. ibid., 1:71, where Ṣadrā cites this tradition as a *ḥadīth qudsī*); 73 (two); 74; 75; 76 (three); 77; 106–7; 107 (two); 108 (two); 109 (two); 119 (three); 125; 128; 130 (three); 147 (two); 150; 152 (two); 153 (three); 156; 158 (three); 168 (two); 171; 176; 179; 181; 182. Indeed, Ṣadrā's heavy reliance on Sunnī Ḥadīth sources is reminiscent of the same practice in earlier Shīʿī *tafsīr*. See Todd Lawson, "Akhbārī Shīʿī Approaches to *tafsīr*," in *Approaches to the Qurʾān*, ed. G. R. Hawting and Abdul-Kader Shareef (London: Routledge, 1993), 173–210 (p. 175 in particular).

17. Ṣadrā, *Tafsīr*, 1:40, 70, 78, 90, 130, 135, 152, 168, 169.

18. Ibid., 1:6, 8, 25, 46, 71, 157, 181.

19. Ibid., 1:76, 123, 153, 168, 169 (two).

20. At ibid., 1:135, Ṣadrā cites a work by Ibn Bābūya (d. 381/991), referring to its author as "The noble Shaykh, Muḥammad b. ʿAlī b. Bābūya al-Qummī."

21. For the passage in context, see Appendix 2 s.v. "God's Words" (*Tafsīr*, 1:166–7).

22. See Hermann Landolt, *Recherches en spiritualité iranienne* (Tehran: Institut français de recherche en Iran, 2005), 364. Cf. Andrew Newman, *Safavid Iran: Rebirth of a Persian Empire* (London: I. B. Tauris, 2008), 69–70; Rizvi, *Mullā Ṣadrā and Metaphysics*, 129–30. It is also interesting to note that although Ṣadrā accepts the long-established tradition in which ʿAlī says that he is the dot under the *bāʾ* of the *basmala* (*Mafātīḥ*, 97–9), he does not develop its implications in any significant manner. This is not to suggest that Ṣadrā's worldview remains uninformed by Shīʿī categories. For the figure of ʿAlī in one of his Persian poems, see Mohammad Ali Amir-Moezzi, *The Spirituality of Shiʿi Islam: Beliefs and Practices*, trans. Hafiz Karmali et al. (London: I. B. Tauris in association with The Institute of Ismaili Studies, 2011), chap. 9.

23. Ṣadrā, *Tafsīr*, 1:4, 9, 10, 33, 69.

24. Ibid., 1:11.

25. Ibid., 1:92 (alluded to), 1:112.

26. Ibid., 1:11. For a translation and study of this work, see *Die Risāla fī l-ḥudūṯ (Die Abhandlung über die Entstehung)*, trans. S. M. Bagher Talgharizadeh (Berlin: Klaus Schwarz, 2000).

27. Ṣadrā, *Tafsīr,* 1:54. This title literally translates as "The Laying Bare of Doctrine."

28. I will thus return to Ṣadrā's treatment of Rāzī later in this chapter, when the different exegetical materials employed in the *Tafsīr Sūrat al-fātiḥa* are surveyed.

29. Ṣadrā, *Tafsīr,* 1:90.

30. See Avicenna, *al-Ishārāt wa-l-tanbīhāt,* ed. Sulaymān Dunyā (Cairo: Dār al-Maʿārif, 1957–60), 4:749–906.

31. For a translation of this section of the *Ishārāt,* see Avicenna, *Avicenna on Mysticism: Remarks and Admonitions, Part 4,* trans. Shams Inati (London: Keagan Paul, 1996). For an argument against the presence of "mysticism" in Avicenna (with an eye specifically on this part of the *Ishārāt*), see Dimitri Gutas, "Intellect without Limits: The Absence of Mysticism in Avicenna," in *Intellect et Imagination dans la Philosophie Médiévale / Intellect and Imagination in Medieval Philosophy / Intelecto e Imaginação na Filosofia Medieval,* ed. Maria Cândida Pacheco and José Francisco Meirinhos (Turnhout: Brepols, 2006), 1:351–72. Although it seems we will never know for certain whether or not Avicenna was a "mystic," it can be pointed out that Gutas overlooks the unmistakable Sufi technical terminology replete throughout the relevant section of the work (as does Inati). Why Avicenna would employ this kind of language remains an open question.

32. See the relevant passage from the *Asfār* translated in Chittick, "Translator's Introduction," xxvi. Yet at *Tafsīr,* 1:90, Ṣadrā explicitly describes Avicenna as someone who has "arrived at the stations of the gnostics and the ranks of the unveilers. . . ."

33. Ibid., 1:89–90.

34. Ibid., 1:48. Ṣadrā also identifies the Stoics and Suhrawardī with "the people of the Real" (*Elixir of the Gnostics,* 96n16). John Walbridge, *The Leaven of the Ancients: Suhrawardī and the Heritage of the Greeks* (Albany: State University of New York Press, 2000), 187–97, views Ṣadrā's identification of the Stoics with Suhrawardī as a way of supporting his claim that his philosophy accorded with Plato's. Morris, on the other hand, says that the term "Stoic" in later Islamic philosophy was commonly misused, and notes the same problem in the crypto-Ismāʿīlī Muḥammad b. ʿAbd al-Karīm al-Shahrastānī (d. 548/1153). See Ṣadrā, *Wisdom of the Throne,* 106, and the corresponding note (n106). Shahrastanī's understanding of the term can be found in Shahrastānī, *al-Milal wa-l-niḥal,* ed. Ṣiḍqī al-ʿAṭṭār (reprint, Beirut: Dār al-Fikr, 2002), 298–9.

35. Ṣadrā, *Tafsīr,* 1:55ff. For a discussion of Suhrawardī's position on rational constructs, see ʿAbd al-Rasūl ʿUbudiyyat, "The Fundamentality of Existence and the Subjectivity of Quiddity," trans. D. D. Sodagar and Muhammad Legenhausen, *Topoi* 26 (2007): 202–4; Walbridge, *The Science of Mystic Lights: Quṭb al-Dīn Shīrāzī and the Illuminationist Tradition in Islamic Philosophy* (Cambridge, MA: Harvard University Press, 1992), 45–6. Earlier (p. 45n3), Walbridge notes that there is a slight difference between rational constructs (what he calls "intellectual fictions") and secondary intelligibles.

With respect to being as a secondary intelligible, Ṣadrā also takes this position, but contra Suhrawardī, understands being to be a secondary intelligible in the "philosophical" sense, not in the logical sense. See Izutsu, *Concept and Reality of Existence,* 82–4.

36. Ṣadrā, *Tafsīr,* 1:75, 78. Hossein Ziai, "The Illuminationist Tradition," in Nasr and Leaman (eds.), *History of Islamic Philosophy,* 1:464–5n39, suggests that Ṣadrā does distinguish between the Stoics and Illuminationists when discussing the latter's "novel" philosophical ideas.

37. See Suhrawardī, *Philosophy of Illumination,* 101ff. Although Suhrawardī has *arbāb al-aṣnām al-nawʿiyya al-falakiyya* here, it is synonymous with *arbāb al-anwāʿ*. See ibid., 182n10.

38. See, for example, Ṣadrā, *Addenda on the Commentary on the Philosophy of Illumination,* ed. Hossein Ziai (Costa Mesa, Mazda: 2010–), 1:434–51. For studies on Ṣadrā's understanding of the Platonic Forms, see Zahra Mostafavi, "Ṣadr-ol-Mota'allahin on Platonic Ideas," *SI* 14, no. 2 (2001): 23–54; Walbridge, "The Background to Mullā Ṣadrā's Doctrine of the Platonic Ideas," in *Islam-West Philosophical Dialogue,* 2:147–75. See also Rahman, *Philosophy of Mullā Ṣadrā,* 47ff., 147ff. Cf. Ṣadrā, *Wisdom of the Throne,* 107, and the corresponding note (n35).

39. This section follows parts of Rāzī's *tafsīr*. It can also be noted that at *Tafsīr,* 1:146, Ṣadrā mentions the Ashʿarites, along with the colleagues of Democritus, in passing. Later in this chapter, we will survey Ṣadrā's use of important *tafsīr*s by Ashʿarite authors in his *Tafsīr Sūrat al-fātiḥa.*

40. Ṣadrā, *Tafsīr,* 1:59. Cf. Rahman, *Philosophy of Mullā Ṣadrā,* 146ff. For Muʿtazilite teachings on the fixity of quiddity, see Abū Rashīd al-Nīsābūrī, *al-Masāʾil fī l-khilāf bayna al-Baṣrīyīn wa-l-Baghdādīyīn,* ed. Riḍwān Sayyid and Maʿn Ziyāda (Tarabulus: Maʿhad al-Inmāʾ al-ʿArabī, 1979), 37ff.; Alnoor Dhanani, *The Physical Theory of Kalām: Atoms, Space, and Void in Basrian Muʿtazilī Cosmology* (Leiden: Brill, 1994), chap. 2; Frank, *al-Maʿdūm wal-mawjūd*: The Non-Existent, the Existent, and the Possible in the Teaching of Abū Hāshim and His Followers," *MIDEO* 14 (1980): 185–209.

41. Like Ṣadrā's treatment of Rāzī (see n28), I will turn to his treatment of Zamakhsharī later in this chapter.

42. I say "directly encounter" since a good deal of Muʿtazilite Qurʾānic exegetical material has historically found its way into the more mainstream Sunnī and Shīʿī *tafsīr* works by way of a complicated process of suppression and integration. See Suleiman Mourad, "The Survival of the Muʿtazilī Tradition of Qurʾanic Exegesis in Shīʿī and Sunnī *tafāsīr,*" *JQS* 12 (2010): 83–108.

43. Ṣadrā, *Tafsīr,* 1:85.

44. Cf. Daniel Gimaret, *Une lecture muʿtazilite du Coran: Le tafsīr d'Abū ʿAlī al-Djubbāʾī (m. 303/915)* (Louvain: Peeters, 1994), 73. For an interesting response to this Muʿtazilite reading, see Rāzī, *al-Maṭālib al-ʿāliya min al-ʿilm al-ilāhī,* ed. Muḥammad ʿAbd al-Salām Shāhīn (Beirut: Dār al-Kutub al-ʿIlmiyya, 1999), 9:186–7.

45. (1) Ṣadrā, *Tafsīr,* 1:38, citing Ibn ʿArabī, *Fuṣūṣ al-ḥikam,* ed. A. E. Afifi (Beirut: Dār al-Kutub al-ʿArabī, 1946), 67 (at *Tafsīr,* 1:39, Ṣadrā goes

on to explain one of the sentences in the passage cited from the *Fuṣūṣ* on the previous page); (2) Ṣadrā, *Tafsīr*, 1:40, citing Ibn ʿArabī, *Fuṣūṣ*, 90; (3) Ṣadrā, *Tafsīr*, 1:71–2, citing Ibn ʿArabī, *al-Futūḥāt al-makkiyya* (reprint, Beirut: Dār Ṣādir, 1968), 2:86–7, which corresponds to Osman Yahia (partial critical edition) (Cairo: al-Hayʾa al-Miṣriyya al-ʿĀmma li-l-Kitāb, 1972–91), 12:395–6; (4) Ṣadrā, *Tafsīr*, 1:110–1, citing Ibn ʿArabī, *Futūḥāt*, 3:470 (Beirut) (cf. Chittick, *Sufi Path of Knowledge*, 338–9); (5) Ṣadrā, *Tafsīr*, 1:114–5, citing Ibn ʿArabī, *Futūḥāt*, 2:629 (Beirut). Of the nine direct citations from Ibn ʿArabī's works, Khwājawī traced four of them, leaving five passages unlocated (which are identified in the following note).

46. (6) Ṣadrā, *Tafsīr*, 1:71, citing Ibn ʿArabī's statement "The end for all is mercy" at *Futūḥāt*, 2:437 (Beirut) (for which, see Chittick, *Sufi Path of Knowledge*, 120, 130, 225, 338; Chittick, *The Self-Disclosure of God: Principles of Ibn al-'Arabī's Cosmology* [Albany: State University of New York Press, 1998], 174); (7) Ṣadrā, *Tafsīr*, 1:101, citing Ibn ʿArabī, *Futūḥāt*, 1:218 (Beirut), 3:335 (Cairo) (cf. Chittick, *Sufi Path of Knowledge*, 170); (8) Ṣadrā, *Tafsīr*, 153–4 (paraphrasing parts of *Asfār*, 9:357–9), closely follows Ibn ʿArabī, *Futūḥāt*, 3:449 (Beirut) (cf. Ibn ʿArabī, "Towards God's Signs," trans. William Chittick in Ibn ʿArabī, *Meccan Revelations*, 1:182; Chittick, *Self-Disclosure of God*, 28); (9) Ṣadrā, *Tafsīr*, 1:154–7, reproducing Ibn ʿArabī, *Futūḥāt*, 3:462–3 (Beirut) (cf. Chittick, *Sufi Path of Knowledge*, 360–1; Chittick, *Self-Disclosure of God*, 174; Chittick, "Ibn al-ʿArabī's Hermeneutics of Mercy," in *Mysticism and Sacred Scripture*, ed. Stephen Katz [New York: Oxford University Press, 2000], 168).

47. (10) Ṣadrā, *Tafsīr*, 1:72, paraphrasing Fakhr al-Dīn ʿIrāqī, *Divine Flashes*, trans. William Chittick and Peter Wilson (Mahwah, NJ: Paulist Press, 1982), 95, who cites Ibn ʿArabī, *Futūḥāt*, 1:210 (Beirut), 3:297–8 (Cairo) (cf. Chittick, *Sufi Path of Knowledge*, 37; see also Chittick *Self-Disclosure of God*, 23).

48. (11) Ṣadrā, *Tafsīr*, 1:144.

49. See n46 # 7.

50. See n46 # 8.

51. See Chapter 7.

52. For the school of Ibn ʿArabī, see Chittick, "The School of Ibn 'Arabī," in *History of Islamic Philosophy*, 1:510–23; Rustom, "Philosophical Sufism."

53. See the apt remarks in Kalin, *Knowledge in Later Islamic Philosophy*, xiv.

54. Ṣadrā, *Tafsīr*, 1:35.

55. Ibid., 1:91.

56. Ibid., 1:100.

57. Ibid., 1:104–5, citing Qūnawī, *Iʿjāz*, 449.

58. Ṣadrā, *Tafsīr*, 1:159–62, reworking Qūnawī, *Iʿjāz*, 475–78.

59. See n3.

60. See Ernst, "Sufism and Philosophy in Mullā Ṣadrā," in *Islam-West Philosophical Dialogue*, 1:173–92. A study outlining the broader relationship between philosophy and mysticism in Ṣadrā's thought can be found in Ešots,

"Mullā Ṣadrā's Teaching on *Wujūd*: A Synthesis of Philosophy and Mysticism" (PhD diss., Tallinn University, 2007).

61. See Ṣadrā, *On the Hermeneutics of the Light Verse*, passim.

62. Ṣadrā, *Tafsīr*, 1:81. Cf. ibid., 4:167; 6:25; Jambet, *Act of Being*, 407. Ṣadrā also relates a version of this *shaṭḥ* in his *ʿArshiyya*, although here Basṭāmī speaks in the first person and says that he would not notice the Throne were it to enter his heart. See Ṣadrā, *Wisdom of the Throne*, 165. For the phenomenon of *shaṭaḥāt* in Sufism, see Ernst, *Words of Ecstasy in Sufism* (Albany: State University of New York Press, 1985). Ṣadrā's likeliest source for this saying is Ibn ʿArabī, *Fuṣūṣ*, 88, 120. For Ibn ʿArabī's treatment of the *shaṭaḥāt*, see "The True Knowledge of Unruly Utterances," trans. William Chittick in *Meccan Revelations*, 1:150–6.

63. See Appendix 2 s.v. "The End for All is Mercy" (*Tafsīr*, 1:70–2) for the incident in translation, and n47 for its sources. See also Ṣadrā, *Tafsīr*, 4:71.

64. For the citation, see ibid., 1:109. I was unable to locate this statement in Anṣārī's writings.

65. Ṣadrā, *Tafsīr*, 1:47.

66. See Chapter 1.

67. Ṣadrā, *Tafsīr*, 1:31.

68. Ibid., 1:47–8.

69. Ghazālī, *Iḥyāʾ*, 4:357ff.

70. Ṣadrā, *Tafsīr*, 1:1.

71. Ibid., 1:74.

72. Ibid., 1:84.

73. Ibid., 1:98.

74. Ibid., 1:143.

75. Ibid., 1:152.

76. Ibid., 1:84.

77. Ibid., 1:98, 142.

78. Ibid., 1:99–100, 125.

79. Ibid., 1:99–100.

80. Ibid., 1:124.

81. Ibid., 1:143.

82. See Meir M. Bar-Asher, *Scripture and Exegesis in Early Imāmī Shiism* (Leiden: Brill, 1999), chap. 2. For ʿAyyāshī, see ibid., 56–63. Bar-Asher's work is the standard account for the development of early Shīʿī *tafsīr*. Ignaz Goldziher's treatment of the subject is still serviceable, although he deals less with figures and schools of Shīʿī exegesis and more with several prominent Shīʿī hermeneutical strategies. See Goldzhier, *Die Richtungen der islamischen Koranauslegung* (Leiden: Brill, 1920), 263–309. The first full-scale survey of Shīʿī *tafsīr* is to be found in al-Dhahabī, *al-Tafsīr wa-l-mufassirūn*, 2:23–234. For a more complete picture of the development of Twelver Shīʿī *tafsīr*, the following works should also be consulted: Mahmoud Ayoub, "The Speaking Qurʾān and the Silent Qurʾān: A Study of the Principles and Development of Imāmī Shīʿī *tafsīr*," in *Approaches to the History of the Interpretation of the*

Qur'ān, ed. Andrew Rippin (Oxford: Clarendon, 1988), 177–98; Corbin, *En islam iranien*, 1:135–219 (inter alia); Robert Gleave, *Scripturalist Islam: The History and Doctrines of the Akhbārī Shī'ī School* (Leiden: Brill, 2007), chap. 7; Lawson, "Akhbārī Shī'ī Approaches to *tafsīr*"; Diana Steigerwald, "Twelver Shī'ī Ta'wīl," in *The Blackwell Companion to the Qur'ān*, ed. Andrew Rippin (Malden, MA: Blackwell, 2006), 373–85.

83. Ṣadrā, *Tafsīr*, 1:168.

84. For a recent study of Ṭabrisī's *tafsīr*, see Bruce Fudge, *Qur'ānic Hermeneutics: Al-Ṭabrisī and the Craft of Commentary* (New York: Routledge, 2011).

85. Ṣadrā, *Tafsīr*, 1:125.

86. Ṣadrā records this work amongst the inventory of books in his personal library. For this inventory, see Ṣadrā, *Yāddāsht-hā-yi Mullā Ṣadrā hamrāh bā fihrist-i kitābkhāna-yi shakhṣī-yi Mullā Ṣadrā*, ed. Muḥammad Barakat (Qum: Intishārāt-i Bīdār, 1998). This inventory of works, although very useful, certainly does not present us with a complete listing of all of the texts in Ṣadrā's possession over the course of his career. This is because a number of important books upon which he draws at one point or another are missing from this list, such as Qūnawī's *I'jāz*, 'Irāqī's *Lama'āt*, and Rāzī's *tafsīr*. According to the editor of the text of Ṣadrā's personal library, the latest he could have drawn up this list would have been around two decades before his death. See Ṣadrā, *Yāddāsht-hā*, 8–9. The entire list is reproduced in English in Rizvi, *Mullā Ṣadrā Shīrāzī*, 117–35 (see pp. 117–8 for the specific reference to Ṭabrisī's *Majma'*).

87. Ṣadrā, *Tafsīr*, 1:124. For an important discussion of Qummī's *tafsīr*, see Bar-Asher, *Scripture and Exegesis*, 33–56.

88. Ṣadrā, *Tafsīr*, 1:67 (implicitly), 98.

89. Cf. Lane, *A Traditional Mu'tazilite Qur'ān Commentary*, 68.

90. Ṣadrā, *Tafsīr*, 1:30.

91. Ibid.

92. See ibid., 1:93. The corresponding section can be found in Bayḍāwī, *Anwār al-tanzīl wa-asrār al-ta'wīl* (Cairo: Dār al-Kutub al-'Arabiyya, 1911), 1:29. Although Ṣadrā had sections of Bayḍāwī's *Anwār* in his possession (see Rizvi, *Mullā Ṣadrā Shīrāzī*, 118–9), a set of glosses upon this *tafsīr* work is wrongfully attributed to him. See ibid., 116.

93. Ṣadrā, *Tafsīr*, 1:79, citing Bayḍāwī, *Anwār*, 1:26.

94. See Ṣadrā, *Tafsīr*, 1:81–2.

95. See Rizvi, *Mullā Ṣadrā Shīrāzī*, 118.

96. See Chapter 4.

97. See Ṣadrā, *Tafsīr*, 1:4–27, which closely follows, at times word-forword, sections from Rāzī, *al-Tafsīr al-kabīr* (Cairo: al-Maṭba'a al-Bahiyya al-Miṣriyya, 1934–8), 1:64ff (especially pp. 64, 68, 73). For a typology of the *isti'ādha*, see Constance Padwick, "I Seek Refuge," *MW* 28 (1938): 372–85. It can be noted that parts of Rāzī's commentary on the *isti'ādha* from his *tafsīr* can be found, albeit in the context of his rebuttal of Mu'tazilite exegeses of the Fātiḥa, in *Maṭālib*, 9:179–82.

98. Ṣadrā, *Tafsīr*, 1:44, reworking Rāzī, *al-Tafsīr al-kabīr*, 1:147. The influence of Rāzī's understanding of the divine names upon later Islamic thought remains unexplored. See the significant discussion in his *al-Tafsīr al-kabīr*, 1:134ff. For a suggested (but highly unlikely) influence of Rāzī upon Ibn ʿArabī in this regard, see Wisnovsky, "One Aspect of the Akbarian Turn in Shīʿī Theology," in *Sufism and Theology*, ed. Ayman Shihadeh (Edinburgh: Edinburgh University Press, 2007), 61–2n10.

99. Ṣadrā, *Tafsīr*, 1:179.

100. Ṣadrā only cites Nīsābūrī once in the text, in the same section where Rāzī is first cited (i.e., *Tafsīr*, 1:47). For a thorough study of Nīsābūrī's "scientific" exegesis of the Qurʾān and its relationship to his theology, see Robert Morrison, *Islam and Science: The Intellectual Career of Niẓām al-Dīn Nīsābūrī* (London: Routledge, 2008), chaps. 6–7.

101. Ṣadrā, *Tafsīr*, 1:46ff.

102. Ibid., 1:48. The text reproduced by Ṣadrā here from Rāzī corresponds to *al-Tafsīr al-kabīr*, 1:151–2, which has an eye on Ghazālī's statement to be found in *The Niche of Lights*, trans. David Buchman (Provo: Brigham Young University Press, 1998), 20. In these two texts, Ghazālī and Rāzī do not mention the point about the invocation *lā huwa illā huwa* corresponding to the station of the "elect of the elect." Rather, they say that the invocation *lā ilāha illā huwa* or "There is no god but He" (cf. Buchman's translation at *Niche of Lights*, 20) corresponds to the station of the "elect" (*khawāṣṣ*).

103. The section is to be found in Ṣadrā, *Tafsīr*, 1:49–64. At ibid., 1:49, Ṣadrā says that he will condense his argument, derived from his other works, into five sections (*fuṣūl*). But at ibid., 1:54, he speaks of several insightful points (*istibṣārāt*) concerning the fundamentality of being which he has already discussed in his books, and which he has incorporated into the *Tafsīr Sūrat al-fātiḥa* as a "single treatise" (*risāla mufrada*). Indeed, Ṣadrā ends the entire section with the type of blessings upon the Prophet and his family which customarily mark the end of a treatise (see ibid., 1:64). In short, all that we can say is that this portion of the *Tafsīr Sūrat al-fātiha* is, in some fashion, based upon some of Ṣadrā's philosophical writings.

104. Ibid., 1:4, 42, 65, 163, 177.

105. Ibid., 1:7, 84.

106. Ibid., 1:41. For Ibn al-Zabʿarī's question, see Ibn Hishām, *al-Sīra al-nabawiyya*, ed. Muṣṭafā al-Saqqā, Ibrāhīm al-Abyārī, and ʿAbd al-Ḥafīẓ Shalabī (Cairo: Muṣṭafā al-Bābī al-Ḥalabī, 1955), 1:359.

107. See Appendix 2 s.v. "Idols of Belief" (*Tafsīr*, 1:40–2).

108. Ṣadrā, *Tafsīr*, 1:42.

109. See Appendix 2 s.v. "The Subsistence of Mercy" (*Tafsīr*, 1:42).

110. For a collection of Ṣadrā's Persian poetry, see *Majmūʿa-yi ashʿār-i Ṣadr al-Dīn Shīrāzī*, ed. Muḥammad Khwājawī (reprint, Tehran: Intishārāt-i Mawlā, 2003). Ṣadrā's citations from Rūmī's *Mathnawī* can be found in *Tafsīr*, 5:287; 6:23–4. For a citation from ʿAṭṭār, see Ṣadrā, *Sih aṣl*, 14.

111. For these poems, see Ṣadrā, *Tafsīr*, 1:30, 73, 78, 81, 86, 119, 130, 147, 158, 164 (2), 171.

112. Ibid., 1:164. For one of these poems, which is also cited in Ṣadrā's other works (i.e., *Asfār*, 3:326, translated in Kalin, *Knowledge in Later Islamic Philosophy*, 271), see Appendix 2 s.v. "The Fātiḥa and the Perfect Man" (*Tafsīr*, 1:163–40). We will return to Ṣadrā's treatment of the Perfect Man in the *Tafsīr Sūrat al-fātiḥa* in Chapter 4.

113. Ṣadrā, *Tafsīr*, 1:78.

114. Ibid., 1:142. For the Banī Salūl, see Michael Lecker, "Salūl," in *EI*[2].

115. Yāqūt al-Ḥamawī, *Muʿjam al-buldān* (reprint, Beirut: Dār Ṣādir, 1977), 5:263.

116. Ṣadrā, *Tafsīr*, 1:30, also cited in *Sih aṣl*, 5. See Chapter 5 for Ṣadrā's use of this couplet. It seems that Ṣadrā's use and even "authorship" of this couplet comes by way of one of the accepted forms of *sariqa* or "plagiarism." For more on this phenomenon in classical Arabic poetry, see Wolfhart Heinrichs, "Sariḳa," in *EI*[2].

117. Ṣadrā was writing for an audience who would have shared his assumptions about textual linearity/non-linearity, and would have been used to the digressive style of philosophical and theological discourse. With that in mind, lengthy digressions in the text should be viewed as supplementary material to the point at hand. In modern scholarship, the function of these digressions would quite literally be equivalent to the function of the footnote/endnote. Since Ṣadrā was writing as a Qurʾān commentator, the normal digressive style of philosophy and theology is further augmented, because, as a commentator on scripture, he had more ground to cover than he normally would in a philosophical or theological treatise.

118. Cf. Morris, "Introduction," in Ṣadrā, *Wisdom of the Throne*, 57–8n63, where he states that these subheadings "indicate the decisive realization of enlightenment or the "unveiling" of Being. . . ." Although this interpretation is open to debate, on p. 99n22, Morris rightly notes the Ishrāqī roots to some of these subheadings. It can be noted that in his edition of Ṣadrā's *tafsīr*, Khwājawī will often insert his own explanatory titles alongside any given subheading. His purpose in doing so is to provide a summary of the heading's contents, although such insertions are far from helpful.

119. To avoid confusion, I summarize each part of the work rather than give the details of the subdivisions in each part, and discuss noteworthy digressions along the way. The most important issues in the *Tafsīr Sūrat al-fātiḥa* will be fully discussed in Chapters 3–5 and 7 of this study.

Chapter 3

1. For a tradition which states that the Fātiḥa is the key to Paradise, see Ghazālī, *The Jewels of the Qurʾān: Al-Ghazālī's Theory*, trans. Muhammad Abul Quasem (Kuala Lumpur: University of Malaya Press, 1977), 73.

2. The phrase "despite its concision" appears frequently in discussions concerning the merits of the Fātiḥa. See, for example, Ghazālī, *Jewels of the Qurʾān*, 66. For its appearance in Ṣadrā's commentary on the *Tafsīr Sūrat al-fātiḥa*, see *Tafsīr*, 1:79, 163–4, 174.

3. Ibid., 1:2.

4. Ibid., 1:1. Cf. ibid., 1:168. Cf. Qūnawī, *Iʿjāz*, 104; Zamakhsharī, *Kashshāf*, 1:35. See also Graham, "Fātiḥa." At *Tafsīr*, 1:165, Ṣadrā states that the Fātiḥa, along with the closing lines of Q 2 (the *khawātīm*), contain "the goal of human perfection." For the interesting parallel drawn by Ibn ʿArabī between the "mother of the book" (*umm al-kitāb*) and the "mother of Qurʾān" and Jesus and Mary, see Gril, "Commentaries on the *Fātiḥa*," 44.

5. See Chapter 1.

6. Ṣadrā, *Tafsīr*, 174–5. Cf. ibid., 1:164.

7. Ibid., 1:174. See also Martin Whittingham, *Al-Ghazālī and the Qurʾān: One Book, Many Meanings* (London: Routledge, 2007), 76, for Ghazālī's division of the verses of the Fātiḥa into theoretical and practical dimensions, although Whittingham's suggestion that this division is essentially Aristotelian should be taken with a grain of salt. For a new inquiry into Ghazālī's understanding of the Qurʾān, see Scott Girdner, "Reasoning with Revelation: The Significance of the Qurʾānic Contextualization of Philosophy in al-Ghazālī's *Mishkāt al-anwār* (*The Niche of Lights*)" (PhD diss., Boston University, 2009). Cf. Alexander Treiger, *Inspired Knowledge in Islamic Thought: Al-Ghazālī's Theory of Mystical Cognition and Its Avicennian Foundation* (New York: Routledge, 2012), chap. 4.

8. A typical linguistic approach to the *basmala* can be found in Rāzī's *tafsīr*: "We have shown that the *bāʾ* in 'In the name of God, the All-Merciful, the Compassionate' attaches to an object of a preposition. We therefore say it is possible for this object of a preposition to accompany a noun or a verb, which can either be precedent or antecedent to it in four ways: (1) when the verb is antecedent to it you say, 'I begin in the name of God'; (2) when the noun is antecedent to it you say, 'The beginning of the discussion is in the name of God'; (3) when the verb is precedent to it you say, 'In the name of God, I begin'; (4) and when the noun is precedent to it you say, 'In the name of God is my beginning'" (Rāzī, *al-Tafsīr al-kabīr*, 1:101).

9. Cf. Muḥammad b. Ḥasan Ṭūsī, *al-Tibyān fī tafsīr al-Qurʾān*, ed. Aḥmad al-Amīn and Aḥmad al-ʿĀmilī (Najaf: al-Maṭbaʿa al-ʿIlmiyya, 1957–64), 1:38; Maḥmūd b. ʿUmar al-Zamakhsharī, *al-Kashshāf ʿan-ghawāmiḍ ḥaqāʾiq al-tanzīl wa-ʿuyūn al-aqāwīl fī wujūh al-taʾwīl* (Beirut: Dār al-Iḥyāʾ al-Turāth al-ʿArabī, 2001), 1:35.

10. A fine summary of the problem in his *tafsīr* can be found in Maḥmūd b. ʿAbd Allāh Ālūsī, *Rūḥ al-maʿānī fī tafsīr al-Qurʾān al-ʿaẓīm wa-l-sabʿ al-mathānī* (Beirut: Dār Iḥyāʾ al-Turāth al-ʿArabī, 1970), 1:52.

11. For a sampling of the Sufi interpretations of the *basmala* offered by Sulamī in his *Ḥaqāʾiq*, see Rustom, "Forms of Gnosis in Sulamī's Sufi Exegesis of the *Fātiḥa*," *ICMR* 16, no. 4 (2005): 340–1. Cf. Paul Nwyia, *Exégèse coranique et langage mystique* (Beirut: Dar El-Machreq, 1970), 166–8 (particularly p. 167); Michael Sells, *Early Islamic Mysticism* (Mahwah, NJ: Paulist Press, 1996), 88–9.

12. With respect to the *basmala*, Maybudī sees in the beginning of this formula a fundamental metaphysical principle, namely the unfolding of the divine hiddenness into the realm of multiplicity through the name "Allah." God's name here becomes the means of access to Him, and must thus be the starting point for any and all human transactions: "'In the Name of

God' means, 'I began in the name of God, so you too begin!' He says, 'I began through My name, was united with My name, and commenced in My name, so begin through My name, unite with My name, and commence in My name'" (Rashīd al-Dīn Maybudī, *Kashf al-asrār wa-ʿuddat al-abrār*, ed. ʿAlī Aṣghar Ḥikmat [Tehran: Chāpkhāna-yi Dānishgāh-i Tihrān, 1952–60], 1:4). For a study of Maybudī's Sufi *tafsīr*, see Keeler, *Ṣūfī Hermeneutics: The Qur'ān Commentary of Rashīd al-Dīn Maybudī* (Oxford: Oxford University Press in association with The Institute of Ismaili Studies), 2007.

13. For a translation and study of his important work, *al-Kahf wa-l-raqīm*, see ʿAbd al-Karīm Jīlī, *Un commentaire ésotérique de la formule inaugurale du Qoran: "Les mystères cryptographiques de Bismi-Llâhi-r-Raḥmâni-Raḥîm,"* trans. Jabir Clément-François (Beirut: Albouraq, 2002).

14. Ṣadrā, *Tafsīr*, 1:182. Here, the *basmala* is given its other title, namely the *tasmiya*.

15. Ibid., 1:39.

16. Ibid., 1:44. Cf. the pertinent remarks in Rizvi, *Mullā Ṣadrā and Metaphysics*, 71–2. For the infinity of the divine Essence, see Frithjof Schuon, *Survey of Metaphysics and Esoterism* (Bloomington: World Wisdom, 1986), chaps. 1–2.

17. For some penetrating analyses of the Absolute from this perspective, see Izutsu, *Sufism and Taoism*, 23–38; Nasr, *The Need for a Sacred Science* (Albany: State University of New York Press, 1993), chap. 1; Qūnawī, *Risālat al-nuṣūṣ*, ed. Jalāl al-Dīn Āshtiyānī (Tehran: Markaz-i Nashr-i Dānishgāhī, 1983), 6–10. Chittick has translated selections from Qūnawī's *Nuṣūṣ* in volume four of *An Anthology of Philosophy in Persia*, ed. Seyyed Hossein Nasr and Mehdi Aminrazavi (London: I. B. Tauris in association with The Institute of Ismaili Studies, 2008–).

18. See Chittick, *Self-Disclosure of God*, 14, and Izutsu, *Concept and Reality of Existence*, 64. It must be noted that the term "God" in this context does not refer to the traditional God of theology. Rather, "God" as used here refers to the Absolute, that is, the God beyond all conception and accessibility. We will return to this crucial point later in the chapter.

19. That we are justified in identifying the reality of being with God is clearly evidenced in the *Mashāʿir*. See, in particular, Ṣadrā, *Mashāʿir*, 8, 44, 46–50.

20. Ṣadrā, *Tafsīr*, 1:36.

21. Ibid.

22. Ibn ʿArabī, *Fuṣūṣ*, 67, cited at Ṣadrā, *Tafsīr*, 1:38.

23. Ibid., 1:39.

24. Ibid. Cf. ibid., 3:46–9. For a related passage from the *Asfār*, see Jambet, *Act of Being*, 182–5.

25. For the term *ghayb al-ghuyūb* in Ṣadrā's writings, see *Asfār*, 2:345ff.; *Elixir of the Gnostics*, 31, 103–4n35; *Tafsīr*, 4:403. For a similar term (*ghayb al-ghayb*), see Muʾayyid al-Dīn Jandī, *Sharḥ Fuṣūṣ al-ḥikam*, ed. Jalāl al-Dīn Āshtiyānī (Mashhad: Dānishgāh-i Mashhad, 1982), 707.

26. See Ibn ʿArabī, *Fuṣūṣ*, 90–4 (for a discussion of *aḥadiyya*); Izutsu, *Sufism and Taoism*, 112, 115n8.

27. See Jandī, *Sharḥ*, 707.

28. See Saʿīd al-Dīn Farghānī, *Muntahā l-madārik* (Cairo, 1876), 1:15ff. Talk of the manifest and non-manifest faces of the Essence is tantamount to speaking about God as the Manifest (*al-ẓāhir*) and the Hidden (*al-bāṭin*). See Chittick, *Sufi Path of Knowledge*, 95; Corbin, *Creative Imagination in the Ṣūfism of Ibn 'Arabī*, trans. Ralph Manheim (Princeton, NJ: Princeton University Press, 1969), 186ff.

29. Ṣadrā also refers to the "pervasiveness" (*shumūl*) of being, which is identical to the manifest face of the Essence. One of his standard philosophical expressions for the pervasiveness of being, which we encountered in Chapter 1, is "expansive being" (or "the expansion of the light of being" (*inbisāṭ nūr al-wujūd*)). Other terms for the manifest face of the Essence (or being) employed by Ṣadrā, the first two of which we have encountered in Chapter 1, are "the Breath of the All-Merciful" (or "the All-Merciful breath" (*al-nafas al-raḥmānī*)), "the Real through whom creation takes place," and "the mercy which encompasses all things" (*al-raḥmat al-latī wasiʿat kull shayʾ*). See Ṣadrā, *Mafātīḥ*, 100; *Mashāʿir*, 8. See also, Jambet, *Act of Being*, 183–4.

30. For a helpful attempt at widening the notion of "theology" in classical Islam, see Winter, "Introduction," 2–4.

31. In rendering *shaʾn* (derived from Q 55:29) as "task," I follow Sachiko Murata, *Chinese Gleams of Sufi Light: Wang Tai-yü's Great Learning of the Pure and Real and Liu Chih's Displaying the Concealment of the Real Realm* (Albany: State University of New York Press, 2000), index s.v. "tasks."

32. Ṣadrā, *Tafsīr*, 1:34. Cf. ibid., 4:42–6. For the "keys to the unseen," see Qūnawī, *Nuṣūṣ*, 57ff.

33. Which explains why Ṣadrā also identifies the Perfect Words, which we encountered in Chapter 1 and shall return to in the following chapter, with the "keys to the unseen." See Ṣadrā, *Sharḥ*, 2:617.

34. For the names of the names, see Chittick, *Sufi Path of Knowledge*, 34–6. See also Ibn ʿArabī, *Fuṣūṣ*, 120; Izutsu, *Sufism and Taoism*, 101.

35. Ṣadrā, *Tafsīr*, 1:34. For the passage in context, see Appendix 2 s.v. "On the Divine Names" (*Tafsīr*, 1:34–6). See also *Tafsīr*, 4:391. For Ibn ʿArabī's understanding of the divine names as relationships (and thus not ontological entities), see *Futūḥāt*, 4:294 (Beirut).

36. For the fixed entities, see Chittick, *Sufi Path of Knowledge*, 83–8 (here Chittick has "immutable entities"). For why "fixed entities" is a more accurate translation than "immutable entities," see Chittick, *Self-Disclosure of God*, xxxviii. Several arguments have been made in favor of alternate translations and (even interpretations) of this expression. Particularly noteworthy in this regard are Caner Dagli's introduction to Ibn ʿArabī, *The Ringstones of Wisdom*, trans. Caner Dagli (Chicago: Kazi, 2004), xviii–xix, and Izutsu, *Sufism and Taoism*, 159ff.

37. See, for example, Qayṣarī, *Sharḥ*, 1:45, which is reproduced in ʿAbd al-Raḥmān Jāmī, *Naqd al-nuṣūṣ fī sharḥ Naqsh al-fuṣūṣ*, ed. William Chittick

(Tehran: Imperial Iranian Academy of Philosophy, 1977), 42. For the passage in translation (cited from Jāmī), see Sachiko Murata, William Chittick, and Tu Weiming, *The Sage Learning of Liu Zhi: Islamic Thought in Confucian Terms* (Cambridge, MA: Harvard University Asia Center, 2009), 209n6.

38. In the *Mashāʿir* (p. 35), Ṣadrā says, "The quiddities are the fixed entities [*al-māhiyyāt hiya al-aʿyān al-thābita*]. . . ." This statement forms part of his famous "conversion" account, that is, when he discarded the position of the "fundamentality of quiddity" (*aṣālat al-māhiyya*) in favor of the "fundamentality of being" (*aṣālat al-wujūd*). The account is also to be found in Ṣadrā, *Asfār*, 1:49; *Masāʾil*, 208 (for a translation of it, see Izutsu, *Concept and Reality of Existence*, 104). For the quiddities as the fixed entities, see also Chittick's note at *Elixir of the Gnostics*, 106–7n15.

39. That is, the existentiated fixed entities or quiddities.

40. It can be argued that, insofar as the divine names are archetypes, the divine names do correspond to the Platonic Forms (see the observation in Chittick, *Sufi Path of Knowledge*, 84). But, with respect to Ṣadrā's thought, such an identification may be problematic, since the Forms for Ṣadrā do have some kind of independent ontological status, whereas the names, as demonstrated in this chapter, strictly speaking, do not. Before making any concrete judgments, a more thorough investigation into Ṣadrā's understanding of the Platonic Forms would have to be undertaken. For some preliminary leads in this direction, see Chapter 2n38.

41. From the perspective that the names denote the Essence, It can also be called the "Named" (*al-musammā*). See Chittick, *Sufi Path of Knowledge*, 385n6.

42. The term *jāmiʿ* in this context is fairly difficult to translate in a completely unambiguous manner. Following Chittick (*Elixir of the Gnostics*, 110n43), I have rendered it as "All-Gathering" in order to convey the sense, when qualifying the term *ism* and describing the function of the name Allah, of "bringing together," "collecting," and "encapsulating" all of God's divine names.

43. See, in particular, Jambet, "L'essence de Dieu est toute chose": Identité et différence selon Ṣadr al-Dīn Shīrāzī (Mullā Ṣadrā)," in *Le shīʿisme imāmite quarante ans après: hommage à Etan Kohlberg*, ed. Mohammad Ali-Amir Moezzi, Meir M. Bar-Asher, and Simon Hopkins (Turnhout, Brepols, 2009), 262–92; Muḥammad ʿAlī Khwursandiyān, "Qāʿida-yi "basīṭ al-ḥaqīqa" wa-kārburd-hā-yi ān dar andīsha-yi Ṣadrāʾī," *FADDS* 23 (2007): 41–64; Ṣadrā, *Asfār*, 2:368–72.

44. Cf. Appendix 2 s.v. "On Ibn ʿArabī's Reference to "the Real"" (*Tafsīr*, 1:39–40).

45. I read a *wāw* here following the Tehran National Library manuscript of the *Tafsīr Sūrat al-fātiḥa* (ms. 263, fol.22a) and a lithographed version of the text (Ṣadrā, *Majmūʿat al-tafāsīr*, lithographed by Aḥmad Shīrāzī [Tehran, 1904], 9). Without the conjunction, the passage is incomprehensible.

46. It will be recalled from the preceding discussion that the loci of God's manifestation, here referred to as "the loci of creation and the engendered Command," are the fixed entities (i.e., the objects of God's knowledge forever

fixed in His "mind") in their state of existentiation through their receiving the divine names, that is, through the particular aspect of the manifest face of the Essence turned toward them.

47. Ṣadrā, *Tafsīr,* 1:34.

48. Chittick, *Sufi Path of Knowledge,* 66.

49. This distinction is important with respect to Ṣadrā's cosmology and soteriology, which will be dealt with in Chapters 4 and 6–7 respectively.

50. See Chittick, *Sufi Path of Knowledge,* 49.

51. Ṣadrā, *Tafsīr,* 1:39. Here Ṣadrā follows Ibn ʿArabī, *Fuṣūṣ,* 67, which is cited at *Tafsīr,* 1:38. Cf. *Tafsīr,* 1:44.

52. It can be noted here that the pronoun *huwa* ("He," "It") which, as Ṣadrā notes, is "that which is praised for His Essence in His Essence" (ibid., 1:44), denotes the Essence in an even more primary sense than does the name Allah. However, Ṣadrā argues, *huwa* does not "define" the Essence in any way, and is the exclusive preserve of the spiritually elect in their invocation of God once they have transcended the particularized names of the Essence, and even the name Allah itself. See Appendix 2 s.v. "The Names "God" and "He"" (*Tafsīr,* 1:42–3).

Chapter 4

1. Ṣadrā's treatment of God's mercy can be found in Chapters 6–7.

2. Ṣadrā also tells us toward the end of the *Tafsīr Sūrat al-fātiḥa* that the *ḥamdala* contains an allusion to the proof of God's existence, and that it also alludes to the beginning of the chain of existents. See Ṣadrā, *Tafsīr,* 1:170 and 174 respectively. I will have a lot more to say about the *ḥamdala*'s relationship to the emergence of existence in this chapter.

3. See Chapter 1 for a discussion of how the Word becomes fragmented into Perfect Words, a point which will resurface in the present chapter.

4. Cf. Ṣadrā, *Tafsīr,* 1:84–5.

5. As was seen in Chapter 1, Ṣadrā refers to the "alphabetical" nature of existents in explaining how the cosmos and its contents form a "text" which is penned by the wise Author. Cf. ibid., 1:135.

6. Ibid., 1:10–1. Cf. ibid., 1:85.

7. For representative discussions of the differences between *ḥamd* and cognate terms, see Rāzī, *al-Tafsīr al-kabīr,* 1:218ff.; and, in the following order, Zamakhsharī, *Kashshāf,* 1:8–11; Bayḍāwī, *Anwār,* 1:25; ʿAbd Allāh b. Aḥmad al-Nasafī, *Madārik al-tanzīl wa-ḥaqāʾiq al-taʾwīl,* ed. Marwān Muḥammad al-Shaʿʿār (Beirut: Dār al-Nafāʾis, 1996), 1:32. Ṣadrā seems to follow the latter quite closely in his discussion of *madḥ* and *thanāʾ*.

8. Ṣadrā, *Tafsīr,* 1:74.

9. Ibid.

10. Ibid.

11. Cf. ibid.

12. Cf. ibid.

13. Ibid., 1:74–5. Cf. Landolt, *Recherches en spiritualité iranienne*, 274–6; Landolt, "Simnânî on *Wahdat al-Wujûd*," in *Collected Papers on Islamic Philosophy and Mysticism*, ed. by Mehdi Mohaghegh and Hermann Landolt (Tehran: McGill University Institute of Islamic Studies, 1971), 104–6.

14. For a fine discussion of this point, see Corbin, *Creative Imagination*, 112–7.

15. Cf. Ṣadrā, *Tafsīr*, 1:76–7.

16. Ibid., 1:75.

17. There is a telling narrative in early Islamic texts which states that Adam's first words were, "Praise is for God, Lord of the worlds" (the same wording as Q 1:2). See Chodkiewicz, "The Banner of Praise," trans. Cecilia Twinch in *Foundations of the Spiritual Life: Praise*, ed. Stephen Hirtenstein (Oxford: Muhyiddin Ibn 'Arabi Society, 1997), 45n1. It is clear how Ṣadrā would understand this tradition. Cf. *Tafsīr*, 1:76–7. See also Ayoub, "The Prayer of Islam," 643.

18. For a subtle treatment of the Muhammadan Reality, see Schuon, "The Spiritual Significance of the Substance of the Prophet," in *Islamic Spirituality*, ed. Seyyed Hossein Nasr (New York: Crossroad, 1987–91), 1:48–63.

19. The "banner of praise" is, in the Islamic tradition, one of a number of special favors which God will confer upon the Prophet on the Day of Judgment. See Tirmidhī, Manāqib 1: "I shall be the master of the children of Adam on the Day of Resurrection, and I boast not; and in my hand shall be the banner of praise, and I boast not. . . ." For the Prophet's special function on the Final Day, particularly the salvific role played by him, see Chodkiewicz, "Banner of Praise," 49–53. Ṣadrā also draws an interesting link between the "banner of praise" and the Prophetic saying, "Whoever is for God, God is for him." See Appendix 2 s.v. "The Specification of Praise" (*Tafsīr*, 1:76–7). For another context in which Ṣadrā cites this *ḥadīth*, see *Tafsīr*, 5:29.

20. Ibid., 1:75. Ṣadrā goes on to explain that the Muhammadan Reality, as the utmost level of praise, does not contradict the Prophet's elemental existence as a part of the macrocosm since all things are stronger than a single denotation, namely a part of the world. Cf. ibid., 1:79–80. See also Ṣadrā, *Asrār*, 110–2. For an important contemporary discussion of the Prophet's relationship to "praise," see Rusmir Mahmutćehajić, *On Love*, trans. Celia Hawkesworth (New York: Fordham University Press, 2007), 101–6.

21. It can also be noted that there has been a long-standing debate in *tafsīr* literature over whether or not the *ḥamdala* formula is a declarative sentence (*al-jumla al-inshāʾiyya*) or an informative sentence (*al-jumla al-khabariyya*). If it is the former, then it is to be understood not as "Praise is for God, Lord of the worlds," but as "Praised be God, Lord of the Worlds." Thus, understood as a declarative sentence, the *ḥamdala* would correspond to God's engendering Command. Although Ṣadrā is silent on this question, Ibn ʿArabī's position is that the *ḥamdala* can only be an informative statement and not a declarative one, although by *inshāʾī* he understands the notion of "declaration" and not necessarily "command." See Chodkiewicz, "Banner of Praise," 45.

22. For the Muhammadan Reality as the First Intellect, see Rustom, "Dāwūd al-Qayṣarī: Notes on His Life, Influence and Reflections on the

Muḥammadan Reality," *JMIAS* 38 (2005): 60–1. Chittick offers a key distinction between the Muhammadan Spirit (*rūḥ Muḥammadī*) and the Muhammadan Reality in *Imaginal Worlds*, chap. 2.

23. For Ṣadrā's citation of Bayḍāwī's explanation of the meaning of this term, see Appendix 2 s.v. "Man is a Macrocosm" (*Tafsīr*, 1:79). See also Ayoub, "The Prayer of Islam," 642–4.

24. Cf. Zamakhsharī, *Kashshāf*, 1:53–4, who limits his treatment of the term *ʿālam* to several basic lexical considerations.

25. Ṣadrā, *Tafsīr*, 1:79.

26. An allusion to Q 41:53, "We will show them Our signs in the horizons and within themselves until it is clear to them that He is the Real." For a discussion of the complementary relationship shared between humans and the cosmos, see Chittick, *Science of the Cosmos, Science of the Soul: The Pertinence of Islamic Cosmology in the Modern World* (Oxford: Oneworld, 2007). For how praise relates to God's signs in the cosmos and the self, see Mahmutćehajić, *On Love*, 101–6.

27. Ṣadrā, *Tafsīr*, 1:79. See also Jambet, *Act of Being*, 412–3, for a useful discussion of the Perfect Man as the microcosm.

28. The text of the tradition (also found in Genesis 1:27) says that "God created Adam in His image." We have another version which says that "God created Adam in the image of the All-Merciful [*al-raḥmān*]." Cf. Ṣadrā, *Asrār*, 158–60; *Tafsīr*, 1:163; 4:390–4.

29. Cf. Qūnawī, *Iʿjāz*, 98, 106. Jambet, *Act of Being*, 492n43, notes that Moshe Idel, *Kabbalah: New Perspectives* (New Haven: Yale University Press, 1988), 210–8, discusses the relationship between the Kabbalah and the Torah, which Jambet connects with the idea of the Perfect Man's identity with the Qurʾān. For the relationship shared between the Sefiroth and the Ten Commandments, see Leo Schaya, *The Universal Meaning of the Kabbalah*, trans. Nancy Pearson (Baltimore: Penguin Books, 1958), 21.

30. Ṣadrā, *Tafsīr*, 1:163–4. Cf. Jambet, *Act of Being*, 413 and 492n43; Jambet, *Se rendre immortel* (Saint-Clément-de-Rivière: Fata Morgana, 2002), 105.

31. Cf. Ṣadrā, *Tafsīr*, 1:164. For an inquiry into the significance of realization or *taḥqīq* in Ṣadrā, see Morris, "The Process of Realization (*taḥqīq*): Mullā Ṣadrā's Conception of the *Barzakh* and the Emerging Science of Spirituality," in *Islam-West Philosophical Dialogue*, 10:93–102.

Chapter 5

1. As we will see in this chapter, Ṣadrā has in mind a hierarchical typology of the different knowers of the Qurʾān. For an earlier example of this type of approach, see Ghazālī, *Niche of Lights*, 36–8. See also Landolt, *Recherches en spiritualité iranienne*, 25–82. A more recent discussion can be found in Whittingham, *Ghazālī and the Qurʾān*, 110ff.

2. Ṣadrā, *Tafsīr*, 1:30.

3. As we saw in Chapter 1, there is a clear correlation between being and the Qurʾān, a point which, although lurking in the background, is made more explicit by Ṣadrā later.

4. Cf. ibid., 1:29.

5. Ibid., 1:28.

6. At ibid., 1:31–2, Ṣadrā says that the one who wants to know the Qur᾽ān's meanings has to go through some very rigorous training. He must know all the *tafsīrs* and, like Ghazālī, be completely conversant with all the different creeds and sects (he recounts here Ghazālī's autobiographical sketch of his quest for truth in his famous *al-Munqidh min al-ḍalāl*—Ṣadrā was fond of this book, as is evidenced, for example, in *Mafātīḥ*, 123–4). This is to be done until the bonds of imitation (*taqlīd*) are broken, which will induce within the seeker of knowledge a sense of deficiency and longing for the truth until God opens up a way for him and he comes to know the secrets of the Qur᾽ān. Yet slightly earlier (*Tafsīr*, 1:29), Ṣadrā says that "the people of God" do not need to bother with accumulating a great deal of knowledge of the exoteric sciences. Judging by the amount of emphasis Ṣadrā places on exoteric learning in his other writings, it seems that the people of God must go through the same process as those advised several pages later. If this is the case, then after having "arrived," they need not busy themselves excessively with formal learning since they now partake in a different mode of knowing—what Ṣadrā, in keeping with many of his predecessors, calls "unveiling" (*kashf*).

7. The distinction appears to have first been made in an early Sufi Qur᾽ānic exegetical maxim, often attributed to Jaʿfar al-Ṣādiq. See, inter alia, Nwyia, *Exégèse coranique et langage mystique*, 175; Sands, *Ṣūfī Commentaries*, 35. The term *ʿibāra* is not to be confused with a word we also encounter in Sufi *tafsīr*, namely *iʿtibār*. This latter term has a positive connotation, and, according to Gril (who renders it as "transposition symbolique" or "symbolic transposition"), is equivalent to *ishāra*, although *iʿtibār* is more explicit than *ishāra* in its reliance on the existence of an intimate relationship between the book, the self, and the cosmos. See Gril, "L'interprétation par transposition symbolique (*iʿtibār*) selon Ibn Barrağān et Ibn ʿArabī," in *Symbolisme et herméneutique dans la pensée de Ibn ʿArabī*, ed. Bakri Aladdin (Damascus: Institut français du Proche-Orient, 2007), 147–61 (he makes the point on p. 147). Cf. Chittick, *Self-Disclosure of God*, 263–5.

8. Ṣadrā, *Tafsīr*, 1:28–9. Cf. ibid., 6:10; Hasan Sa'idi, "Illumination, Unveiling and Intuition in Mullā Ṣadrā's Qur᾽ānic Commentary," 10:532.

9. Ṣadrā, *Tafsīr*, 1:30. Cf. ibid., 1:36.

10. For an excellent exposition of this point, see Izutsu, *Creation and the Timeless Order of Things: Essays in Islamic Mystical Philosophy* (Ashland: White Cloud Press, 1994), 38–65.

11. See ʿAbd Allāh al-Ḥārith b. Asad al-Muḥāsibī, *al-Riʿāya li-ḥuqūq Allāh*, ed. ʿAbd al-Qādir Aḥmad ʿAṭā᾽ (Cairo: Dār al-Kutub al-Ḥadītha, 1971), 177–355.

12. Jalāl al-Dīn Rūmī, *Mathnawī-yi maʿnawī*, ed. and trans. R. A. Nicholson as *The Mathnawí of Jalálu'ddín Rúmí* (London: Luzac, 1924–40), 1:710 (book 1, line 710):

Go, strive toward meaning, O form worshipper!
For meaning is the wing of form's body.

13. ʿAyn al-Quḍāt, *Tamhīdāt*, ed. ʿAfīf ʿUsayrān, 4th ed. (Tehran: Intishārāt-i Manūchihrī, 1994), 98: "O friend! If you want the secrets of the unseen to be manifest before you, then desist from habit worship, for habit worship is idol worship [*but-parast*]." For the ontological dimension of this form of idolatry, see the discussion in Shah-Kazemi, *The Other in the Light of the One: The Universality of the Qurʾān and Interfaith Dialogue* (Cambridge: Islamic Texts Society, 2006), 119ff.

14. See Chittick, *Imaginal Worlds*, 162–5; Chittick, *Sufi Path of Knowledge*, 335–44; Corbin, *Creative Imagination*, 124, 195–200.

15. Ibn ʿArabī, *Fuṣūṣ*, 121.

16. Cited in Chittick, *Imaginal Worlds*, 150. See also the pertinent remarks in Shah-Kazemi, *Other in the Light of the One*, 195–9.

17. For an excellent study of Shabistarī's life and thought, see Leonard Lewisohn, *Beyond Faith and Infidelity: The Sufi Poetry and Teachings of Maḥmūd Shabistarī* (Richmond: Curzon, 1995). See also Izutsu, *Creation and the Timeless Order of Things*, 38–65; Lewisohn, "The Transcendent Unity of Polytheism and Monotheism in the Sufism of Shabistarī," in *The Heritage of Sufism*, 2:379–406. Some striking parallels between Ibn ʿArabī's position and a ninth/fifteenth century Ismāʿīlī author are highlighted in Shafique Virani, *The Ismailis in the Middle Ages: A History of Survival, a Search for Salvation* (Oxford: Oxford University Press, 2007), 148–54.

18. For the Oneness of Being in Ṣadrā, see *Asfār*, 1:53, 433; 2:291, 300, 335, 339; 4:183; 6:18, 24, 335, 348; *al-Shawāhid al-rubūbiyya*, ed. Jalāl al-Dīn Āshtiyānī (Mashhad: Chāpkhāna-yi Dānishgāh-i Mashhad, 1967), 51. See also Muhammad Reza Juzi, "The Influence of Ibn ʿArabī's Doctrine of the Unity of Being on the Transcendental Theosophy of Ṣadr al-Dīn Shīrāzī," in *The Heritage of Sufism*, 3:266–72; Nasr, *Islamic Life and Thought*, chap. 16. For the Perfect Man in Ṣadrā, see *Asfār*, 6:296; 7:7, 181–3, 188–91; 8:140; 9:61, 284. A thorough index of books, names of figures and schools, technical terms, and scriptural references in the *Asfār* can be found in Sayyid Muḥsin Mīrī and Muḥammad Jaʿfar ʿAlī (ed.), *Fihrist-i mawḍūʿī-yi Kitāb al-Ḥikma al-mutaʿāliya fī l-asfār al-arbaʿa* (Tehran: Intishārāt-i Ḥikmat, 1995).

19. Ṣadrā, *Tafsīr*, 1:40, citing ibid., 4:49.

20. See Q 37:95, where Abraham says to his people, "Do you worship what you carve [*tanḥitūna*]?" According to Chittick (*Imaginal Worlds*, 185n7), Ibn ʿArabī clearly has this verse in mind when he says that "Every believer has a Lord in his heart that he has brought into existence, so he believes in Him. . . . They worship nothing but what they themselves have carved" (cited in ibid., 151).

21. See Ṣadrā, *Tafsīr*, 1:41.

22. See ibid., 1:40, drawing on ibid., 4:50.

23. Ibid., 1:40–1, citing ibid., 4:50. Cf. ibid., 1:6, 30.

24. Ibid., 1:42, citing ibid., 4:50.

25. This is an allusion to Q 2:144.

26. Ṣadrā, *Tafsīr*, 1:30. Ibn ʿArabī is more explicit on this point: "If God were to take people to account for error, He would take every possessor of a belief to account. Every believer has delimited his Lord with his reason

and consideration and has thereby restricted Him. But nothing is worthy of God except nondelimitation. . . . [S]o He delimits, but He does not become delimited. Nevertheless, God pardons everyone" (cited in Chittick, *Imaginal Worlds,* 153).

27. His position in this regard is similar to Ibn ʿArabī. See Ṣadrā, *Tafsīr,* 1:151–5.

28. Ibid., 1:30. Cf. the inquiry into the role played by "love" in readers' approaches to the Qurʾān in Chittick, *In Search of the Lost Heart: Explorations in Islamic Thought,* ed. Mohammed Rustom, Atif Khalil, and Kazuyo Murata (Albany: State University of New York Press, 2012), chap. 7.

29. An allusion to Q 3:39, which Ṣadrā cites at *Tafsīr,* 1:30.

30. Ibid.

31. *Madhāhib shattā li-l-muḥibbīn fī l-hawā / wa-lī madhhab fard aʿīshu bihi waḥdī* (ibid.). Ḥamawī's text has *madhāhib shattā li-l-muḥibbīn fī l-hawā / wa-lī madhhab fīhim aqūlu bihi waḥdī.* For the reference to the couplet in the *Muʿjam al-buldān,* see Chapter 2n115.

32. In theoretical Sufism, *mawṭin* and *maẓhar* function as hendiadys.

33. Ṣadrā, *Tafsīr* 1:41–2.

34. That is, "idolâtrie métaphysique." For Corbin's most extensive treatment of this idea, see his *Le paradoxe du monothéisme* (Paris: L'Herne, 1981), 7–17. See also Corbin, *En islam iranien,* 1:289, where he uses this phrase to render the Arabic term *tashbīh.*

35. I take this phrase from a title of one of Ṣadrā's treatises on the spiritual life in which he criticizes false Sufis. See Ṣadrā, *Kasr aṣnām al-jāhiliyya,* ed. Muḥammad Taqī Dānishpazhū (Tehran: University of Tehran Press, 1962). An English translation of the book is also available: *Breaking the Idols of Ignorance: Admonition of the Soi-Disant Sufi,* trans. Mahdi Dasht Bozorgi and Fazel Asadi Amjad (London: ICAS Press, 2008).

36. For this phenomenon in Sufism, see Rustom, "Rumi's Metaphysics of the Heart," *MRR* 1, no. 1 (2010): 69–79. See also the insightful points in Corbin, *En islam iranien,* 1:234.

37. Ṣadrā, *Tafsīr,* 1:153–4. This passage is a reworking of Ibn ʿArabī, *Futūḥāt,* 3:449 (Beirut) (translated in Chittick, *Self-Disclosure of God,* 28). Cf. Ṣadrā, *Shawāhid,* 143ff. For a complete translation of the passage, a part of which I have followed here, see Ibn ʿArabī, "Towards God's Signs." For Ibn ʿArabī's treatment of this idea, see *Fuṣūṣ,* 68–74. See also Chittick, *Imaginal Worlds,* chap. 9; Chittick, *Sufi Path of Knowledge,* 356–81; Chittick, *Self-Disclosure of God,* 86–7; Corbin, *Creative Imagination,* 184ff. For Ṣadrā's understanding of beauty, see ʿAlī-Akbar Afrāsiyābpūr, "Zībāʾī az dīdgāh-i Mullā Ṣadrā," *KHNṢ* 51 (2008): 91–107; ʿAlī Bābāʾī, *Zībāʾī-shināsī dar maktab-i Ṣadrā: parīchihra-yi ḥikmat* (Tehran: Intishārāt-i Mawlā, 2006).

38. We can also say that the Perfect Man glorifies God through every act of glorification to be found in the cosmos, since the Perfect Man himself is a transcription (*nuskha*) of the cosmos. Thus, the very act of glorification becomes "inscribed" upon the Perfect Man's being, and he therefore glorifies God by his very nature in every one of his modes. Cf. Ibn ʿArabī, *Futūḥāt,* 3:77 (Beirut).

Chapter 6

1. See Binyamin Abrahamov, "The Creation and Duration of Paradise and Hell in Islamic Theology," *DI* 79 (2002): 87–102 (particularly p. 99); Georges Vajda, "A propos de la perpétuité de la rétribution d'outre-tombe en théologie musulmane," *SIs* 11 (1959): 29–38. Cf. Josef Van Ess, "Das Begrenzte Paradies," in *Mélanges d'islamologie: volume dédié à la mémoire de Arman Abel par ses collègues, ses élèves et ses amis*, ed. Pierre Salmon (Leiden: Brill, 1974), 108–27. See also the forthcoming study by Feras Hamza: *To Hell and Back: The Prophet's Intercession and the Making of Temporary Hellfire in Sunni Orthodoxy* (Leiden: Brill).

2. But cf. the observation made in Jane Smith and Yvonne Haddad, *The Islamic Understanding of Death and Resurrection* (Albany: State University of New York Press, 1981), 95. One of the most sophisticated attempts at providing a rational defense of the eternal nature of punishment in Hell, despite the time-bound and therefore supposedly finite consequences of human actions, can be found in the writings of the Baṣran Muʿtazilites. See Sophia Vasalou, *Moral Agents and their Deserts: The Character of Muʿtazilite Ethics* (Princeton: Princeton University Press, 2008), chap. 5. For a standard presentation of the eternal nature of chastisement in Hell, see Nerina Rustomji, *The Garden and the Fire: Heaven and Hell in Islamic Culture* (New York: Columbia University Press, 2009), 79–83. An interesting discussion of Hell's "topography" can be found in Christian Lange, *Justice, Punishment, and the Medieval Muslim Imagination* (Cambridge: Cambridge University Press, 2008), 122–33.

3. We will outline Ibn ʿArabī's treatment of this question, along with its influence upon Ṣadrā, in the present chapter and in Chapter 7.

4. See Jon Hoover, "Islamic Universalism: Ibn Qayyim al-Jawziyya's Salafī Deliberations on the Duration of Hell-Fire," *MW* 99, no. 1 (2009): 181–201 (particularly pp. 183–9); Mohammad Hassan Khalil, *Islam and the Fate of Others: The Salvation Question* (New York: Oxford University Press, 2012), chap. 3. Khalil's study examines the soteriologies of Ghazālī, Ibn ʿArabī, Ibn Taymiyya, Ibn Qayyim, and Rashīd Riḍā.

5. See Hoover, "Islamic Universalism"; Khalil, *Islam and the Fate of Others*, chap. 3. Some insightful observations on Ibn ʿArabī's influence upon Ibn Taymiyya and Ibn Qayyim in this regard (as well as their points of divergence with Ibn ʿArabī) can be found in ʿĀʾisha al-Mannāʿī, "ʿAqīdat fanāʾ al-nār bayna Ibn ʿArabī wa-Ibn Taymiyya wa-Ibn al-Qayyim," *MBSS* 11 (2002): 86–141 (particularly pp. 96–121, 125–34).

6. See Winter, "Ibn Kemāl (d. 940/1534) on Ibn ʿArabī's Hagiology," in *Sufism and Theology*, 157n97.

7. Chittick, *Ibn 'Arabi: Heir to the Prophets* (Oxford: Oneworld, 2005), chap. 9 (see chapter title).

8. Winter, "Ibn Kemāl (d. 940/1534) on Ibn ʿArabī's Hagiology," 157n97.

9. See Khalil, *Islam and the Fate of Others*, chap. 2.

10. See Willemien Otten, *The Anthropology of Johannes Scottus Eriugena* (Leiden: Brill, 1991), 210–9; Panayiotis Tzamalikos, *Origen: Philosophy of*

History and Eschatology (Leiden: Brill, 2007), pt. 3. For an interesting discussion of the reception of Origen's teachings in the medieval period, see Henri De Lubac, *Medieval Exegesis (Vol. 1: The Four Senses of Scripture)*, trans. Mark Sebanc (Grand Rapids: Wm. B. Eerdmans Publishing Co., 1998), chap. 4. This is not to say that restoration in God negates torment in the next life. See, for example, Donald Duclow and Paul Dietrich, "Hell and Damnation in Eriugena," in *History and Eschatology in John Scottus Eriugena and His Time*, ed. James McEvoy and Michael Dunne (Louvain: Louvain University Press, 2002), 347–66.

11. The point is made in Moshe Idel, "Kabbalah," in *EJ*[2]. Idel goes on to note that this position is implied in the Zohar.

12. See, in particular, Jalāl al-Dīn Āshtiyānī, *Maʿād-i jismānī: Sharḥ bar Zād al-musāfir* (Mashhad: Muʾassasa-yi Chāp wa-Intishār wa-Grāfīk-i Dānishgāh-i Firdawsī, 1976); Corbin, *En islam iranien*, 4:84–115; Kamada, "Transmigration of Soul (*tanāsukh*) in Shaykh al-Mufīd and Mullā Ṣadrā," *Orient* 44 (2009): 105–119; Zailan Moris, *Revelation, Intellectual Intuition and Reason in the Philosophy of Mulla Sadra: An Analysis of the al-Hikmah al-ʻArshiyyah* (London: RoutledgeCurzon, 2002), 154–65. For translations from relevant texts in Ṣadrā, see Jambet, *Mort et résurrection en islam: L'au-delà selon Mullâ Sadrâ* (Paris: Albin Michel, 2008), 225–85; Ṣadrā, *Elixir of the Gnostics*, pt. 4; *Traité de la résurrection* (in Jambet, *Se rendre immortel*, 119–71); *Wisdom of the Throne*, pt. 2 (c).

13. Nasr, *Islamic Intellectual Tradition in Persia*, 292. This study was originally published in 1966.

14. See Āshtiyānī, *Maʿād-i jismānī*, 193.

15. See Chapter 7.

16. Khwājawī, *Lawāmiʿ*, 96–8.

17. Cf. Bīdārfar, "Taqdīm," 1:46–50, which closely follows Khwājawī. Khwājawī also does not attempt to account for the rhetorical function of talk of "eternal chastisement" in Islamic texts in general, and in Ṣadrā's thought in particular. It would, for example, be quite easy to read Ṣadrā as supporting eternal punishment in Hell by selectively drawing on isolated passages within his oeuvre. See, for example, *Tafsīr*, 1:236; 4:222; 6:98. As will be seen in Chapter 7, Ṣadrā's most comprehensive treatment of the problem of the eternal nature of Hell is to be found in his *Tafsīr Sūrat al-fātiḥa* (which, ironically, was edited by Khwājawī himself).

18. Jad Hatem, "Pure Love in Mulla Sadra," in *Timing and Temporality in Islamic Philosophy and Phenomenology of Life*, ed. Anna-Teresa Tymieniecka (Dordrecht: Springer, 2007), 298–9.

19. Naṣīrī, *Maktab-i tafsīrī*, 298–308 (his critique of Ṣadrā's soteriology is on pp. 306–8). For an assessment of this work in general, see the Introduction to the present study (n21).

20. See Chapter 7 for a critique of Naṣīrī's argument.

21. The works in question will be surveyed in this chapter and in Chapter 7.

22. Rizvi, *Mullā Ṣadrā Shīrāzī*, 64.

23. We know that Ṣadrā underwent his conversion to the position of the fundamentality of being some time during his stay in Kahak. According to Rizvi, *Mullā Ṣadrā Shīrāzī*, 14, the Kahak period is likely to have lasted for a period of five years. Judging from our knowledge of Ṣadrā's whereabouts in 1010/1601–2, we can safely estimate that the Kahak period was from 1013/1604 to 1018/1609. If this is the case, then we can assume that his conversion took place before 1013/1604.

24. Ṣadrā, *al-Mabdaʾ wa-l-maʿād*, ed. Jalāl al-Dīn Āshtiyānī (Tehran: Imperial Iranian Academy of Philosophy, 1976), 460–1. Cf. Ṣadrā, *Tafsīr*, 7:374.

25. For the identification of *wujūd* with *raḥma*, see ibid., 1:70 (cited later in this chapter); *Sharḥ*, 3:249–50. See also the pertinent remarks in Qūnawī, *Iʿjāz*, 319. It can also be noted here that in the previous chapter the Essence (*dhāt*) was identified with *wujūd*. This is because God's Essence, insofar as we can and cannot speak about It, is nothing other than *raḥma*. Cf. Ṣadrā, *Tafsīr*, 1:48.

26. Ṣadrā, *Tafsir*, 4:305–21.

27. See Rustom, "Nature and Significance," 130.

28. A summary of this work's structure and content can be found in ibid., 120–1.

29. He returns to this issue in his *Tafsīr Sūrat al-baqara* (*Tafsīr*, 1:376–7). See Chapter 7.

30. Ibid., 1:309.

31. Ibid., 4:305–6.

32. Ibid., 4:314–21. The following forms the basis for ibid., 1:348–9. See Chapter 7.

33. Ibid., 4:314. See n52 for this tradition and one of its other versions.

34. Dāwūd b. Maḥmūd al-Qayṣarī, *Maṭlaʿ khuṣūṣ al-kalim fī maʿānī Fuṣūṣ al-ḥikam (Sharḥ Fuṣūṣ al-ḥikam)* (Qum: Instishārāt Anwār al-Hudā, 2002), 2:26, cited by Ṣadrā at *Tafsīr*, 4:314–5. For Qayṣarī's life and work, see Mehmet Bayrakdar, *La philosophie mystique chez Dawud de Kayseri* (Ankara: Ministère de la Culture, 1990).

35. Qayṣarī, *Sharḥ*, 2:26, cited by Ṣadrā at *Tafsīr*, 4:314.

36. Ibn ʿArabī, *Fuṣūṣ*, 169–70, cited by Ṣadrā at *Tafsīr*, 3:314–5. For the fire becoming cool for Abraham, see Q 21:69.

37. Ṣadrā, *Tafsīr*, 4:315. This is, in a sense, a soteriological version of the well-known idiom, "one man's trash is another man's treasure."

38. See Q 96:18.

39. Ṣadrā, *Tafsīr*, 4:315–6.

40. Ibid., 4:316.

41. Ibid., 4:316–7.

42. Qayṣarī, *Sharḥ*, 1:433–6, cited by Ṣadrā at *Tafsīr*, 4:418–21.

43. Qayṣarī, *Sharḥ*, 1:436, cited by Ṣadrā at *Tafsīr*, 4:321.

44. Ṣadrā, *Asfār*, 9:346–62, which is also abridged in *Shawāhid*, 313–9. For an English translation of this section of the *Asfār*, see *Spiritual Psychology:*

The Fourth Intellectual Journey in Transcendent Philosophy: Volumes VIII & IX of the Asfar, trans. Latimah Peerwani (London: ICAS Press, 2008), 666–80. If we were to assume that the book's structure reflects the order of its chronological composition, then this would place Ṣadrā's treatment of this problem closer toward 1037/1628, roughly two decades after he dealt with the issue in his *Mabdaʾ*.

45. Ṣadrā, *Asfār*, 9:346–7.

46. The Aristotelian notion that love moves all things in the cosmos is in a sense commensurate with Ṣadrā's understanding of substantial motion, since motion can be defined as the inclining (*mayl*) of one thing toward another. Since the Ṣadrian doctrine of substantial motion posits that all things in existence are in an upward flow of motion back to their Source and thereby increasing in intensity, their very inclination to and arrival at their Source necessitates that they increase in love at every stage of their upward ascent, and, at the time of their arrival, become reabsorbed into their Source of love once again.

47. Ibid., 9:347. Cf. Ṣadrā, *Wisdom of the Throne*, 235–6.

48. "Whoever loves to encounter [*liqāʾ*] God, God loves to encounter him; and whoever detests to encounter God, God detests to encounter him." See Bukhārī, Riqāq 41.

49. Ṣadrā, *Asfār*, 9:347. Nevertheless, there are people who do not like to meet God. Concerning them, Ṣadrā states the position that after some time in which the sicknesses in their souls are cleansed through chastisement, they will either return to their original disposition or, after their chastisement, will return to their sickness but with the difference that the chastisement and pain will be removed in place of a second disposition which will be a form of despair (*qunūṭ*) over God's mercy, although God's general mercy will be available to all. Ṣadrā does not develop this position here, and it remains somewhat unclear until he discusses the notion of disparity in Hell in his *Tafsır Sūrat al-fātiḥa*, for which, see Chapter 7.

50. Ṣadrā, *Asfār*, 9:348. Cf. Ṣadrā, *Wisdom of the Throne*, 236–8.

51. Ṣadrā, *Asfār*, 9:348–9.

52. *Inna raḥmatī taghlibu ghaḍabī*. See Bukhārī, Tawḥīd 15. The present study's title is derived from this tradition. The other version, already alluded to in this chapter, has God say, "My mercy outstrips My wrath [*inna raḥmatī sabaqat ghaḍabī*]." For variations on these traditions, see Graham, *Divine Word and Prophetic Word*, 184–5.

53. Ṣadrā, *Asfār*, 9:349, citing Ibn ʿArabī, *Futūḥāt*, 3:648 (Beirut). Cf. Ṣadrā, *Wisdom of the Throne*, 239. Below, we will return to Ibn ʿArabī's argument—reproduced by Ṣadrā in the *Asfār* as well as the *Tafsīr Sūrat al-fātiḥa* (but with one very important difference)—concerning the manner in which chastisement in Hell becomes a form of pleasure for its inhabitants.

54. Ibn ʿArabī, *Futūḥāt*, 2:207 (Beirut), 14:214 (Cairo) (cited in Chittick, "Ibn al-ʿArabī's Hermeneutics of Mercy," 165). Cf. Ibn ʿArabī, *De la mort à la resurrection: chapitres 61 à 65 des Ouvertures Spirituelles Mekkoises*, trans. Maurice Gloton (Beirut: Albouraq, 2009), 217–8. Roberto Tottoli offers an inquiry into the reception of *zamharīr* in medieval Islamic literature in his

article, "The Qur'an, Qur'anic Exegesis and Muslim Traditions: The Case of *zamharīr* (Q. 76:13) Among Hell's Punishments," *JQS* 10, no. 1 (2008): 142–52.

55. Ṣadrā, *Asfār,* 9:349–50. The idea that punishment is a form of cleansing is not unique to Qayṣarī. For similar points made by other Muslim thinkers, see Hoover, "Islamic Universalism" (Ibn Qayyim); Khalil, *Islam and the Fate of Others,* chaps. 1 (Ghazālī) and 3 (Ibn Taymiyya and Ibn Qayyim).

56. Ṣadrā, *Asfār,* 9:350 (cf. *Spiritual Psychology,* 669). Cf. *Wisdom of the Throne*, 237n238; Nasr, *Islamic Intellectual Tradition in Persia,* 292, 301n71.

57. See Gershom Scholem, "Gilgul," in *EJ*[2].

58. Ṣadrā, *Asfār,* 9:353 (cf. *Spiritual Psychology,* 672), citing Qayṣarī, *Sharḥ,* 1:436.

59. Ṣadrā, *Asfār,* 9:350–51, citing Ibn ʿArabī, *Futūḥāt,* 3:24 (Beirut) (translated in Chittick, "Ibn al-ʿArabī's Hermeneutics of Mercy," 162). Cf. Ibn ʿArabī, *Futūḥāt,* 3:465 (Beirut) (translated in Chittick, *Sufi Path of Knowledge,* 338). For the concept of *fiṭra* in Islam, see Geneviève Gobillot, *La conception originelle: ses interprétations et fonctions chez les penseurs musulmans: la fiṭra* (Cairo: Institut français d'archéologie orientale, 2000).

60. For Ibn ʿArabī's argument as laid out in the *Futūḥāt,* see Chittick, *Sufi Path of Knowledge,* 342–3, 381.

61. Cf. Ṣadrā, *Asfār,* 9:353, where he cites Ibn ʿArabī, *Futūḥāt,* 2:225 (Beirut), 14:361 (Cairo). See also Chittick, *Self-Disclosure of God,* 86–7.

62. Ṣadrā, *Asfār,* 9:351.

63. Ibid. (cf. *Spiritual Psychology,* 671). This, Ṣadrā explains, is the sense in which they will have "eternal" punishment, since they will suffer from "the punishment of compound ignorance [*ʿadhāb al-jahl al-murakkab*]." Cf. Chittick, *Imaginal Worlds,* 101–2.

64. Ṣadrā, *Asfār,* 9:352, citing Ibn ʿArabī, *Futūḥāt,* 3:24 (Beirut) (translated in Chittick, *Self-Disclosure of God,* 188).

65. Ṣadrā, *Asfār,* 9:352.

66. Ibid.

67. Ibid. (cf. *Spiritual Psychology,* 671). Cf. Hatem, "Pure Love in Mulla Sadra," 298.

68. Ṣadrā, *Asfār,* 9:352 (cf. *Spiritual Psychology,* 671–2).

69. Ṣadrā, *Asfār,* 9:355–6.

70. See also ibid., 9:357.

71. It is unlikely that the manuscript of the *Futūḥāt* in Ṣadrā's possession offered this alternate reading. For one thing, of all of Ibn ʿArabī's books, the *Futūḥāt* has historically been the best-preserved and the one most faithfully transmitted throughout the generations. See Chodkiewicz, "Towards Reading the *Futūḥāt Makkiyya,*" in Ibn ʿArabī, *Meccan Revelations,* 1:5–7; Osman Yahia, *Histoire et classification de l'oeuvre d'Ibn ʿArabī* (Damascus: Institut Français de Damas, 1964), 1:201–35, for the text's mss. and their accompanying *samāʿ* certificates. Secondly, other parts of the *Futūḥāt* are cited by Ṣadrā elsewhere in the same discussion in the *Asfār,* and in all cases his citations are almost identical to the text of the *Futūḥāt* that has come down to us. See *Asfār* 9:349 → *Futūḥāt,* 3:648 (Beirut); *Asfār,* 9:350 → *Futūḥāt,* 3:24 (Beirut); *Asfār,* 9:353–5 → *Futūḥāt,* 2:225 (Beirut), 14:361 (Cairo); *Asfār,* 3:357–9 → *Futūḥāt,* 3:462–3 (Beirut).

72. Except in cases where Ṣadrā's reading differs from Ibn ʿArabī's, I have reproduced (with slight modifications) the passages in both cases from Chittick, *Self-Disclosure of God,* 188–9.

73. For a different translation of this passage, see Ṣadrā, *Spiritual Psychology,* 672.

74. Another possible reading of the passage could be, "For if God has decreed it in His creation, then He will remove the attribute of chastisement in the cosmos." In both cases, the Arabic particle *law,* which indicates an impossible or unlikely hypothetical clause, is to be read in conjunction with *bi-ḥayth,* thus losing its sense of impossibility / improbability. The construction *ḥattā law* in the *Futūḥāt* to be found in place of Ṣadrā's *bi-ḥayth law* also carries the effect of the *law* losing its sense of impossibility / improbability, and is thus translated by Chittick as "even if . . . ."

75. That Ṣadrā in the *Asfār* conscientiously reworded the soteriological passage in question from Ibn ʿArabī's *Futūḥāt* in order to drive home a particular point should not come as a surprise. This is a feature we find in his other writings as well, and not in matters of soteriology only. See, in particular, Kamada, "Mullā Ṣadrā's *imāma / walāya*: An Aspect of His Indebtedness to Ibn ʿArabī," *JIP* 6 (2010): 67–78.

Chapter 7

1. For references to the essential nature of mercy and the accidental nature of wrath which are particularly germane to the present chapter, see Chittick, *Imaginal Worlds,* 113; Ibn ʿArabī, *Fuṣūṣ,* 177–80; Izutsu, *Sufism and Taoism,* 99ff; Ṣadrā, *Wisdom of the Throne,* 217.

2. Along with Q 7:156, another important verse which Ṣadrā does not draw upon in the *Tafsīr Sūrat al-fātiḥa* is Q 6:12 (cf. v. 54), part of which says, "He has written mercy upon Himself" (*kataba ʿalā nafsihi al-raḥma*). A variety of medieval and modern Muslim interpretations of this verse can be found in Feras Hamza, Sajjad Rizvi with Farhana Mayer (eds.), *An Anthology of Qur'anic Commentaries (Volume 1: On the Nature of the Divine)* (Oxford: Oxford University Press in association with The Institute of Ismaili Studies, 2008), chap. 3.

3. Ṣadrā, *Tafsīr,* 1:70–1. Cf. *Tafsīr,* 1:151–2. This passage might be inspired by, if not directly based on, Ibn ʿArabī, *Fuṣūṣ,* 177. It also seems to have been reworked into Ṣadrā's *Sharḥ uṣūl al-kāfī* (see Jambet, *Act of Being,* 411). Cf. Rizvi, "The Existential Breath of *al-raḥmān* and the Munificent Grace of *al-raḥīm*: The *Tafsīr sūrat al-fātiḥa* of Jāmī and the School of Ibn ʿArabī," *JQS* 8, no. 1 (2006): 70.

4. See Appendix 2 s.v. "Man is a Macrocosm" (*Tafsīr,* 1:79). Cf. the passage from the *Asfār* translated in Chittick, "Translator's Introduction," xxiv.

5. For a discussion of the philosophical and mythic underpinnings of the doctrine of the Breath of the All-Merciful, both in terms of how it relates to the unfolding of God's Self-knowledge and the existentiation from, and return of all things to mercy, see Rustom, "Philosophical Sufism." For the Breath to the All-Merciful in Ṣadrā's Qurʾānic hermeneutics, see Chapter 1.

6. Ṣadrā, *Tafsīr*, 1:151–2. On p. 152, Ṣadrā cites a telling saying from ʿAlī: "Glory to the one whose mercy embraces His friends in the intensity of His vengeance, and whose vengeance is intensified towards His enemies in the embrace of His mercy" (for the statement in context, see Appendix 2 s.v. "The Preponderance of Mercy" [*Tafsīr*, 1:151–2]). Ṣadrā also cites it at *Tafsīr*, 7:179–80. The saying comes from ʿAlī's famous *Nahj al-balāgha* ("The Path of Eloquence"). See Maytham b. ʿAlī al-Baḥrānī, *Sharḥ Nahj al-balāgha* (Tehran: Manshūrāt-i Muʾassasat-i Naṣr, 1959), sermon # 88.

7. Ṣadrā, *Tafsīr*, 1:71. For the statement in Ibn ʿArabī, see Chittick, *Sufi Path of Knowledge*, 120, 130, 226, 338.

8. The relevant section in the *Tafsīr Sūrat al-fātiḥa* is 1:111–23, which is based on *Asfār*, 9:284–90. The latter itself serves as the basis for a similar discussion in Ṣadrā, *Wisdom of the Throne*, 191–7.

9. Ṣadrā, *Tafsīr*, 1:111, based on *Asfār*, 9:284; *Mafātīḥ*, 732–4. Ṭūsī, *Āghāz*, 7, may be an indirect source.

10. Ṣadrā, *Tafsīr*, 1:122, based on *Asfār*, 9:289. See also Ṣadrā, *Wisdom of the Throne*, 196. See also Dakake, "The Soul as *Barzakh*: Substantial Motion and Mullā Ṣadrā's Theory of Human Becoming," *MW* 94 (2004): 107–30. Ṣadrā may derive his teaching on Hell's correspondence with the earth from Neoplatonic sources. Cf. Ṣadrā, *Risālat al-ḥashr*, ed. and trans. Muḥammad Khwājawī (Tehran: Intishārāt-i Mawlā, 1983), 110–1 (Arabic text). As Rizvi notes (*Mullā Ṣadrā Shīrāzī*, 100), this treatise was completed in 1032/1623.

11. See Ṭūsī, *Āghāz*, 129 (section containing Āmulī's *Taʿlīqāt*). Cf. Nāṣir-i Khusraw, *Knowledge and Liberation*, 104–6.

12. See Corbin, *En islam iranien*, 1:302.

13. For substantial motion in Ṣadrā, see Mahdi Dehbashi, *Transubstantial Motion and the Natural World: With a Translation of Volume III, Stage 7, Chapters 18–32 of the Asfar of Mulla Sadra* (London: ICAS Press, 2011); Kalin, "Between Physics and Metaphysics: Mullā Ṣadrā on Nature and Motion," *IS* 1, no. 1 (2003): 59–90. See also Corbin's comments in *En islam iranien*, 4:84–95, and Ṣadrā, *Le livre des pénétrations métaphysiques*, 227–8n117.

14. See Ṣadrā, *Asfār*, 8:333–4, 350.

15. Ṣadrā, *Tafsīr*, 1:112.

16. Ibid. Cf. *Wisdom of the Throne*, 193.

17. Cf. Ṣadrā, *Tafsīr*, 1:80, 113. See also Jambet, *Act of Being*, 414.

18. See Ṣadrā, *Asfār*, 9:356.

19. Ṣadrā, *Tafsīr*, 1:175. Since the Perfect Man is the original end purpose of creation, Ṣadrā says that he is guided, blessed, and under God's solicitude from his beginning to his end. He also makes it clear that those who do not receive this solicitude are afflicted (ibid., 1:102–3). See also Appendix 2 s.v. "The Path of the Perfect Man" (*Tafsīr*, 1:108).

20. Ṣadrā, *Tafsīr*, 1:113. He goes on to cite Ibn ʿArabī to prove substantial motion. See *Tafsīr*, 1:114. See also Jambet, *Act of Being*, 185, where the author suggests that Ṣadrā's doctrine of substantial motion was intuited on the basis of Ibn ʿArabī's "theosophy."

21. Ṣadrā, *Tafsīr*, 1:116. Cf. Chittick, *Imaginal Worlds*, 113–9.

22. Ṣadrā, *Tafsīr*, 1:117.

23. Ibid., 1:111.

24. Ibid., 1:118. Ṣadrā also anticipates another objection: why is there preference/priority in rank and difference in the *fiṭra* itself, and does that not compromise God's justice? He begins by answering that, firstly, this question has given many thinkers a particularly hard time. The differences exist as a result of the very structure and order of being. If there were no gradation, there would not be a multiplicity of things. So it is because of God's justice and equanimity that grades exist. See ibid., 1:118–22, and Appendix 2 s.v. "Why People's Natures Differ" (*Tafsīr*, 1:118–21). For the logic underlying this position, see Kalin, "Mullā Ṣadrā on Theodicy and the Best of All Possible Worlds," *JIS* 18, no. 2 (2007): 183–207.

25. Ṣadrā, *Tafsīr*, 1:108.

26. Recall the famous Sufi dictum which tells us that there are as many paths to God as there are children of Adam.

27. Ṣadrā, *Tafsīr*, 1:42.

28. Cf. ibid., 1:166.

29. Ibid., 1:42, citing ibid., 4:51–2.

30. Cf. ibid., 1:47–8.

31. See Ṣadrā's use of this tradition at ibid., 1:72, 157–8; 3:338. Cf. Chittick, *Sufi Path of Knowledge*, 396n24. For the text of the *ḥadīth*, see Graham, *Divine Word and Prophetic Word*, 190.

32. Ṣadrā, *Tafsīr*, 1:42. As noted in Chapter 2, Ṣadrā says that God's name *al-raḥmān* takes precedence over *al-raḥīm*, which reflects a common understanding of these two terms. One of the most interesting interpretations for why this is the case is to be found in Shahrastānī's commentary upon the Fātiḥa. In the introduction to his translation of this text (*Keys to the Arcana*, 12), Toby Mayer explains it in this way: "*Raḥmān* is exclusive in predicability (used only of God) but inclusive in operation (extending to all existents) while *Raḥīm* is inclusive in predicability (used of God and creature) but exclusive in operation (extending only to believers). Or as he [i.e., Shahrastānī] himself puts this: '*Raḥmān* is specific as a name (*khāṣṣ al-ism*) but general in meaning (*ʿāmm al-maʿnā*) and *Raḥīm* is general as a name (*ʿāmm al-ism*) but specific in meaning (*khāṣṣ al-maʿnā*).' "

33. In yet another passage toward the end of the *Tafsīr Sūrat al-fātiḥa*, Ṣadrā elucidates the point he made earlier. Meditating on Q 1:7, which speaks of those with whom God is angry (*al-maghḍūb ʿalayhim*), Ṣadrā, most likely under the influence of Ibn ʿArabī (although I have been unable to locate the passage in Ibn ʿArabī's writings), states that there will come a point when even those with whom God is angry will eventually be pardoned because God will transmute (*taḥawwala*) Himself in the form of bliss. Since the return for all is back to God, the God with whom they will abide eternally will be one who is pleased with them by virtue of the preponderance of the ruling property of His contentment (*riḍāʾ*). See Appendix 2 s.v. "The Transmutations of God" (*Tafsīr*, 1:154).

34. Ṣadrā refers to this famous tradition at *Tafsīr*, 1:149.

35. Ibid.

36. Ibid. The last part of the closing sentence literally reads, "is in opposition to the other from the standpoint of their owners." Cf. this passage with Chittick, *Sufi Path of Knowledge*, 156–61.

37. See Chapter 6 for Ṣadrā's use of this image.

38. Ṣadrā, *Tafsīr*, 1:151.

39. Cf. ibid., 1:157. Cf. also ibid., 1:159–61, where Ṣadrā follows Qūnawī, *Iʿjāz*, 475–8, in his discussion of how chastisement exists either to protect or purify the servant.

40. Ṣadrā, *Tafsīr*, 1:151.

41. Cf. ibid.

42. According to Qayṣarī, the Throne is the seat upon which the Muhammadan Reality is established, and from which mercy is distributed throughout the cosmos. This reading is in keeping with the Qurʾānic idea of the All-Merciful being seated upon the Throne, for the Muhammadan Reality is the locus of manifestation for the name *al-raḥmān*. See Rustom, "Dāwūd al-Qayṣarī," 57ff. See also Jambet, *Act of Being*, 414.

43. Cf. Chittick, *Imaginal Worlds*, 111–2; Chittick, *Sufi Path of Knowledge*, 359–61.

44. Ṣadrā, *Tafsīr*, 1:154–5.

45. Cf. ibid., 1:149, where he takes his lead from Ibn ʿArabī and his followers when discussing God's feet. See Appendix 2 s.v. "God's Hands and Feet" (*Tafsīr*, 1:149–50). Cf. Murata, *The Tao of Islam: A Sourcebook on Gender Relationships in Islamic Thought* (Albany: State University of New York Press, 1992), 85–8.

46. Ibn ʿArabī, *Futūḥāt*, 3:462 (Beirut).

47. Ṣadrā, *Tafsīr*, 1:155, paraphrasing Ibn ʿArabī, *Futūḥāt*, 3:462 (Beirut) (for a partial translation of the original, see Chittick, *Sufi Path of Knowledge*, 360–1), also cited in slightly altered fashion in Ṣadrā, *Asfār*, 9:357.

48. Ṣadrā, *Tafsīr*, 1:155, paraphrasing Ibn ʿArabī, *Futūḥāt*, 3:462 (Beirut), also cited in Ṣadrā, *Asfār*, 9:357–8.

49. Ṣadrā, *Tafsīr*, 1:155. At *Futūḥāt*, 3:462 (Beirut), Ibn ʿArabī simply has "reflection" (*naẓar*). For the two texts in translation and in juxtaposition with one another, see Appendix 3, text III.

50. Ṣadrā, *Tafsīr*, 1:155.

51. See ibid.

52. See also the summary of positions in al-Mannāʿī, "ʿAqīdat fanāʾ al-nār," 96–121.

53. With this question in mind, Martin Lings remarks, "God knows that the worst sinners in Hell are totally innocent of one thing, namely their own existence, for which He alone is responsible" (*A Return to the Spirit: Questions and Answers* [Louisville: Fons Vitae, 2005], 77).

54. Ibn ʿArabī says that in the expression *khālidīna fīhā*, the feminine pronoun *hāʾ* always goes back to the word Fire (*nār*) and not to chastisement (*ʿadhāb*), which is masculine at any rate. In other words, Ibn ʿArabī argues, there will indeed be people who abide in Hell forever, but they will not abide in their state of punishment forever. See Chittick, *Imaginal Worlds*, 113;

Ibn ʿArabī, *Futūḥāt*, 3:77 (Beirut). Cf. Abrahamov, "Creation and Duration," 94, as well as the discussion on *khālidīna fīhā abadan* in James Robson, "Is the Moslem Hell Eternal?," *MW* 28 (1938): 386–93 (pp. 386–8 in particular). For an unnuanced approach to the question, see Rosalind Gwynne, "Hell and Hellfire," in *EQ*.

55. See Ibn Qayyim al-Jawziyya, *Shifāʾ al-ʿalīl fī l-masāʾil al-qaḍāʾ wa-l-qadar wa-l-ḥikma wa-l-taʿlīl*, ed. Muṣṭafā al-Shalabī (Jeddah: Maktabat al-Sawādī li-l-Tawzīʿ, 1991), 2:228, 39, cited in Khalil, *Islam and the Fate of Others*, chap. 3. It can further be noted that the two verses in question (Q 10:15 and 32:14) explicitly speak of "tasting" eternal punishment. Thus, the argument can be put forward that these verses favor the reading that punishment in Hell cannot be eternal: Hell is so intense and painful that even just a "taste" of eternal punishment in it would suffice as requital.

56. Another argument that Ibn ʿArabī gives, and which Ṣadrā does not draw upon in his writings when discussing soteriology, is that the belief in God's universal mercy in the afterlife is in keeping with a *ḥadīth qudsī* which states that God's servant should have a good opinion of Him. See Ibn ʿArabī, *Futūḥāt*, 2:206 (Beirut). See also al-Mannāʿī, "ʿAqīdat fanāʾ al-nār," 125. The *ḥadīth qudsī* which Ibn ʿArabī has in mind (and which he cites a number of times—i.e., *Futūḥāt*, 1:473, 2:185, 3:377, 4:446 [Beirut], etc.) reads, "I am with My servant according to his opinion of Me. So let him think well of Me." For variations of this *ḥadīth qudsī*, see Graham, *Divine Word and Prophetic Word*, 130.

57. See Chapter 6 and the earlier parts of the present chapter for the logic underlying this perspective.

58. See Ṣadrā, *Tafsīr*, 1:345–6, 347–8. For the *Tafsīr Sūrat al-baqara*'s dates, see Rustom, "Nature and Significance," 129–30.

59. Ṣadrā, *Tafsīr*, 1:346–9, following ibid., 4:314–21.

60. Ibid., 2:188–9.

61. Ibid., 3:328ff.

62. Ibid., 3:336.

63. Ibid., 3:338.

64. Ibid., 1:363–5.

65. Ibid., 1:375–6.

66. Ibid., 1:365–72.

67. See ibid., 1:365–75.

68. See ibid., 1:372–4. See also ibid. 1:348–9, which closely follows Qayṣarī. For Ṣadrā's use of Qayṣarī's soteriology in the *Tafsīr Āyat al-kursī*, see Chapter 6.

69. See Qūnawī, *Iʿjāz*, 317. At ibid., 469, Qūnawī alludes to the fact that God's wrath must come to an end. Cf. Jāmī, *Naqd*, 189–90. It is also interesting to note that in his Sufi Qurʾān commentary, the famous member of the school of Ibn ʿArabī, ʿAbd al-Razzāq Kāshānī (d. 736/1335), upholds a belief in the non-eternality of Hell, although he is not as explicit as Ibn ʿArabī in this regard. See Lory, *Les commentaires ésotériques*, 129–32. But, as expected, in his commentary upon the seventh chapter of Ibn ʿArabī's *Fuṣūṣ*, he makes

his stance clear. See Kāshānī, *Sharḥ Fuṣūṣ al-ḥikam* (Cairo: Al-Maktaba al-Azhariyya li-l-Turāth, 2003), 144–158.

70. Ṣadrā, *Wisdom of the Throne*, 240.

71. Ibid., 135.

72. This point was communicated to me by the late Hossein Ziai in an email correspondence dated February 11th, 2008. The specific reference would be in the second volume of Ṣadrā's *Addenda*, which is yet to be published.

73. See Khwājawī's note at Ṣadrā, *Tafsīr*, 4:321n1. Cf. Āshtiyānī's gloss at *Shawāhid*, 778–9.

74. For a discussion of his treatment of this issue, see Chapter 6.

75. See Naṣīrī, *Maktab-i tafsīrī*, 308, which approvingly cites Khwājawī's note at Ṣadrā, *Tafsīr*, 4:321n1.

76. See Naṣīrī, *Maktab-i tafsīrī*, 308.

77. Which is what Naṣīrī does. See Chapter 6.

78. See Chodkiewicz, "The *Futūḥāt Makkiyya* and its Commentators: Some Unresolved Enigmas," trans. Peter Kingsley in *The Heritage of Sufism*, 2:221.

79. See John Cooper, "Some Observations on the Religious Intellectual Milieu of Safawid Persia," in *Intellectual Traditions in Islam*, ed. Farhad Daftary (London: I. B. Tauris in association with The Institute of Ismaili Studies, 2000), 146–59; Nasrollah Pourjavady, "Opposition to Sufism in Twelver Shiism," in *Islamic Mysticism Contested: Thirteen Centuries of Controversies and Polemics*, ed. Frederick De Jong and Bernd Radtke (Leiden: Brill, 1999), 614–24. An overview of the interaction between different intellectual and spiritual currents in the Safavid period can be found in Nasr, "Spiritual Movements, Philosophy and Theology in the Safavid Period," in *The Cambridge History of Iran*, ed. Peter Jackson and Laurence Lockhart (Cambridge: Cambridge University Press, 1986), 6:656–97.

80. Perhaps the earliest source which mentions the opposition of Ṣadrā's son to his father can be found in the *Lu'lu'at al-Baḥrayn* ("The Pearl of Bahrain") by the Akhbārī scholar Aḥmad b. Ibrāhīm al-Baḥrānī (d. 1186/1772). Although I did not have access to this text, the relevant section is reproduced in Maʿṣūm ʿAlī Shāh, *Ṭarā'iq al-ḥaqā'iq*, ed. Muḥammad Jaʿfar Maḥjūb (Tehran: Kitābkhāna-yi Sanā'ī, 1960), 1:181–2. For the opposition of Ṣadrā's son to his father's mystical and philosophical teachings, see also Sayyid Muḥsin al-Amīn, *Aʿyān al-shīʿa* (Beirut: Dār al-Taʿāruf li-l-Maṭbūʿāt, 1983), 2:202. Given the *Aʿyān*'s general attitude toward Ṣadrā (see *Aʿyān*, 9:321–30), the point about Ṣadrā's son may have a polemical function here.

81. Ṣadrā, *Wisdom of the Throne*, 237n283.

82. See Morris, "Introduction," 43. As noted by Rizvi, *Mullā Ṣadrā Shīrāzī*, 33, one of Ṣadrā's positions which was later condemned by the famous author of the *Biḥār al-anwār* Muḥammad Bāqir Majlisī (d. 1111/1699) was his belief in the non-eternality of Hell. At the same time, as Corbin points out, Majlisī's attitude toward Mullā Ṣadrā remains ambiguous. See Corbin, *En islam iranien*, 4:20–1, as well as Newman, *Safavid Iran*, 96–100. We are also told

that some scholars had accused Ṣadrā of infidelity (*kufr*), presumably after his death, because of statements he made in his commentary upon al-Kulaynī's *Kāfī*. See Maʿṣūm ʿAlī Shāh, *Ṭarāʾiq*, 1:182. As for Ṣadrā's own attitude toward the exoteric *ʿulamāʾ* of his day, it would be an understatement to say that he did not view them too favorably. See, for example, the introduction to his *Sih aṣl*. Al-Amīn takes particular issue with Ṣadrā's condemnation of the *ʿulamāʾ* at *Aʿyān*, 9:329–30.

83. Cf. Chittick, "Ibn al-ʿArabī's Hermeneutics of Mercy," 166. After this point, Ṣadrā makes it clear that he is reporting a text from Ibn ʿArabī, but does not note that what had preceded this and what is to follow is also from the latter's pen.

84. For this *ḥadīth*, which speaks of God (as *al-jabbār*) extinguishing the flames of Hell by placing His foot in Hell, see Chittick, *Sufi Path of Knowledge*, 361; Murata, *Tao of Islam*, 86. Cf. the perplexing remark in Naṣīrī, *Maktab-i tafsīrī*, 183, which occurs in the context of his discussion of Ṣadrā's use of this *ḥadīth qudsī* in the *Tafsīr Sūrat al-fātiḥa*.

85. Ibn ʿArabī has *tanazzul al-ilāhī al-laṭīf*. See Chittick, *Sufi Path of Knowledge*, 361; Murata, *Tao of Islam*, 86.

86. Ṣadrā, *Tafsīr*, 1:156, reworked from Ibn ʿArabī, *Futūḥāt*, 3:463 (Beirut), also cited in Ṣadrā, *Asfār*, 9:358–9 (cf. *Spiritual Psychology*, 677). Cf. Chittick, "Ibn al-ʿArabī's Hermeneutics of Mercy," 166; Chittick, *Self-Disclosure of God*, 174; Murata, *Tao of Islam*, 86. For a lengthy passage from Qayṣarī's commentary upon the *Fuṣūṣ* in which he explains how punishment is sweetness, see Ibn ʿArabī, *Ringstones of Wisdom*, 85–6n29. See also the nuanced explanation of this position in Jīlī, *al-Insān al-kāmil* (Beirut: Muʾassasat al-Tārīkh al-ʿArabī, 2000), 179–90. This section of the work (i.e., chapter 58) deserves closer study.

87. Cf. Ṣadrā, *Tafsīr*, 1:71–2, citing Ibn ʿArabī, *Futūḥāt*, 2:86–7 (Beirut), 12:395–6 (Cairo). For the text, see Appendix 2 s.v. "The End for All is Mercy" (*Tafsīr*, 1:71–2). For this passage in ʿIrāqī, see *Divine Flashes*, 95. For Ibn ʿArabī's reply, see Chittick, *Sufi Path of Knowledge*, 37; Chittick, *Self-Disclosure of God*, 23.

88. See, for example, Jambet, *Act of Being*, 211, 386–98, 470n44; Ṣadrā, *Asfār*, 8:135–6, translated in Chittick, "Translator's Introduction," xxvi.

89. Rizvi, *Mullā Ṣadrā Shīrāzī*, 11–3, makes it clear that Mīr Dāmād and Ṣadrā had great affection for one another. At the same time, Mīr Dāmād's position concerning the existence/essence debate was that essence was real and principial and existence unreal and accidental. There is no doubt therefore that Ṣadrā's conversion to the position of the fundamentality of being was a direct consequence of his reaction to his teacher's ideas. In the case of Ibn ʿArabī, Ṣadrā seems to side with him almost unequivocally on every issue. But see Chapter 6 for Ṣadrā's slight disagreement with Ibn ʿArabī, as well as Ṣadrā's *Risālat al-ḥashr*, 112–4 (Arabic text). One can aver that Ṣadrā almost always sees eye-to-eye with Ibn ʿArabī for the simple reason that his position concerning the fundamentality of being, although worked out by him in its philosophical form against the backdrop of his highly original dynamic metaphysics, is nothing other than *waḥdat al-wujūd* or the Oneness of Being. For Ṣadrā, the notion of *wujūd*'s dynamism and hence its "act" is a natural

corollary to his doctrine of *wujūd*'s gradational nature. Cf. Rizvi, *Mullā Ṣadrā and Metaphysics*, 45–6.

90. It can be noted here that few if any readers familiar with Ibn ʿArabī's writings would not notice Ṣadrā's borrowings from the former. See Chodkiewicz, "*Futūḥāt Makkiyya* and its Commentators," 221, where he notes that even when Ṣadrā had to conceal his borrowings from Ibn ʿArabī for reasons of prudence, they "are easily identifiable nonetheless."

91. Cf. Morris, "Introduction," 35–6.

Bibliography

Works by Mullā Ṣadrā

Addenda on the Commentary on the Philosophy of Illumination. Edited by Hossein Ziai. Costa Mesa, Mazda: 2010–.

al-ʿArshiyya. Reprint. Beirut: Muʾassasat al-Tārīkh al-ʿArabī, 2000.

Asrār al-āyāt wa-anwār al-bayyināt. Edited by Sayyid Muḥammad Mūsawī. Tehran: Intishārāt-i Ḥikmat, 2006.

Breaking the Idols of Ignorance: Admonition of the Soi-Disant Sufi. Translated by Mahdi Dasht Bozorgi and Fazel Asadi Amjad. London: ICAS Press, 2008.

The Elixir of the Gnostics. Edited and translated by William Chittick. Provo: Brigham Young University Press, 2003.

al-Ḥikma al-mutaʿāliya fī l-asfār al-ʿaqliyya al-arbaʿa. Edited by Riḍā Luṭfī, Ibrāhīm Amīnī, and Fatḥ Allāh Ummīd. Beirut: Dār Iḥyāʾ al-Turāth al-ʿArabī, 1981.

Kasr aṣnām al-jāhiliyya. Edited by Muḥammad Taqī Dānishpazhū. Tehran: University of Tehran Press, 1962.

Kitāb al-Mashāʿir. Edited and translated by Henry Corbin as *Le livre des penetrations métaphysiques*. Tehran: Département d'iranologie de l'Institut franco-iranien, 1964.

al-Mabdaʾ wa-l-maʿād. Edited by Jalāl al-Dīn Āshtiyānī. Tehran: Imperial Iranian Academy of Philosophy, 1976.

Mafātīḥ al-ghayb. Edited by Muḥammad Khwājawī. Reprint. Beirut: Muʾassasat al-Tārīkh al-ʿArabī, 2002.

Majmūʿat al-tafāsīr. Lithographed by Aḥmad Shīrāzī. Tehran, 1904.

Majmūʿa-yi ashʿār-i Ṣadr al-Dīn Shīrāzī. Edited by Muḥammad Khwājawī. Reprint. Tehran: Intishārāt-i Mawlā, 2003.

al-Masāʾil al-qudsiyya. In Ṣadrā, *Sih risāla-yi falsafī*, 185–254.

Mutashābihāt al-Qurʾān. In Ṣadrā, *Sih risāla-yi falsafī*, 257–84.

On the Hermeneutics of the Light Verse of the Qurʾān. Translated by Latimah Peerwani. London: ICAS Press, 2004.

Die Risāla fī l-ḥudūṯ (Die Abhandlung über die Entstehung). Translated by S. M. Bagher Talgharizadeh. Berlin: Klaus Schwarz, 2000.

Risālat al-ḥashr. Edited and translated into Persian by Muḥammad Khwājawī. Tehran: Intishārāt-i Mawlā, 1983.

Sharḥ Uṣūl al-kāfī. Edited by Muḥammad Khwājawī. Tehran: Muʾassasa-yi Muṭālaʿāt wa-Taḥqīqāt-i Farhangī, 1987.

al-Shawāhid al-rubūbiyya. Edited by Jalāl al-Dīn Āshtiyānī. Mashhad: Chāpkhāna-yi Dānishgāh-i Mashhad, 1967.

Sih aṣl. Edited by Seyyed Hossein Nasr. Tehran: University of Tehran Press, 1961.

Sih risāla-yi falsafī. Edited by Jalāl al-Dīn Āshtiyānī. 2nd ed. Tehran: Markazī-yi Intishārāt-i Daftar-i Tablīghāt-i Islāmī, 2000.

Spiritual Psychology: The Fourth Intellectual Journey in Transcendent Philosophy: Volumes VIII & IX of the Asfar. Translated by Latimah Peerwani. London: ICAS Press, 2008.

Tafsīr al-Qurʾān al-karīm. Edited by Muḥammad Khwājawī. Qum: Intishārāt-i Bīdār, 1987–90.

Tafsīr Sūrat al-fātiḥa. Ms. Tehran National Library 263.

The Three Principles of Mullā Ṣadrā: Divine Gnosis, Self-Realisation and the Dangers of Pseudo-Knowledge in Islam. Translated by Colin Turner. London: Routledge, forthcoming.

The Wisdom of the Throne. Translated by James Morris. Princeton, NJ: Princeton University Press, 1981.

Yāddāsht-hā-yi Mullā Ṣadrā hamrāh bā fihrist-i kitābkhāna-yi shakhṣī-yi Mullā Ṣadrā. Edited by Muḥammad Barakat. Qum: Intishārāt-i Bīdār, 1998.

Primary Sources

Afandī, Mīrzā ʿAbd Allāh. *Riyāḍ al-ʿulamāʾ wa-ḥiyāḍ al-fuḍalāʾ*. Edited by Sayyid Aḥmad Ḥusaynī. Qum: Maṭbaʿat al-Khayyām, 1981.

Ālūsī, Maḥmūd b. ʿAbd Allāh al-. *Rūḥ al-maʿānī fī tafsīr al-Qurʾān al-ʿaẓīm wa-l-sabʿ al-mathānī*. Beirut: Dār Iḥyāʾ al-Turāth al-ʿArabī, 1970.

ʿĀmilī, Muḥammad b. al-Ḥasan al-Ḥurr al-. *Amal al-āmil*. Edited by Sayyid Aḥmad Ḥusaynī. Baghdad: Maktabat al-Andalus, 1965.

Aristotle. *The Complete Works of Aristotle: The Revised Oxford Translation*. Edited by Jonathan Barnes. Princeton, NJ: Princeton University Press, 1984.

Āshtiyānī, Jalāl al-Dīn, ed. *Tafsīr Fātiḥat al-kitāb*. Mashhad: Chāpkhāna-yi Dānishgāh-i Mashhad, 1978.

Averroës. *Decisive Treatise and Epistle Dedicatory*. Translated by Charles Butterworth. Provo: Brigham Young University Press, 2001.

Avicenna. *Ibn Sīnā on Mysticism: Remarks and Admonitions, Part 4*. Translated by Shams Inati. London: Keagan Paul, 1996.

———. *al-Ishārāt wa-l-tanbīhāt*. Edited by Sulaymān Dunyā. Cairo: Dār al-Maʿārif, 1957–60.

———. *al-Risāla al-nayrūziyya fī maʿānī al-ḥurūf al-hijāʾiyya*. In Avicenna, *Tisʿ rasāʾil*, 92–7.

———. *Tisʿ rasāʾil*. Constantinople: Maṭbaʿat al-Jawāʾib, 1880.

Ayoub, Mahmoud, trans. *The Qur'an and Its Interpreters*. Albany: State University of New York Press, 1984–92.

Baḥrānī, Maytham b. ʿAlī al-. *Sharḥ Nahj al-balāgha*. Tehran: Manshūrāt-i Muʾassasat-i Naṣr, 1959.

Bayḍāwī, ʿAbd Allāh b. ʿUmar. *Anwār al-tanzīl wa-asrār al-taʾwīl*. Cairo: Dār al-Kutub al-ʿArabiyya, 1911.

Bukhārī, Muḥammad b. Ismaʿīl al-. *al-Ṣaḥīḥ*. N. p.: Maṭābiʿ al-Shuʿab, 1958–9.

Farghānī, Saʿīd al-Dīn. *Muntahā l-madārik*. Cairo, 1876.

Ghazālī, Abū Ḥāmid Muḥammad al-. *Iḥyāʾ ʿulūm al-dīn*. Beirut: Dār al-Jayl, 1997.

———. *The Jewels of the Qurʾān: Al-Ghazāli's Theory*. Translated by Muhammad Abul Quasem. Kuala Lumpur: University of Malaya Press, 1977.

———. *The Niche of Lights*. Translated by David Buchman. Provo: Brigham Young University Press, 1998.

Hamadānī, ʿAyn al-Quḍāt. *Nāmahā*. Edited by ʿAlī Naqī Munzawī (vols. 1–3) and ʿAfīf ʿUsayrān (vols. 1–2). Tehran: Intishārāt-i Asāṭīr, 1998.

———. *Tamhīdāt*. Edited by ʿAfīf ʿUsayrān. 4th ed. Tehran: Intishārāt-i Manūchirī, 1994.

Ḥamawī, Yāqūt al-. *Muʿjam al-buldān*. Reprint. Beirut: Dār Ṣādir, 1977.

Hamza, Feras, and Sajjad Rizvi with Farhana Mayer, eds. *An Anthology of Qur'anic Commentaries (Volume 1: On the Nature of the Divine)*. Oxford: Oxford University Press in association with The Institute of Ismaili Studies, 2008.

Heidegger, Martin. "Qu'est-ce que la métaphysique?" Translated by Henry Corbin. *Bifur* 8 (1931): 5–27.

Ibn ʿArabī. *De la mort à la resurrection: chapitres 61 à 65 des Ouvertures Spirituelles Mekkoises*. Translated by Maurice Gloton. Beirut: Albouraq, 2009.

———. *Fuṣūṣ al-ḥikam*. Edited by A. E. Afifi. Beirut: Dār al-Kutub al-ʿArabī, 1946.

———. *al-Futūḥāt al-makkiyya*. Reprint. Beirut: Dār Ṣādir, n. d.; partial critical edition edited by Osman Yahia. Cairo: al-Hayʾa al-Miṣriyya al-ʿĀmma li-l-Kitāb, 1972–91.

———. *The Meccan Revelations*. Edited by Michel Chodkiewicz. New York: Pir Press, 2002–4.

———. *The Ringstones of Wisdom*. Translated by Caner Dagli. Chicago: Kazi, 2004.

Ibn Hishām, ʿAbd al-Malik. *al-Sīra al-nabawiyya*. Edited by Muṣṭafā al-Saqqā, Ibrāhīm al-Abyārī, and ʿAbd al-Ḥafīẓ Shalabī. Cairo: Muṣṭafā al-Bābī al-Ḥalabī, 1955.

ʿIrāqī, Fakhr al-Dīn Ibrāhīm. *Divine Flashes*. Translated by William Chittick and Peter Wilson. Mahwah, NJ: Paulist Press, 1982.

Jaʿfar al-Ṣādiq. *Spiritual Gems: The Mystical Qurʾān Commentary Ascribed by the Sufis to Imām Jaʿfar al-Ṣādiq (d. 148/765)*. Translated by Farhana Mayer. Louisville: Fons Vitae, 2011.

Jāmī, ʿAbd al-Raḥmān. *Naqd al-nuṣūṣ fī sharḥ Naqsh al-fuṣūṣ*. Edited by William Chittick. Tehran: Imperial Iranian Academy of Philosophy, 1977.

Jandī, Muʾayyid al-Dīn. *Sharḥ Fuṣūṣ al-ḥikam*. Edited by Jalāl al-Dīn Āshtiyānī. Mashhad: Dānishgāh-i Mashhad, 1982.

Jawziyya, Ibn Qayyim al-. *Shifāʾ al-ʿalīl fī l-masāʾil al-qaḍāʾ wa-l-qadar wa-l-ḥikma wa-l-taʿlīl*. Edited by Muṣṭafā al-Shalabī. Jeddah: Maktabat al-Sawādī li-l-Tawzīʿ, 1991.

Jīlī, ʿAbd al-Karīm. *Un commentaire ésotérique de la formule inaugurale du Qoran: "Les mystères cryptographiques de Bismi-Llâhi-r-Raḥmâni-Raḥîm"*. Translated by Jabir Clément-François. Beirut: Albouraq, 2002.

———. *al-Insān al-kāmil*. Beirut: Muʾassasat al-Tārīkh al-ʿArabī, 2000.

Kāshānī, ʿAbd al-Razzāq. *Sharḥ Fuṣūṣ al-ḥikam*. Cairo: Al-Maktaba al-Azhariyya li-l-Turāth, 2003.

Khusraw, Nāṣir-i. *Knowledge and Liberation: A Treatise on Philosophical Theology*. Edited and translated by Faquir Hunzai. London: I. B. Tauris in association with The Institute of Ismaili Studies, 1998.

Khwānsarī, Muḥammad Bāqir. *Rawḍāt al-jannāt fī aḥwāl al-ʿulamāʾ wa-l-sādāt*. Tehran: Kitābfurūshī-yi Islāmī, 1976–81.

Majlisī, ʿAllāma Muḥammad Bāqir. *Biḥār al-anwār*. Qum, 1956–72.

Maybudī, Rashīd al-Dīn. *Kashf al-asrār wa-ʿuddat al-abrār*. Edited by ʿAlī Aṣghar Ḥikmat. Tehran: Chāpkhāna-yi Dānishgāh-i Tihrān, 1952–60.

Muḥāsibī, ʿAbd Allāh al-Ḥārith b. Asad al-. *al-Riʿāya li-ḥuqūq Allāh*. Edited by ʿAbd al-Qādir Aḥmad ʿAṭāʾ. Cairo: Dār al-Kutub al-Ḥadītha, 1971.

Nasafī, ʿAbd Allāh b. Aḥmad al-. *Madārik al-tanzīl wa-ḥaqāʾiq al-taʾwīl*. Edited by Marwān Muḥammad al-Shaʿʿār. Beirut: Dār al-Nafāʾis, 1996.

Nasr, Seyyed Hossein and Mehdi Aminrazavi, eds. *An Anthology of Philosophy in Persia*. London: I. B. Tauris in association with The Institute of Ismaili Studies, 2008–.

Nīsābūrī, Abū Rashīd al-. *al-Masāʾil fī l-khilāf bayna al-Baṣrīyīn wa-l-Baghdādīyīn*. Edited by Riḍwān Sayyid and Maʿn Ziyāda. Tarabulus: Maʿhad al-Inmāʾ al-ʿArabī, 1979.

Plato. *Complete Works*. Edited by John Cooper and D. S. Hutchinson. Indianapolis: Hackett, 1997.

Qayṣarī, Dāwūd b. Maḥmūd al-. *Maṭlaʿ khuṣūṣ al-kalim fī maʿānī Fuṣūṣ al-ḥikam (Sharḥ Fuṣūṣ al-ḥikam)*. Qum: Instishārāt Anwār al-Hudā, 2002.

Qūnawī, Abū l-Maʿālī Ṣadr al-Dīn al-. *Risālat al-nuṣūṣ*. Edited by Jalāl al-Dīn Āshtiyānī. Tehran: Markaz-i Nashr-i Dānishgāhī, 1983.

———. *al-Tafsīr al-ṣūfī li-l-Qurʾān (Iʿjāz al-bayān fī taʾwīl umm al-Qurʾān)*. Edited by ʿAbd al-Qādir Aḥmad ʿAṭāʾ. Cairo: Dār al-Kutub al-Ḥadītha, 1969.

Rāzī, Fakhr al-Dīn Muḥammad b. ʿUmar al-. *al-Maṭālib al-ʿāliya min al-ʿilm al-ilāhī*. Edited by Muḥammad ʿAbd al-Salām Shāhīn. Beirut: Dār al-Kutub al-ʿIlmiyya, 1999.

———. *al-Tafsīr al-kabīr*. Cairo: al-Maṭbaʿa al-Bahiyya al-Miṣriyya, 1934–8.

Rāzī, Najm al-Dīn al-. *Mirṣād al-ʿibād*. Edited by Muḥammad Amīn Riyāḥī. Tehran: Bungāh-i Tarjama wa-Nashr-i Kitāb, 1973.

Rūmī, Jalāl al-Dīn. *Mathnawī-yi maʿnawī*. Edited and translated by R. A. Nicholson as *The Mathnawí of Jalálu'ddín Rúmí*. London: Luzac, 1924–40.

Sabziwārī, Mullā Hādī. *The Metaphysics of Sabzavārī*. Translated by Mehdi Mohaghegh and Toshihiko Izutsu. Delmar: Caravan, 1977.

———. *Sharḥ-i Manẓūma*. Edited by Mehdi Mohaghegh and Toshihiko Izutsu. Tehran: McGill University Institute of Islamic Studies, 1969.

Shāh, Maʿṣūm ʿAlī. *Ṭarāʾiq al-ḥaqāʾiq*. Edited by Muḥammad Jaʿfar Maḥjūb. Tehran: Kitābkhāna-yi Sanāʾī, 1960.

Shahrastānī, Muḥammad b. ʿAbd al-Karīm al-. *Keys to the Arcana: Shahrastānī's Esoteric Commentary on the Qurʾān*. Translated by Toby Mayer. Oxford: Oxford University Press in association with The Institute of Ismaili Studies, 2009.

———. *al-Milal wa-l-niḥal*. Edited by Ṣidqī al-ʿAṭṭār. Reprint. Beirut: Dār al-Fikr, 2002.

Shīrāzī, Ibn Maʿṣūm. *Sulāfat al-ʿaṣr fī maḥāsin al-shuʿarāʾ bi-kull miṣr*. Cairo: Maktabat al-Wafd, 1906.

Suhrawardī, Shihāb al-Dīn. *Āyat-i ishrāq: Tafsīr wa-taʾwīl-i āyāt-i Qurʾān-i karīm dar āthār-i Suhrawardī*. Edited by Sīmā Nūrbakhsh. Tehran: Mihr Niyūshā, 2008.

———. *Majmūʿa-yi muṣannafāt-i Shaykh-i Ishrāq*. Edited by Henry Corbin (vols. 1–2) and Seyyed Hossein Nasr (vol. 3). Reprint. Tehran: Imperial Iranian Academy of Philosophy, 1976–7.

———. *The Philosophy of Illumination*. Edited and translated by John Walbridge and Hossein Ziai. Provo: Brigham Young University Press, 1999.

Tirmidhī, Muḥammad b. ʿIsā al-. *al-Jāmiʿ al- ṣaḥīḥ*. Edited by A. M. Shākir. Cairo: al-Maktabat al-Islāmiyya, 1938.

Ṭūsī, Muḥammad b. Ḥasan al-. *al-Tibyān fī tafsīr al-Qurʾān*. Edited by Aḥmad al-Amīn and Aḥmad al-ʿĀmilī. Najaf: al-Maṭbaʿa al-ʿIlmiyya, 1957–64.

Ṭūsī, Naṣīr al-Dīn. *Āghāz wa-anjām*. Edited by Ḥasanzādah Āmulī. Tehran: Wizārat-i Farhang wa-Irshād-i Islāmī, 1987.

———. *The Paradise of Submission: A Medieval Treatise on Ismaili Thought*. Edited and translated by S. J. Badakhchani. London: I. B. Tauris in association with The Institute of Ismaili Studies, 2005.

———. *Shi'i Interpretations of Islam: Three Treatises on Islamic Theology and Eschatology*. Edited and translated by S. J. Badakhchani. London: I. B. Tauris in association with The Institute of Ismaili Studies, 2010.

Zamakhsharī, Maḥmūd b. ʿUmar al-. *al-Kashshāf ʿan-ghawāmiḍ ḥaqāʾiq al-tanzīl wa-ʿuyūn al-aqāwīl fī wujūh al-taʾwīl*. Beirut: Dār al-Iḥyāʾ al-Turāth al-ʿArabī, 2001.

Secondary Sources

Aavani, Gholamreza and Nāṣir Muḥammadī. "Zabān-i Qurʾān wa-zabān-i tamthīl az dīdgāh-i Ṣadr al-mutaʾallihīn." *KHNṢ* 54 (2008): 4–17.

Abdul Haq, Muhammad. "Ibn Sīnā's Interpretation of the Qurʾān." *IQ* 32, no. 1 (1988): 46–56.

Abrahamov, Binyamin. "The Creation and Duration of Paradise and Hell in Islamic Theology." *DI* 79 (2002): 87–102.

Adamson, Peter. *Abū Bakr al-Rāzī*. Oxford: Oneworld, forthcoming.

———. *The Arabic Plotinus: A Philosophical Study of the 'Theology of Aristotle.'* London: Duckworth, 2002.

———. *Al-Kindī*. New York: Oxford University Press, 2007.

Afrāsiyābpūr, ʿAlī-Akbar. "Zībāʾī az dīdgāh-i Mullā Ṣadrā." *KHNṢ* 51 (2008): 91–107.

Akbarian, Reza. *The Fundamentals of Mulla Sadra's Transcendent Philosophy*. London: Xlibris, 2009.

Akhlāqī, Marḍiya. "Sirisht-i maʿnāʾī wa-zabān-i waḥy az dīdgāh-i Ṣadr al-mutaʾallihīn." *KHNṢ* 52 (2008): 70–86

Ali-de-Unzaga, Omar. "The Use of the Qurʾān in the Epistles of the Pure Brethren (*Rasāʾil Ikhwān al-Ṣafāʾ*)." PhD diss., University of Cambridge, 2004.

Amīn, Sayyid Muḥsin al-. *Aʿyān al-shīʿa*. Beirut: Dār al-Taʿāruf li-l-Maṭbūʿāt, 1983.

Amir-Moezzi, Mohammad Ali. *The Spirituality of Shiʿi Islam: Beliefs and Practices*. Translated by Hafiz Karmali, David Bachrach, Amy Jacobs, and David Streight. London: I. B. Tauris in association with The Institute of Ismaili Studies, 2011.

Ārānī, Fāṭima. Taṭābuq-i madārij-i Qurʾān wa-maʿārij-i insān az manẓar-i Ṣadr-i mutaʾallihīn." *KHNṢ* 32 (2002): 46–52.

Āshtiyānī, Jalāl al-Dīn. *Maʿād-i jismānī: Sharḥ bar Zād al-musāfir*. Mashhad: Muʾassasa-yi Chāp wa-Intishār wa-Grāfīk-i Dānishgāh-i Firdawsī, 1976.

ʿĀṣī, Ḥasan. *al-Tafsīr al-Qurʾānī wa-l-lugha al-ṣūfiyya fī falsafat Ibn Sīnā*. Beirut: al-Muʾassasa al-Jāmiʿa li-l-Dirāsa wa-l-Nashr wa-l-Tawzīʿ, 1983.

Ayoub, Mahmoud. "The Prayer of Islam: A Presentation of Sūrat al-Fātiḥa in Muslim Exegesis." *JAAR* 47S (1979): 635–47.

———. "The Speaking Qurʾān and the Silent Qurʾān: A Study of the Principles and Development of Imāmī Shīʿī *tafsīr*." In *Approaches to the History of the Interpretation of the Qurʾān*, edited by Andrew Rippin, 177–98. Oxford: Clarendon Press, 1988.

Bābāʾī, ʿAlī. *Zībāʾī-shināsī dar maktab-i Ṣadrā: parīchihra-yi ḥikmat*. Tehran: Intishārāt-i Mawlā, 2006.

Baffioni, Carmela. "Metaphors of Light and the 'Verse of Light' in the Brethren of Purity." In *In the Age of al-Farābī: Arabic Philosophy in the Fourth/Tenth Century*, edited by Peter Adamson, 163–77. London: The Warburg Institute of Advanced Study, 2008.

Ballanfat, Paul. "Considérations sur la conception du coeur chez Mullâ Sadrâ." *KN* 5 (1999): 33–46, 67–84.

Bar-Asher, Meir M. *Scripture and Exegesis in Early Imāmī Shiism*. Leiden: Brill, 1999.

Bayrakdar, Mehmet. *La philosophie mystique chez Dawud de Kayseri*. Ankara: Ministère de la Culture, 1990.

Bīdārfar, Muḥsin. "Taqdīm." In Ṣadrā, *Tafsīr*, 1:1–131.

Bonmariage, Cécile. *Le Réel et les réalités: Mullā Ṣadrā Shīrāzī et la structure de la réalité*. Paris: Vrin, 2008.

Böwering, Gerhard. *The Classical Vision of Existence in Islam: The Qurʾānic Hermeneutics of the Ṣūfī Sahl al-Tustarī (d. 283/896)*. Berlin: de Gruyter, 1979.

Chittick, William. *The Heart of Islamic Philosophy: The Quest for Self-Knowledge in the Writings of Afḍal al-Dīn Kāshānī*. New York: Oxford University Press, 2001.

———. "Ibn al-ʿArabī's Hermeneutics of Mercy." In *Mysticism and Sacred Scripture*, edited by Stephen Katz, 153–68. New York: Oxford Univeristy Press, 2000.

———. *Ibn 'Arabi: Heir to the Prophets*. Oxford: Oneworld, 2005.

———. *Imaginal Worlds: Ibn al-'Arabī and the Problem of Religious Diversity*. Albany: State University of New York Press, 1994.

———. *In Search of the Lost Heart: Explorations in Islamic Thought*. Edited by Mohammed Rustom, Atif Khalil, and Kazuyo Murata. Albany: State University of New York Press, 2012.

———. "The School of Ibn 'Arabī." In Nasr and Leaman (eds.), *History of Islamic Philosophy*, 1:510–23.

———. *Science of the Cosmos, Science of the Soul: The Pertinence of Islamic Cosmology in the Modern World*. Oxford: Oneworld, 2007.

———. *The Self-Disclosure of God: Principles of Ibn al-'Arabī's Cosmology*. Albany: State University of New York Press, 1998.

———. *The Sufi Path of Knowledge: Ibn al-'Arabī's Metaphysics of Imagination*. Albany: State University of New York Press, 1989.

———. "Translator's Introduction." In Ṣadrā, *Elixir of the Gnostics*, xvii–xxvii.

Chodkiewicz, Michel. "The Banner of Praise." Translated by Cecilia Twinch. In *Foundations of the Spiritual Life According to Ibn 'Arabi: Praise*, edited by Stephen Hirtenstein, 45–58. Oxford: Muhyiddin Ibn 'Arabi Society, 1997.

———. "The *Futūḥāt Makkiyya* and its Commentators: Some Unresolved Enigmas." Translated by Peter Kingsley. In Lewisohn (ed.), *Heritage of Sufism*, 2:219–32.

———. *An Ocean Without Shore: Ibn 'Arabî, the Book, and the Law*. Translated by David Streight. Albany: State University of New York Press, 1993.

———. "Towards Reading the *Futūḥāt Makkiyya*." In Ibn ʿArabī, *The Meccan Revelations*, 2:3–55.

Cooper, John. "Some Observations on the Religious Intellectual Milieu of Safawid Persia." In *Intellectual Traditions in Islam*, edited by Farhad Daftary, 146–59. London: I. B. Tauris in association with The Institute of Ismaili Studies, 2000.

Corbin, Henry. *Avicenna and the Visionary Recital*. Translated by Willard Trask. Irving: Spring Publications, 1980.

———. *Creative Imagination in the Ṣūfism of Ibn 'Arabī*. Translated by Ralph Manheim. Princeton, NJ: Princeton University Press, 1969.

———. *En islam iranien*. Paris: Gallimard, 1971–2.

———. *Le paradoxe du monothéisme*. Paris: L'Herne, 1981.

———. *La philosophie iranienne islamique aux XVIIe et XVIIIe siècles*. Paris: Buchet/Chastel, 1981.

Corbin, Henry, with Seyyed Hossein Nasr and Osman Yahia. *Histoire de la philosophie islamique*. Reprint. Paris: Gallimard, 1986.

Dakake, David. "Defining Ambiguity: Early and Classical Commentary on the *Mutashābih* Verses of the Qurʾān." PhD diss., Temple University, in progress.

Dakake, Maria. *The Charismatic Community: Shiʿite Identity in Early Islam*. Albany: State University of New York Press, 2007.

———. "Hierarchies of Knowing in Mullā Ṣadrā's Commentary on *al-Kāfī*." *JIP* 6 (2010): 5–44.

———. "The Soul as *Barzakh*: Substantial Motion and Mullā Ṣadrā's Theory of Human Becoming." *MW* 94, no. 1 (2004): 107–30.

Dāmād, Muṣṭafā Muḥaqqiq. "The Quran and Schools of Islamic Theology and Philosophy." Translated by Seyyed Hossein Nasr. In *The HarperCollins Study Quran*, edited by Seyyed Hossein Nasr, Caner Dagli, Maria Dakake, Joseph Lumbard, and Mohammed Rustom, chap. 7. San Francisco: HarperOne: forthcoming.

Dehbashi, Mahdi. *Transubstantial Motion and the Natural World: With a Translation of Volume III, Stage 7, Chapters 18-32 of the Asfar of Mulla Sadra*. London: ICAS Press, 2011.

De Lubac, Henri. *Medieval Exegesis (Vol. 1: The Four Senses of Scripture)*. Translated by Mark Sebanc. Grand Rapids: Wm. B. Eerdmans Publishing Co., 1998.

De Smet, Daniel. "'Illiyyûn et Sijjîn" in *DC*.

———. "Le Souffle du Miséricordieux (*Nafas ar-Rahmán*): un élément pseudo–empédoclée dans la métaphysique de Mullá Sadrá aš-Šírázi." *DSTFM* 10 (1999): 467–86.

De Smet, Daniel and Meryem Sebti. "Avicenna's Philosophical Approach to the Qur'an in the Light of His *Tafsīr Sūrat al-Ikhlāṣ*." *JQS* 11, no. 2 (2009): 134–148.

Dhahabī, Muḥammad Ḥusayn al-. *al-Tafsīr wa-l-mufassirūn*. Cairo: Dār al-Kutub al-Ḥadītha, 1961–2.

Dhanani, Alnoor. *The Physical Theory of Kalām: Atoms, Space, and Void in Basrian Muʿtazilī Cosmology*. Leiden: Brill, 1994.

Dihqānpūr, ʿAlī-Riḍā. "Ruykard-i ḥikmat-i Ṣadrāʾī ba-tafsīr-i Qurʾān." *KHNṢ* 56 (2009): 54–68.

Dobie, Robert. *Logos and Revelation: Ibn 'Arabi, Meister Eckhart, and Mystical Hermeneutics*. Washington: The Catholic University of America Pres, 2010.

Duclow, Donald and Paul Dietrich. "Hell and Damnation in Eriugena." In *History and Eschatology in John Scottus Eriugena and His Time*, edited by James McEvoy and Michael Dunne, 457–66. Louvain: Louvain University Press, 2002.

Elias, Jamal. *The Throne Carrier of God: The Life and Thought of ʿAlāʾ ad-Dawla as-Simnānī*. Albany: State University of New York Press, 1995.

Endress, Gerhard and Dimitri Gutas, eds. *A Greek and Arabic Lexicon*. Leiden: Brill, 1992–.

Ernst, Carl. "Sufism and Philosophy in Mullā Ṣadrā." In *Islam-West Philosophical Dialogue*, 1:173–92.

———. *Words of Ecstasy in Sufism*. Albany: State University of New York Press, 1985.

Eschraghi, Armin. "'I Was a Hidden Treasure': Some Notes on a Commentary Ascribed to Mullā Ṣadrā Shīrāzī: *Sharh ḥadīth: 'Kuntu kanzan makhfīyyan* (sic).'" In *Islamic Thought in the Middle Ages: Studies in Text, Transmission and Translation, in Honour of Hans Daiber*, edited by Wim Raven and Anna Akasoy, 91–100. Leiden: Brill, 2008.

Ešots, Janis. "Mullā Ṣadrā's Teaching on *Wujūd*: A Synthesis of Philosophy and Mysticism." PhD diss., Tallinn University, 2007.

———. "Speech, Book, and Healing Knowledge: The Qur'anic Hermeneutics of Mullā Ṣadrā." In *Esoteric Approaches to the Interpretation of the Qur'ān* (working title), edited by Annabel Keeler and Sajjad Rizvi. Oxford: Oxford University Press in association with The Institute of Ismaili Studies, forthcoming.

Fakhry, Majid. *Al-Fārābī, Founder of Islamic Neoplatonism: His Life, Works and Influence*. Oxford: Oneworld, 2002.

———. "Philosophy and the Qur'ān" in *EQ*.

———. "Philosophy and Scripture in the Theology of Averroes." *MS* 30 (1968): 78-89.

Falāḥpūr, Majīd. *Mabānī-yi uṣūl wa-rawish-i tafsīrī-yi Mullā Ṣadrā*. Tehran: SIPRIn, 2010.

Frank, Richard. "The Origin of the Arabic Philosophical Term *'anīya*." *CB* 6 (1956): 181–201.

———. "*al-Ma'dūm wal-mawjūd*: The Non-Existent, the Existent, and the Possible in the Teaching of Abū Hāshim and His Followers." *MIDEO* 14 (1980): 185–209.

Fudge, Bruce. *Qur'ānic Hermeneutics: Al-Ṭabrisī and the Craft of Commentary*. New York: Routledge, 2011.

Gimaret, Daniel. *Une lecture mu'tazilite du Coran: Le tafsīr d'Abū 'Alī al-Djubbā'ī (m. 303/915)*. Louvain: Peeters, 1994.

Girdner, Scott. "Reasoning with Revelation: The Significance of the Qur'ānic Contextualization of Philosophy in al-Ghazālī's *Mishkāt al-anwār* (*The Niche of Lights*)." PhD diss., Boston University, 2009.

Gleave, Robert. *Scripturalist Islam: The History and Doctrines of the Akhbārī Shī'ī School*. Leiden: Brill, 2007.

Gobillot, Geneviève. *La conception originelle: ses interprétations et fonctions chez les penseurs musulmans: la fiṭra*. Cairo: Institut français d'archéologie orientale, 2000.

Goldzhier, Ignaz. *Die Richtungen der islamischen Koranauslegung*. Leiden: Brill, 1920.

Graham, William. *Divine Word and Prophetic Word in Early Islam*. The Hague: Mouton, 1977.

———. "Fātiḥa" in *EQ*.

Griffel, Frank. *Al-Ghazālī's Philosophical Theology*. New York: Oxford University Press, 2009.

Gril, Denis. "Commentaries on the *Fātiḥa* and Experience of Being According to Ibn 'Arabī." Translated by Josip Rainer. *JMIAS* 20 (1996): 33–52.

———. "L'interprétation par transposition symbolique (*i'tibār*) selon Ibn Barraǧān et Ibn 'Arabī." In *Symbolisme et herméneutique dans la pensée de Ibn 'Arabī*, edited by Bakri Aladdin, 147–61. Damascus: Institut français du Proche-Orient, 2007.

Gutas, Dimitri. *Avicenna and the Aristotelian Tradition: Introduction to Reading Avicenna's Philosophical Works*. Leiden: Brill, 1988.

———. "Intellect without Limits: The Absence of Mysticism in Avicenna." In *Intellect et Imagination dans la Philosophie Médiévale / Intellect and Imagination in Medieval Philosophy / Intelecto e Imaginação na Filosofia Medieval*, edited by Maria Cândida Pacheco and José Francisco Meirinhos, 1:351–72. Turnhout: Brepols, 2006.

———. "The Study of Arabic Philosophy in the Twentieth Century: An Essay on the Historiography of Arabic Philosophy." *BJMES* 29, no. 1 (2002): 5–25.

Gwynne, Rosalind. "Hell and Hellfire" in *EQ*.

Habil, Abdurrahman. "Traditional Esoteric Commentaries on the Qurʾān." In Nasr (ed.), *Islamic Spirituality*, 1:24–47.

Hadot, Pierre. *Philosophy as a Way of Life: Spiritual Exercises from Socrates to Foucault*. Edited by Arnold Davidson, translated by Michael Chase. Malden, MA: Blackwell, 1995.

Hamza, Feras. *To Hell and Back: The Prophet's Intercession and the Making of Temporary Hellfire in Sunni Orthodoxy*. Leiden: Brill, forthcoming.

Hatem, Jad. "Pure Love in Mulla Sadra." In *Timing and Temporality in Islamic Philosophy and Phenomenology of Life*, edited by Anna-Teresa Tymieniecka, 295–309. Dordrecht: Springer, 2007.

Heath, Peter. "Creative Hermeneutics: A Comparative Analysis of Three Islamic Approaches." *Arabica* 36, no. 2 (1989): 173–210.

Heinrichs, Wolfhart. "Sariḳa" in *EI*[2].

Hoover, Jon. "Islamic Universalism: Ibn Qayyim al-Jawziyya's Salafī Deliberations on the Duration of Hell-Fire." *MW* 99, no. 1 (2009): 181–201.

Horten, Max. *Die Gottesbeweise bei Schirázi (1640†)*. Bonn: Friedrich Cohen, 1912.

———. *Das philosophische System von Schirázi (1640†)*. Strasbourg: Trübner, 1913.

Ḥusayn-Dūst, Abū l-Qāsim. "Ḥurūf-i munqaṭiʿa-yi Qurʾān dar ḥikmat-i mutaʿāliya-yi Mullā Ṣadrā." *KHNṢ* 36 (2004): 58–63.

Idel, Moshe. "Kabbalah" in *EJ*[2].

———. *Kabbalah: New Perspectives*. New Haven: Yale University Press, 1988.

Iqbal, Muhammad. *The Development of Metaphysics in Persia*. London: Luzac, 1908.

Islam-West Philosophical Dialogue: The Papers Presented at the World Congress on Mullā Ṣadrā (May, 1999, Tehran). Tehran: SIPRIn, 2001–5.

Izutsu, Toshihiko. *The Concept and Reality of Existence*. Tokyo: The Keio Institute of Cultural and Linguistic Studies, 1971.

———. *Creation and the Timeless Order of Things*. Ashland: White Cloud Press, 1994.

———. "Revelation as a Linguistic Concept in Islam." *SMT* 5 (1962): 122–67.

———. *Sufism and Taoism: A Comparative Study of Key Philosophical Concepts*. 2nd ed. Berkeley: University of California Press, 1984.

Jaʿfarī, ʿAlī Aṣghar. "Sharḥ-i ḥadīth 'kuntu kanzan makhfiyyan.'" *KHNṢ* 32 (2002): 61–3.

Jambet, Christian. *The Act of Being: The Philosophy of Revelation in Mullā Sadrā*. Translated by Jeff Fort. New York: Zone Books, 2006.

———. "L'essence de Dieu est toute chose": Identité et différence selon Ṣadr al-Dīn Shīrāzī (Mullā Ṣadrā)." In *Le shīʿisme imāmite quarante ans après: hommage à Etan Kohlberg*, edited by Mohammad Ali-Amir Moezzi, Meir M. Bar-Asher, and Simon Hopkins, 269–92. Turnhout, Brepols, 2009.

———. *Mort et résurrection en islam: L'au-delà selon Mullâ Sadrâ*. Paris: Albin Michel, 2008.

———. *Se rendre immortel*. Saint-Clément-de-Rivière: Fata Morgana, 2002.

Janssens, Jules. "Avicenna and the Qurʾān: A Survey of His Qurʾānic Commentaries." *MIDEO* 25–26 (2004): 177–192.

———. "Al-Kindī: The Founder of Philosophical Exegesis of the Qurʾān." *JQS* 9, no. 2 (2007): 1–21.

Juzi, Muhammad Reza. "The Influence of Ibn ʿArabī's Doctrine of the Unity of Being on the Transcendental Theosophy of Ṣadr al-Dīn Shīrāzī." In Lewisohn and Morgan (eds.), *Heritage of Sufism*, 3:266–72.

Kalin, Ibrahim. "An Annotated Bibliography of the Works of Mullā Ṣadrā with a Brief Account of His Life." *ISt* 42, no. 1 (2003): 21–62.

———. "Between Physics and Metaphysics: Mullā Ṣadrā on Nature and Motion." *IS* 1, no. 1 (2003): 59–90.

———. *Knowledge in Later Islamic Philosophy: Mullā Ṣadrā on Existence, Intellect and Intuition*. New York: Oxford University Press, 2010.

———. "Mullā Ṣadrā on Theodicy and the Best of All Possible Worlds." *JIS* 18, no. 2 (2007): 183–207.

Kamada, Shigeru. "Mullā Ṣadrā Between Mystical Philosophy and Qurʾān Interpretation through His Commentary on the "Chapter of the Earthquake"." *IJAS* 2, no. 2 (2005): 275–89.

———. "Mullā Ṣadrā's *imāma/walāya*: An Aspect of His Indebtedness to Ibn ʿArabī." *JIP* 6 (2010): 67–78.

———. "Transmigration of Soul (*tanāsukh*) in Shaykh al-Mufīd and Mullā Ṣadrā." *Orient* 44 (2009): 105–119.

Karāmatī, Muḥammad Taqī. *Taʾthīr-i mabānī-yi falsafī dar tafsīr-i Ṣadr al-mutaʾallihīn*. Tehran: SIPRIn, 2006.

Keeler, Annabel. "Mullā Ṣadrā's Commentary on *Sūrat al-Sajda*." In *Islam-West Philosophical Dialogue*, 10:343–56.

———. *Ṣūfī Hermeneutics: The Qurʾān Commentary of Rashīd al-Dīn Maybudī*. Oxford: Oxford University Press in association with The Institute of Ismaili Studies, 2007.

Kennedy-Day, Kiki. *Books of Definition in Islamic Philosophy: The Limits of Words*. London: RouledgeCurzon, 2003.

Khalil, Mohammad Hassan. *Islam and the Fate of Others: The Salvation Question*. New York: Oxford University Press, 2012.

Khamenei, Muhammad. *The Qur'anic Hermeneutics of Mulla Sadra*. Tehran: SIPRIn, 2006.

Khwājawī, Muḥammad. *Lawāmiʿ al-ʿārifīn fī sharḥ aḥwāl Ṣadr al-mutaʾallihīn*. Tehran: Āriyan Press, 1987.

Khwursandiyān, Muḥammad ʿAlī. "Qāʿida-yi "basīṭ al-ḥaqīqa" wa-kārburd-hā-yi ān dar andīsha-yi Ṣadrāʾī." *FADDS* 23 (2007): 41–64.

Knysh, Alexander. "Multiple Areas of Influence." In *The Cambridge Companion to the Qurʾān*, edited by Jane McAuliffe, 211–33. Cambridge: Cambridge University Press, 2006.

Lagarde, Michel. *Les secrets de l'invisible: essai sur le Grand commentaire de Faḫr al-Dîn al-Râzî (1149–1209)*. Beirut: Albouraq, 2008.

Landolt, Hermann. *Recherches en spiritualité iranienne*. Tehran: Institut français de recherche en Iran, 2005.

———. "Simnânî on Wahdat al-Wujûd." In *Collected Papers on Islamic Philosophy and Mysticism*, edited by Mehdi Mohaghegh and Hermann Landolt, 93–111. Tehran: McGill University Institute of Islamic Studies, 1971.

Lane, Andrew. *A Traditional Muʿtazilite Qurʾān Commentary: The Kashshāf of Jār Allāh al-Zamakhsharī (d. 538/1144)*. Leiden: Brill, 2006.

Lange, Christian. *Justice, Punishment, and the Medieval Muslim Imagination*. Cambridge: Cambridge University Press, 2008.

Langhade, Jacques. *Du Coran a la philosophie: la langue arabe et la formation du vocabulaire philosophique de Farabi*. Damascus: Institut Français de Damas, 1994.

Lawson, Todd. "Akhbārī Shīʿī Approaches to *tafsīr*." In *Approaches to the Qurʾān*, edited by G. R. Hawting and Abdul-Kader Shareef, 173–210. London: Routledge, 1993.

Leaman, Oliver. "Orientalism and Islamic Philosophy." In Nasr and Leaman (eds.), *History of Islamic Philosophy*, 2:1143–8.

Lecker, Michael. "Salūl" in *EI*².

Leemhuis, Frederik. "ʿIlliyyūn" in *EQ*.

Lewisohn, Leonard. *Beyond Faith and Infidelity: The Sufi Poetry and Teachings of Maḥmūd Shabistarī*. Richmond: Curzon, 1995.

———. "The Transcendent Unity of Polytheism and Monotheism in the Sufism of Shabistarī." In Lewisohn (ed.), *Heritage of Sufism*, 2:379–406.

Lewisohn, Leonard (vols. 1–3) and David Morgan (vol. 3), eds. *The Heritage of Sufism*. Oxford: Oneworld, 1999.

Lings, Martin. *A Return to the Spirit: Questions and Answers*. Louisville: Fons Vitae, 2005.

Lory, Pierre. *Les commentaires ésotériques du Coran d'après 'Abd al-Razzâq al-Qâshânî*. Paris: Les Deux Océans, 1980.

———. *La science des lettres en islam*. Paris: Dervy, 2004.

Mahdi, Muhsin. "Orientalism and the Study of Islamic Philosophy." *JIS* 1, no. 1 (1990): 73–98.

Mahmutćehajić, Rusmir. *On Love*. Translated by Celia Hawkesworth. New York: Fordham University Press, 2007.

Mannāʿī, ʿĀʾisha al-. "ʿAqīdat fanāʾ al-nār bayna Ibn ʿArabī wa-Ibn Taymiyya wa-Ibn al-Qayyim." *MBSS* 11 (2002): 86–141.

Mangabadi, Dihqan. "Mullā Ṣadrā's Method of Qur'ān Commentary." In *Islam-West Philosophical Dialogue*, 10:429–44.

Marquet, Yves. *La philosophie des Iḫwān al-Ṣafā'*. 2nd ed. Paris: Société d'études de l'histoire de l'alchimie, 1999.

Mayer, Toby. "Anniyya" in *EI*3.

McGinnis, Jon. *Avicenna*. New York: Oxford University Press, 2010.

Meisami, Sayeh. *Mulla Sadra*. Oxford: Oneworld, forthcoming.

Mīrī, Sayyid Muḥsin and Muḥammad Ja'far 'Alī, eds. *Fihrist-i mawḍū'ī-yi Kitāb al-Ḥikma al-muta'āliya fī l-asfār al-arba'a*. Tehran: Intishārāt-i Ḥikmat, 1995.

Mohaghegh, Mehdi. *Bīst guftār*. Tehran: Naqsh-i Jahān, 1971.

Moris, Zailan. *Revelation, Intellectual Intuition and Reason in the Philosophy of Mulla Sadra: An Analysis of the al-Hikmah al-'Arshiyyah*. London: RoutledgeCurzon, 2002.

Morris, James. "Introduction." In Ṣadrā, *Wisdom of the Throne*, 3–85.

———. "The Process of Realization (*taḥqīq*): Mullā Ṣadrā's Conception of the Barzakh and the Emerging Science of Spirituality." In *Islam-West Philosophical Dialogue*, 10:93–102.

Morrison, Robert. *Islam and Science: The Intellectual Career of Niẓām al-Dīn Nīsābūrī*. London: Routledge, 2008.

Mostafavi, Zahra. "Ṣadr-ol-Mota'allahin on Platonic Ideas." *SI* 14, no. 2 (2001): 23–54.

Mourad, Suleiman. "The Survival of the Mu'tazilī Tradition of Qur'anic Exegesis in Shī'ī and Sunnī *tafāsīr*." *JQS* 12 (2010): 83–108.

Murata, Sachiko. *Chinese Gleams of Sufi Light: Wang Tai-yü's Great Learning of the Pure and Real and Liu Chih's Displaying the Concealment of the Real Realm*. Albany: State University of New York Press, 2000.

———. *The Tao of Islam: A Sourcebook on Gender Relationships in Islamic Thought*. Albany: State University of New York Press, 1992.

Murata, Sachiko, William Chittick, and Tu Weiming. *The Sage Learning of Liu Zhi: Islamic Thought in Confucian Terms*. Cambridge, MA: Harvard University Asia Center, 2009.

Naṣīrī, 'Alī. *Maktab-i tafsīrī-yi Ṣadr al-muta'allihīn*. Tehran: SIPRIn, 2007.

Nasr, Seyyed Hossein. *The Garden of Truth: The Vision and Promise of Sufism, Islam's Mystical Tradition*. New York: HarperOne, 2007.

———. *The Islamic Intellectual Tradition in Persia*. Edited by Mehdi Aminrazavi. Richmond: Curzon, 1996.

———. *Islamic Life and Thought*. Albany: State University of New York Press, 1981.

———. *Islamic Philosophy from Its Origins to the Present: Philosophy in the Land of Prophecy*. Albany: State University of New York Press, 2006.

———, ed. *Islamic Spirituality*. New York: Crossroad, 1987–1991.

———. *The Need for a Sacred Science*. Albany: State University of New York Press, 1993.

———. "The Place of the School of Iṣfahān in Islamic Philosophy and Sufism." In Lewisohn and Morgan (eds.), *Heritage of Sufism*, 3:3–15.

———. "The Qur'ān and Ḥadīth as Source and Inspiration of Islamic Philosophy." In Nasr and Leaman (eds.), *History of Islamic Philosophy*, 1:27–39.

———. *Ṣadr al-Dīn Shīrāzī and His Transcendent Theosophy*. 2nd ed. Tehran: Institute for Humanities and Cultural Studies, 1997.

———. "Spiritual Movements, Philosophy and Theology in the Safavid Period." In *The Cambridge History of Iran*, edited by Peter Jackson and Laurence Lockhart, 6:656–97. Cambridge: Cambridge University Press, 1986.

Nasr, Seyyed Hossein and Oliver Leaman, eds. *History of Islamic Philosophy*. New York: Routledge, 1996.

Netton, Ian Richard. *Allāh Transcendent: Studies in the Structure and Semiotics of Islamic Philosophy, Theology, and Cosmology*. London: Routledge, 1989.

Newman, Andrew. *Safavid Iran: Rebirth of a Persian Empire*. London: I. B. Tauris, 2008.

Nwyia, Paul. *Exégèse coranique et langage mystique*. Beirut: Dar El-Machreq, 1970.

Otten, Willemien. *The Anthropology of Johannes Scottus Eriugena*. Leiden: Brill, 1991.

Padwick, Constance, ""I Seek Refuge."" *MW* 28 (1938): 372–85.

Peerwani, Latimah. "Qur'ānic Hermeneutics: The Views of Ṣadr al-Dīn Shīrāzī." *PBSMS* (1991): 468–77.

———. "Translator's Introduction." In Ṣadrā, *On The Hermeneutics of the Light Verse of the Qur'ān*, 9–32.

Pfannmüller, Gustav. *Handbuch der Islam-Literatur*. Berlin: De Gruyter, 1923.

Pourjavady, Nasrollah. "Opposition to Sufism in Twelver Shiism." In *Islamic Mysticism Contested: Thirteen Centuries of Controversies and Polemics*, edited by Frederick De Jong and Bernd Radtke, 614–24. Leiden: Brill, 1999.

Pourjavady, Reza. *Philosophy in Early Safavid Iran: Najm al-Dīn Maḥmūd al-Nayrīzī and His Writings*. Leiden: Brill, 2011.

Rahman, Fazlur. *The Philosophy of Mullā Ṣadrā*. Albany: State University of New York Press, 1975.

Rizvi, Sajjad. "'Au-delà du miroir' or Beyond Discourse and Intuition: Pedagogy and Epistemology in the Philosophy of Mullā Ṣadrā Šīrāzī [ca. 1571–1635]." In *Miroir et savoir: la transmission d'un thème platonicien des Alexandrins à la philosophie arabo-musulmane*, edited by Daniel De Smet and Meryem Sebti, 251–71. Louvain: Peeters, 2008.

———. "The Existential Breath of *al-raḥmān* and the Munificent Grace of *al-raḥīm*: The *Tafsīr sūrat al-fātiḥa* of Jāmī and the School of Ibn ʿArabī." *JQS* 8, no. 1 (2006): 58–87.

———. *Mullā Ṣadrā and Metaphysics: Modulation of Being*. London: Routledge, 2009.

———. *Mullā Ṣadrā Shīrāzī: His Life and Works and the Sources for Safavid Philosophy*. Oxford: Oxford University Press, 2007.

Robson, James. "Is the Moslem Hell Eternal?" *MW* 28 (1938): 386–93.

Rustom, Mohammed. "Approaching Mullā Ṣadrā as Scriptural Exegete: A Survey of Scholarship on His Quranic Works." *CIS* 4, no. 1-2 (2008): 75–96.

———. "Dāwūd al-Qayṣarī: Notes on His Life, Influence and Reflections on the Muḥammadan Reality." *JMIAS* 38 (2005): 51–64.

———. "Forms of Gnosis in Sulamī's Sufi Exegesis of the *Fātiḥa*." *ICMR* 16, no. 4 (2005): 327–44.

———. "The Nature and Significance of Mullā Ṣadrā's Qur'ānic Writings." *JIP* 6 (2010): 109–30.

———. "Philosophical Sufism." In *The Routledge Companion to Islamic Philosophy*, edited by Richard Taylor and Luis Xavier López-Farjeat. New York: Routledge, forthcoming.

———. "Psychology, Eschatology, and Imagination in Mullā Ṣadrā Shīrāzī's Commentary on the *Ḥadīth* of Awakening." *IS* 5, no. 1 (2007): 9–22.

———. "Rumi's Metaphysics of the Heart." *MRR* 1, no. 1 (2010): 69–79.

———. "Story-Telling as Philosophical Pedagogy: The Case of Suhrawardī." In *Knowledge and Education in Classical Islam*, edited by Sebastian Günther. Leiden: Brill, forthcoming.

Rustomji, Nerina. *The Garden and the Fire: Heaven and Hell in Islamic Culture*. New York: Columbia University Press, 2009.

Sa'idi, Hasan. "Illumination, Unveiling and Intuition in Mullā Ṣadrā's Qur'ānic Commentary." In *Islam-West Philosophical Dialogue*, 10:519–38.

Saleh, Walid. "Preliminary Remarks on the Historiography of *tafsīr* in Arabic: A History of the Book Approach." *JQS* 12 (2010): 6–40.

Sands, Kristin. *Ṣūfī Commentaries on the Qur'ān in Classical Islam*. London: Routledge, 2006.

Schaya, Leo. *The Universal Meaning of the Kabbalah*. Translated by Nancy Pearson. Baltimore: Penguin Books, 1958.

Schimmel, Annemarie. *Deciphering the Signs of God: A Phenomenological Approach to Islam*. Edinburgh: Edinburgh University Press, 1994.

Scholem, Gershom. "Gilgul" in *EJ*².

Schuon, Frithjof. "The Spiritual Significance of the Substance of the Prophet." In Nasr (ed.), *Islamic Spirituality*, 1:48–63.

———. *Survey of Metaphysics and Esoterism*. Bloomington: World Wisdom, 1986.

Sells, Michael. *Early Islamic Mysticism*. Mahwah, NJ: Paulist Press, 1996.

Shah-Kazemi, Reza. *Justice and Remembrance: Introducing the Spirituality of Imam ʿAlī*. London: I. B. Tauris in association with The Institute of Ismaili Studies, 2006.

———. *The Other in the Light of the One: The Universality of the Qur'ān and Interfaith Dialogue*. Cambridge: Islamic Texts Society, 2006.

———. *Spiritual Quest: Reflections on Qur'ānic Prayer According to the Teachings of Imam ʿAlī*. London: I. B. Tauris in association with The Institute of Ismaili Studies, 2011.

Shihadeh, Ayman, ed. *Sufism and Theology*. Edinburgh: Edinburgh University Press, 2007.

Smith, Jane and Yvonne Haddad. *The Islamic Understanding of Death and Resurrection.* Albany: State University of New York Press, 1981.

Steigerwald, Diana. "Twelver Shīʿī *Taʾwīl.*" In *The Blackwell Companion to the Qurʾān,* edited by Andrew Rippin, 373–85. Malden, MA: Blackwell, 2006.

Tottoli, Roberto. "The Qur'an, Qur'anic Exegesis and Muslim Traditions: The Case of *zamharīr* (Q. 76:13) Among Hell's Punishments." *JQS* 10, no. 1 (2008): 142–52.

Treiger, Alexander. *Inspired Knowledge in Islamic Thought: Al-Ghazālī's Theory of Mystical Cognition and Its Avicennian Foundation.* New York: Routledge, 2012.

Tzamalikos, Panayiotis. *Origen: Philosophy of History and Eschatology.* Leiden: Brill, 2007.

ʿUbudiyyat, ʿAbd al-Rasūl. "The Fundamentality of Existence and the Subjectivity of Quiddity." Translated by D. D. Sodagar and Muhammad Legenhausen. *Topoi* 26 (2007): 201–12.

Vajda, Georges. "A propos de la perpétuité de la rétribution d'outre-tombe en théologie musulmane." *SIs* 11 (1959): 29–38.

Van Ess, Josef. "Das Begrenzte Paradies." In *Mélanges d'islamologie: volume dédié à la mémoire de Arman Abel par ses collègues, ses élèves et ses amis,* edited by Pierre Salmon, 108–27. Leiden: Brill, 1974.

Vasalou, Sophia. *Moral Agents and their Deserts: The Character of Muʿtazilite Ethics.* Princeton, NJ: Princeton University Press, 2008.

Virani, Shafique. *The Ismailis in the Middle Ages: A History of Survival, a Search for Salvation.* Oxford: Oxford University Press, 2007.

Walbridge, John. *The Leaven of the Ancients: Suhrawardī and the Heritage of the Greeks.* Albany: State University of New York Press, 2000.

———. "The Background to Mullā Ṣadrā's Doctrine of the Platonic Ideas." In *Islam-West Philosophical Dialogue,* 2:147–75.

———. *The Science of Mystic Lights: Quṭb al-Dīn Shīrāzī and the Illuminationist Tradition in Islamic Philosophy.* Cambridge, MA: Harvard University Press, 1992.

Whittingham, Martin. *Al-Ghazālī and the Qurʾān: One Book, Many Meanings.* London: Routledge, 2007.

Winter, Tim. "Introduction." In *The Cambridge Companion to Classical Islamic Theology,* edited by Tim Winter, 1–16. Cambridge: Cambridge University Press, 2008.

———. "Ibn Kemāl (d. 940/1534) on Ibn ʿArabī's Hagiology." In Shihadeh (ed.), *Sufism and Theology,* 137–57.

Wisnovsky, Robert. "The Nature and Scope of Arabic Philosophical Commentary in Post-Classical (ca. 1100-1900 AD) Islamic Intellectual History: Some Preliminary Observations." In *Philosophy, Science and Exegesis in Greek, Arabic and Latin Commentaries,* edited by Peter Adamson, Han Baltussen, and M. W. F. Stone, 2:149–91. London: Institute of Classical Studies, 2004.

———. "One Aspect of the Akbarian Turn in Shīʿī Theology." In Shihadeh (ed.), *Sufism and Theology*, 49–62.

Wohlman, Avital. *Al-Ghazali, Averroës and the Interpretation of the Qur'an: Common Sense and Philosophy in Islam*. Translated by David Burrell. London: Routledge, 2010.

Yahia, Osman. *Histoire et classification de l'oeuvre d'Ibn ʿArabī*. Damascus: Institut Français de Damas, 1964.

Ziai, Hossein. "The Illuminationist Tradition." In Nasr and Leaman (eds.), *History of Islamic Philosophy*, 1:465–96.

Index of Qurʾānic Passages

Index of Ḥadīths and Sayings

Index of Names and Terms